KAIZEN

ROBERT MILLER

© **Copyright 2021 - All rights reserved.**

The content contained within this book may not be reproduced, duplicated, or transmitted without direct written permission from the author or the publisher.

Under no circumstances will any blame or legal responsibility be held against the publisher, or author, for any damages, reparation, or monetary loss due to the information contained within this book, either directly or indirectly.

Legal Notice:

This book is copyright protected. It is only for personal use. You cannot amend, distribute, sell, use, quote or paraphrase any part, or the content within this book, without the consent of the author or publisher.

Disclaimer Notice:

Please note the information contained within this document is for educational and entertainment purposes only. All effort has been executed to present accurate, up to date, reliable, complete information. No warranties of any kind are declared or implied. Readers acknowledge that the author is not engaging in the rendering of legal, financial, medical, or professional advice. The content within this book has been derived from various sources. Please consult a licensed professional before attempting any techniques outlined in this book.

By reading this document, the reader agrees that under no circumstances is the author responsible for any losses, direct or indirect, that are incurred as a result of the use of the information contained within this document, including, but not limited to, errors, omissions, or inaccuracies.

Table of Contents

Kaizen

*A Comprehensive Beginner's Guide
to Learn the Realms of Kaizen from A-Z*

Introduction 3

Chapter One: What is Kaizen? 5

Chapter Two: History of Kaizen 8
    Continuous Improvement 8
    Understanding History 9
    Toyota Production System 13
    Kaizen Comes to the West 17
    Kaizen Practices Are Context-Specific 19

Chapter Three: Effectiveness of Kaizen 22
    How is Kaizen Effective? 22
    PDCA or Kaizen Process 23
    5S 24
    How to Identify Problems: The Kaizen Way 25
    What are the New Standards? 26
    Kaizen and TPS or Toyota Production System 31

Chapter Four: Kaizen and Personal Life 34
- Kaizen and Perfection 36
- Kaizen and Difficulties of Day to Day Life 39
- Kaizen and Long-Term Improvement 41

Chapter Five: Using Kaizen to Improve Personal Workflow 42
- Personal Kaizen 42

Chapter Six: Goals – How to Achieve Them 59
- SMART Goals 60
- Benefits and Drawbacks 66
- Mistakes of SMART Goals 70
- SMART Goals - Example 72
- Email Subscription Goal 73
- Landing Page Performance Goal 75
- Tips and Tricks 76
- Kaizen and Perfectionists 78

Chapter Seven: Habits and Kaizen 80
- Examples of Kaizen in Personal Life and Habits 82

Chapter Eight: Kaizen Events 89
- Types of Kaizen Events 90
- When to Use Kaizen Events 94
- How to Use Kaizen Events 96
- Why you Should Choose Kaizen 97
- Planning a Kaizen Event 98
- The Seven Wastes or Seven Mudas 102

Additional Wastes 110

Eliminating the Seven Wastes... 111

Chapter Nine: Basics of 5S 117

What is 5S?.. 117

Chapter Ten: How to Lead a Kaizen Event 124

Conclusion.. 130

References 132

Kaizen
Japanese Tips, Tricks and Strategies Using Kaizen and Ikigai Theories and Principles

Introduction 139

Chapter One: Basics of Kaizen.. 141

Core of Kaizen 145

History of Kaizen 149

Kaizen's Pillars 158

Chapter Two: Kaizen and Business 165

Expanding your Company 167

Kaizen Event 171

Creating and Training Kaizen Leaders................................... 177

Chapter Three: Kaizen's Benefits.. 185

Chapter Four: Kaizen and Startups 201
    Applying Kaizen 202
    Tips and Tricks 205
    Guide to Instilling Kaizen Changes 207

Chapter Five: Ikigai 215
    Defining Ikigai 220

Chapter Six: Other Applications of Kaizen 229
    Dietary Habits 232
    Tips 248
    How to Fight 254

Conclusion 259

References 261

Kaizen
Advanced Guide of Effective Kaizen Methods and Strategies in the Information Era

Introduction 267

Chapter 1: What Is Kaizen? 271
    Types of Kaizen 274
    The History of Kaizen 280

Chapter 2: How Does Kaizen Work? 291
    The Basic Effects of Kaizen 293

    The "Waste" Takes Several Different Forms 294

    Toyota's Kaizen 296

    The Lean Six Sigma 304

Chapter 3: How Can Kaizen Help My Business? 308

    How Can Kaizen Help You? 310

Chapter 4: Kaizen In Everyday Life 319

    Kaizen in Your Professional Life 327

    A Rarely Spoken Of Benefit 332

Chapter 5: Implementing Kaizen 334

Chapter 6: Kaizen Events 346

    The Benefits of Kaizen Events 357

Chapter 7: Kaizen And Self Reflection 362

    The Hansei Process 362

    Working On Kaizen And Self-Reflection 365

Conclusion 379

KAIZEN

A Comprehensive Beginner's Guide to Learn the Realms of Kaizen from A-Z

ROBERT MILLER

Introduction

Kaizen is one of the most famous exports in Japan. It won't be an exaggeration if you say that it is a gift that keeps on giving. It is no wonder that Kaizen has become so popular all around the world. Incorporating Kaizen in your life can really help you change it around for good.

Kaizen, while popular, is still considered to be a complex topic by many. This is because of the sheer amount of information available online and offline regarding the subject. Due to this excess influx of information, it might be quite difficult for a lot of beginners to find a starting point. If you are one such beginner, this book will help you bring Kaizen to your life with ease.

This book will help you understand the basics and core principles of Kaizen. This way, you will be able to understand what this term means and why it is so important. You will also learn how to use Kaizen to improve your personal and professional life. This book will also help you learn how to achieve your personal goals with the help of Kaizen. Another factor that this book will help you learn is how to pursue a satisfying and happy life just with Kaizen.

Ultimately, this book contains proven strategies and steps that will help you understand what Kaizen is and will teach you how to use this Japanese style of management in your day-to-day life to improve it significantly.

With some simple changes, you will be able to change your life for good, forever.

Chapter One

What is Kaizen?

Before moving on to the incorporation of Kaizen in your day-to-day life, it is necessary to learn the basics of the system. This chapter will cover all the basics of Kaizen, which will help you create a base for the system.

Kaizen is a combination of two Japanese words- Kai, which means continuous or change, and Zen, which means improvement or good. So, Kaizen stands for continuous change or improvement, which is considered to be good. This system believes that it is necessary to change for the good.

Some other sources report a slightly different translation of the term. Still, regardless of the translation, the ultimate essence of Kaizen is 'change,' and it has become one of the most popular words and concepts in Japan. Nowadays, you can find it being discussed almost everywhere, including print media, television media, radio, the internet, social media, etc.

There are so many different iterations of Kaizen now. Kaizen is now used in many different scenarios and fields, including business, education, etc. In the corporate world, the principles of this system have become so ingrained that now managers and workers both follow them naturally.

'Change' as a concept is seen through a variety of points of view in the world. Each culture views it differently. Change is not only an acceptable but also a highly celebrated concept in Japanese culture, which is why Kaizen is so popular. Most Japanese people don't even need to follow the principles of Kaizen consciously; they just do it naturally. This is why businesses and individuals keep on changing in Japan. The same cannot be said about other cultures, including the USA. For Americans, change is a rather difficult thing to cope with.

While following Kaizen, it is believed that not even a day should go without changing or transforming something in your life. Japan suffered a lot of pain and destruction in World War II. A lot of her businesses crumbled along with the economy. It looked like Japan would never rise again, but it did and that too at a surprisingly rapid pace. Many businesses rose once again, literally from ashes. As most of the resources and capital had vanished in the aftermath of the war, the workers, the employers, and the managers, everyone had to face a new challenge every other day. Even staying in business was difficult and nerve-wracking. It was a cyclic process, and everyone had to work with total dedication to keeping everything afloat. This is where the Kaizen principle helped the businesses and the Japanese people. Without Kaizen, the Japanese would have found it difficult, if not impossible, to come out of the shock of the Great War.

Kaizen can surely help you change your life around. Many people believe that Kaizen means making drastic changes in your life instantly. This is a myth. Kaizen involves changing your life slowly and doing it one by one. Before moving on to the theory itself, let us have a look at the history of Kaizen. By understanding the history and origin of the philosophy, you will be able to incorporate it into your life with ease.

Chapter Two

History of Kaizen

Kaizen is now considered to be one of the most important concepts that form the base of agile and lean business practices.

Kaizen (改善) stands for constant improvement. In business, it means improvements that are continuous, ongoing, and incremental.

Continuous Improvement

In Kaizen, constant changes are utilized to boost the efficiency of the business. It is used to bring down inefficiency in 3 significant forms. These forms are Muri (excessive or burdening work), Muda (waste), and Mura (inconsistent work).

Kaizen involves constant tweaks that are used to make the operations of the business better constantly. Each small step taken to improve the business is holistic. Kaizen is focused on products, processes, individuals, and the work culture and environment. It is highly focused on the quality of work and the desire for better efficiency.

Kaizen does not believe in haphazard and 'big moves.' It believes that changes should happen iteratively. It believes that small changes are necessary and should be made from time to time for the greater good. These kinds of changes are participative and inclusive. This is why, in this system, each person of the enterprise is involved. Kaizen uses the intrinsic psychological motivations along with the brainpower of all the team members, including CEO to frontline workers.

Along with regular Kaizen, there exists a related concept known as Kaizen blitz. This concept is also known as Kaizen events. In this concept, a small team is chosen, and they are supposed to participate in an even that can boost profits and hard work. This is supposed to be a period of high focus.

Some people believe that Kaizen is nothing but a glorified version of Six Sigma, but this is a myth. Six Sigma focuses on the quality of the final product only, while Kaizen is focused on the quality of the whole business.

Understanding History

The history of Kaizen can be traced back to the pre-World War II United States of America. Then, it traveled to the post-World War II Japan. Ultimately, it spread all over the world.

Walter Shewhart, an American statistician, and engineer were working at the Bell Labs in the 1930s. He was working on the 'Shewhart Cycle' or Plan-Do-Study-Act (PDSA) plan or PDCA (Plan Do Check Act). It was supposed to be a plan designed in such a way that it could check the honesty and utility of the changes in the organization and whether they could bring in some form of improvements or not. PDSA or the 'Shewhart Cycle' can be labeled as the ancestor of the current Kaizen.

In the 'Shewhart cycle' or the PDCA/PDSA cycle, you are supposed to be with 'Plan.' In this step, you need to plan what you want to do. This includes an analysis of the problem that needs to be solved immediately. This is followed by the best way to solve the problem and the resources that are necessary to solve it.

The next step in the cycle is 'do' in which you are supposed to apply the plan that you decided in the last step.

After some time has passed, you follow the third step, 'Study,' in which you see whether the plan that you followed and used really worked or not. You are also supposed to analyze whether there were some things that you could have modified or made better for the plan to work better.

The last step is the 'Act' in which you are supposed to implement the plan. Suppose the plan delivers the results that you wanted, congratulations. If not, then the last step becomes 'Adjust,' where you need to readjust and reassess your plans once again.

PDSA or 'Shewhart Cycle' is an important method of solving problems because it does so with the help of critical thinking and employee engagement. It uses the collective brainpower of the whole company.

It has been used for the last five decades in various clinical laboratories and is considered to be the standard protocol for maintaining and testing quality control.

Shewhart was the teacher and mentor of W. Edwards Deming. Another statistician and engineer, Deming are considered to be an important figure in the world of Kaizen. He carried forward Shewhart's ideas to make something even more radical and useful in the next (the 1940s) decade.

The most basic concept that Demings was 'Total Quality Management.' In this concept, you are supposed to stay focused on the quality of the management and the product. The costs of management and production are supposed to drop with time while the productivity rate is supposed to grow constantly in this method. According to Deming, it is always recommended to focus on creating a better system than bringing down the costs just to be 'cheap.' In the long-term, the company can make a lot more profit by cutting costs and get a bigger market share.

The best method to have good quality management is to understand the information in variation. According to Deming, there are two causes of variation, which are 'special' causes and 'common' causes.

Special causes happen due to big changes that are not part of the current system. These include changes in which the whole management is changed, external situations such as natural disasters, etc. It may also include fluctuations in the international trade policy.

In the common causes, they only happen in the existing system. These include all small, everyday details and events that may be difficult to see unless you really look for them.

The bases of the variations are often only seen by workers. This is because they are directly in touch with the micro-level and nitty-gritty details of the business all the time. This is why Deming believed that most of the problems that happen in companies are caused due to management. When the management does not pay any attention to the workers and the problems they identify, they potentially ruin the future of the company.

While Deming was a citizen of the United States of America, his ideas did not fly off well with Americans, at least in the beginning. The main reason behind this was that America possessed the mentality of getting there as soon as possible. After the war, a consumerist boom took place in the United States of America, which lasted for years. The same ethos continued. The US did not understand the necessity of quality control and carefulness.

In a surprising move, Deming was able to use his idea in still-recovering and still-rising Japan. He worked in the American occupation government in Japan in the mid-1940s.

The US helped in the speedy recovery of Japan because it had a lot of vested interests in it. This is why a lot of visionary, brainy, and intellectual academics were sent to the nation to help you get it back on track. Deming was one of these many geniuses. His presence and work inspired and helped Japan in such a significant way that in the

1960s, Nobsuke Kishi, the then Prime Minister of Japan, honored him with The Order of the Sacred Treasure, Second Class. Later Japan named a prize after him.

Thus, it is clear that Kaizen and the Japanese Miracle was influenced, helped, and abetted by an American economist. This is because he was given independence to do and choose whatever he wanted to do. This freedom allowed him to come up with a way that was smart and intelligent. Japanese managers utilized his ideas and cultivated them to form a new practice known as Kaizen.

The GDP of the nation continued to grow significantly almost every year. Similarly, the quality of the exports increased too. It was around the 1970s when the Japanese economy started to boom significantly, and by the next decade, it had become the second-largest GDP of the world.

Deming's practices worked so well in Japan because the nation and the culture were already renowned for its focused, intricate, and detailed craftsmanship and production techniques. Deming's practices and methods allowed the Japanese companies to go beyond the Western ones on all levels, including supply chain, manufacturing process, and the cost of production too.

Toyota Production System

The next important name that arrived on the scene of Kaizen and changed it forever was an industrial engineer and businessman, Taiichi Ohno. He was the first Japanese entrepreneur who chose to use the methodology of Deming and modified it according to his needs and requirements.

Ohno began to develop the TPS or the Toyota Production System around the year 1945. He continued to work on it until 1965. This form of production of manufacturing is also known as "just-in-time" manufacturing. This system is beneficial because it focuses on maximizing efficiency. It also concentrates on reducing waste and increase improvement continuously. As it is clear, it is just another form of the Kaizen system.

It is also considered to be a good case study of the Lean manufacturing method and lean business strategy. In the initial stages, TPS was devised as the last minute survival strategy. It was supposed to be the last option. The company was in a dire state, and it was facing the after-effects of the Great War. Toyota was almost dead and had no future because resources were low; most of the manufacturing units had been damaged, etc. It was just because of the combination of the necessity and ingenuity that the company thrived. Ohno realized that he did not have a lot of material, so he tried to utilize whatever he had. His best assets proved to be highly intelligent and skillful employees who were ready to do hard work to save the company and their jobs.

To make things easier, Ohno devised 'Ten Commandments' of his theory which were as follows:

1. Reduce or eliminate waste. You are a cost as well.

2. Always believe that you can do it if you try hard enough.

3. You can always find your answers in the workplace, as it is like a teacher.

4. The best and only way to win is to start right away. If you plan to do something, do not wait for too long.

5. Perseverance is a must. If you begin something, finish it. Do not leave it in the middle.

6. Try to explain difficult concepts in a simple and easy to understand way. If the concept is already simple, then repeat it a couple of times.

7. Discuss your problems openly.

8. Any action, which doesn't have a value, is pointless.

9. Always try hard to improve your productivity. Try to improve things that have already been improved.

10. Share and practice the wisdom that you have earned. Never hoard it.

Ohno was a white-collar manager who was quite reluctant. He tried to focus on situations where the action was. He also tried to incorporate this philosophy into all walks of life. His method, i.e., TPS, focused on the visibility of the process. This allowed him to check the minute details of the basics of the manufacturing right on the factory floor. It included asking many different questions to all the workers, including the assembly line workers. These talks, along with other strategies, were used to find hidden processes that often hid a lot of waste.

The TPS system worked wonders for the company. Toyota continued to grow consistently, and its sales went up significantly every year. In the year 2008, Toyota crossed the global sales position of General Motors. This was a huge deal in the world of automobiles as General Motors or GM had been holding the position for around 77 long years. This all happened thanks to the mentorship of Ohno, which promoted person-to-person contact.

He mentored students and other people who further went on to become mentors. This cycle continued, and soon TPS became the core of the company. By looking at the eye-catching progress of Toyota, other companies, too, started to follow suit. They passed on their knowledge to other students until it became a common concept in the company. Other Japanese companies then adapted this method.

Ohno's methodology and innovations, with time, brought forth the wrong notion/cliché that Japanese cars are cheap. This went on and but now people have realized that this just a myth.

TPS and all other related systems that were used by other companies worked extremely well. Nissan, Honda, and Suzuki all became dramatically successful on all levels, including costs, quality, and output. This proves how Kaizen can bring a lot of changes everywhere.

Kaizen Comes to the West

The third important name in the journey of Kaizen is Masaaki Imai. He is considered to be the person who brought Kaizen to the West almost single-handedly. A Japanese management advisor, Imai has been working with joint ventures and foreign companies all over the world since the 1960s.

It was Imai's book Kaizen: The Key to Japan's Competitive Success, published in 1986 that made people aware of Kaizen in the western world. Soon he came out with another book in the next decade called Gemba Kaizen: A Commonsense, Low-cost Approach to Management, which was published in 1997.

Another important factor that made Imai the Kaizen guru of the West was that he started the Kaizen Institute in 1986. The main focus of this institute is to help enterprises to use Kaizen practices in their business by following the local business practices and culture.

Imai's Kaizen, too, believes in slow and continuous changes. It focuses on improving things and then maintaining them. He believes that good changes happen gradually. He also believes that a business should always provide value because customers value 'value' a lot.

Another factor that is crucial for Imai is Gemba. Gemba means the place where the work is done. So for instance, in a company it is the factory or the workstation, in a doctor's clinic, it is his or her office, etc. Imai believes that all the managers need to spend a lot of time on Gemba instead of just focusing on the 'outer' details only. Production is much more important than marketing and the reputation of R&D.

This means the managers need to defeat and outgrow the fear of being labeled as ignorant. They need to learn how to focus on the smaller aspects of their company by asking simple and often childlike questions.

One of the major aspects of Imai's book Kaizen: The Key to Japan's Competitive Success is that he showed how the American culture and companies are result-oriented while the Japanese ones are process-oriented. He showed how the success of Japanese companies lies in the improvement and quality control of things. He discovered that process-oriented thinking is good for transparency. He believed that the company should be run using a holistic system.

It is true that Japan, around the 1950s and 1960s, was considered to be a nation that produced affordable, cost-efficient, and 'cheap' products that were either below average or just average. Still, many companies continued to use Kaizen principles and kept changing the future.

This perseverance helped a lot because, by the 1980s, Japan's name became almost synonymous with high quality and durability. This proves that Kaizen management led to results. This is why almost all major Japanese companies, including Honda, Fuji, Xerox, Canon, Toyota, etc. used it. By the 1980s, all these companies started to perform better as compared to their Western counterparts. Ultimately, Western, especially American companies, had to pay a lot of price for not paying attention to Deming at the right time.

Deming was reintroduced to the Western world, particularly America, in 1980, when NBC aired a segment called "If Japan Can, Why Can't We?" It was an immensely popular segment and was originally viewed by millions of people. The very next year, Ford hired Deming because the company had suffered a hefty loss of $3 billion in just three years.

Deming saved the company and was awarded the National Medal of Technology by President Reagan in 1987. His innovations led to an economic comeback.

The year 1997 saw the foundation of the Lean Enterprise Institute through which Deming's ideas were carried forward all over.

Kaizen Practices Are Context-Specific

Kaizen is not a one-fit-for-all solution. It changes according to the situation and condition of the organization and its business environment as well. The plan and its implementation both vary significantly. It is a method that burns slow, but it produces excellent results in the long-term. It is a method that should be used to improve yourself slowly and steadily.

It is a cost-effective method because it is always better to work on how to retain your current customers instead of focusing on getting new ones all the time. In this process, you are supposed to change your current assets in such a way that performance can be enhanced. Kaizen can help you save money, time, and energy.

There are many different methods of how you can incorporate Kaizen in your personal and professional life. Many of these methods will be discussed in the later chapters.

The first thing that any company needs to do to implement the Kaizen method is to document everything, especially the work processes. This will allow you to have a look at the workflow step-by-step. There are different methods of doing this. Many people prefer to use visualization tools such as Kanban to make this process easy and interactive.

While doing this, the people in a leadership position need to bring down the corporate culture significantly. Instead of behaving like 'bosses,' they need to learn how to behave like everyone else. This will create a personal connection with people and will usher in an atmosphere of openness. It will also create an environment of positivity, and most people get motivated by positive reinforcement. This is why it is necessary to create a culture of good and motivating incentives. An atmosphere of mutual respect is necessary, as well. All these factors need to be followed by every member of the group.

Your team members should be able to suggest improvements and discuss problems without any hesitation. They can only do this why they feel personally invested and interested in the success of the company. An employee will only care about the company when she sees that the company cares for her.

While Kaizen is great on its own, it becomes even better when the team members can align their interests, Kaizen, and the interests of the company with each other. This is why Kaizen needs to be initiated around problems that will bring satisfying solutions. This satisfaction will boost the morale of the company personnel.

Kaizen is most suitable for situations where goals are modest, but for many people, modest is boring. For long-term success and improvement, sometimes it is better to take modest, comfortable, but successful steps. This way, you will be able to avoid big yet potentially risky steps.

Nowadays, many African companies are using various Kaizen approaches and are enjoying a sustained and comfortable success.

Chapter Three

Effectiveness of Kaizen

The previous two chapters covered the basics and history of Kaizen. Kaizen is indeed a supremely effective and efficient method that can work wonders if implemented correctly. This chapter will focus on how Kaizen is so effective and why it should be used.

How is Kaizen Effective?

Kaizen is highly effective because it can bring down the waste or the 'muda' and can bring down the processes, which are bad for the business. Thus, it is considered to be an integral tool of lean business too. Kaizen becomes extremely beneficial when all the people present in the group become involved in it. When all the people are involved in the process, they can freely express what they feel, observe, and recommend. They can freely discuss the minor changes that they would like to see happening in the company. These minor changes, over time, will improve the overall condition of the company gradually.

It is necessary to understand right from the initial stages that all recommendations presented under Kaizen will be accepted. There will be no repercussions or negative effects for airing doubts, problems, or suggesting changes. In fact, instead of negative effects, the employees who present the problems will actually be praised because they want to improve the company. For example, Toyota continues to encourage its workers by presenting them with small perks for bringing in good changes.

PDCA or Kaizen Process

As stated above, PDCA stands for Plan-Do-Check-Act method. By using this method, you can bring in changes that will create a continuous cycle of change. This cycle will keep track of all the changes and will continue to improve simultaneously. The four steps of PDCA are as follows:

Plan
Identify the problem and try to find the solution for it.

Do
Act on the decided solution.

Check

Check the results and see whether the solution has really worked or not.

Act

If the solution has worked, implement it for all other sections of the organization. If the solution did not work, start from the 'Plan' section again.

Kaizen is a simple and easy to understand philosophy. It solely focuses on a few things that make it easy to follow too. You just need to check how to improve things, act on them, and then continue to improve slowly but constantly. As the concept is quite broad, it is relevant to a lot of businesses and methodologies. This can be done to improve the process of production and other various processes continuously.

Many business tools are considered to be a part of the Kaizen clout. They include:

5S

The 5S system is used for constant improvement and to keep the facility clean and well-functioning.

Kanban

This is used to reduce waste production by getting only the things that you need and when you need them.

TPM

This brings down the downtime, and improves the total production. It is also known as the Total Productive Maintenance process.

As Kaizen is extremely flexible, it can be used in a variety of ways and can be combined with lean tools that are the most suitable for your enterprise.

How to Identify Problems: The Kaizen Way

The first step of Kaizen is to reach an agreement and accept the fact that you have a problem in your organization. All the members of your team need to understand that you have a problem. If you do not accept or acknowledge the problem, you will never be able to improve.

A problem in an organization can be anything. It can include minor inconveniences faced by people while working, or troubles faced by the end-users, etc. The most significant standpoint of Kaizen is that the theory believes that the people who generally create the problem are rarely affected by it. This is why they are often insensitive about it and simply do not care for it. In regular management and workings, the best way to deal with such problems is to hide them or ignore them instead of facing them. This is how most of the employees work and continue to suffer in silence.

The biggest reason why this practice continues is that no one wants to be the person who will talk about problems. It is only through the power of positive thinking that you can convert each of your problems into an opportunity to change, grow, and improve. If there exists a problem, there also exists an opportunity to grow and improve. If you find a problem, you need to solve it. If the problem is solved, you need to standardize the solution so that next time whenever a similar problem arises, you will have a ready-made solution.

What are the New Standards?

As stated above, when you find a solution to a problem, you need to assess it and then standardize it. No amount of improvement is possible if standards will help you if you do not try to learn from them. You need to understand your current position carefully if you want to move on and improve. Each specific criterion requires a different tool and parameter to measure it. This means there are different tools to measure the managers, the personnel, etc.

Kaizen is all about improving constantly. It is a continuous process that is also a continuous challenge. Establishing new standards may sound quite difficult in the beginning, but with time, practice, and patience, you will learn how to do so. In Kaizen, the future standards should always be better and an improved version of the current standards. This is why Kaizen is also known as a method of constant upgrade and revision. Only the important details and elements need to be measured and standardized.

Setting up standards is a great way to bring in improvement throughout the company. Each staff member should understand and implement the new standards in his or her work. This includes everyone from CEO to workers. This is how the company will achieve discipline. Always remember that discipline is the foundation of Kaizen, and without discipline, Kaizen can never survive.

The System of Suggestions

As stated earlier, if you want to implement Kaizen in your organization successfully, you need to allow everyone right from the topmost boss to the lowest ranking worker to make suggestions. In Kaizen, suggestions are not only accepted; they are welcome as well. In Kaizen in the initial stages, suggestions are promoted by giving some monetary incentive. This is not a regular practice, though. It is just used in the initial stages to boost morale. Making Kaizen popular in the company is a must because it can help every member of the team. Kaizen believes that improvement can only happen when problems are solved. If people do not bring in problems, they will never get solved, and ultimately the company will either shut down or become stagnant for a long time. This is why a lot of companies in Japan believe that a large number of suggestions mean the manager of the firm is skillfully managing the company.

The manager and the supervisors are supposed to promote and create a culture of understanding and encouragement so that the employees can bring forth their suggestions with ease. Management needs to understand the efforts put in by the workers to bring forth the suggestions. The number of suggestions brought in by various departments and employees should be put and updated every day. This will increase the competition, and people will begin to bring in new suggestions.

Most of the Japanese companies have a reserved corner in their workplaces where they can publicize the activities of the company. Other features that are included in this corner include the level of suggestions received, the achievements that various teams achieved recently, etc. Often new and different strategies, suggestions, and tools that enhanced a particular work or process are posted too. This can help other people to learn about these new tools and incorporate them into their day-to-day work. While these tools cannot be incorporated or copied directly from one team to another, they can be modified accordingly and made suitable for all the departments. They can also serve as a starting point for the departments.

When used and implemented properly, each suggestion can bring in a new and improved standard. The best thing about this new standard is that it will be based on the suggestions recommended by the workers. This way, they will appreciate the new standard better and will proud and honored to follow it. This will create an atmosphere of friendliness and will make the culture of the whole office a bit more positive and friendly.

Compared to this, if the standard is set by only following the instructions of the managers and is imposed directly, the employers may feel uncomfortable following it. This is because the team of managers may or may not know the problems of the employees. Their new standard may even prove to be counterproductive. This is why Kaizen promotes and forces every team member to join the process and welcomes all kinds of suggestions from everyone. This way, the decision is made democratically, and everyone ends up feeling happy.

Companies and managers who use the Kaizen system understand the importance of it. Implementing the Kaizen system has a lot of benefits, including:

- It can reduce the dullness from work
- It can make the work easy to do
- It can reduce or get rid of the nuisance associated with work
- It can increase production
- It can increase safety
- It can bring down the resources required including cost and time

Focus on the Process

Kaizen promotes 'focus on the process' because the philosophy believes that the results can only improve when the process is improved. The process is also highly focused on the people as it rises from their suggestions and helps the people who make the suggestions. This is quite the opposite of the result-oriented mindset that is popular in the West. In the West, the means do not matter; only the result does, while in Japanese companies, the process is as important as a result. In Western, especially American companies, it does not matter if you put in a lot of inputs and efforts; if the results are unsatisfactory, the whole situation will be rated poorly. The staff and their contribution are only valued if they can produce tangible results. Otherwise, the whole process is considered to be useless.

Kaizen believes that by focusing on the process, you can improve a lot of things, including:

- Discipline in the work

- Proper utilization of resources

- Morale

- Development of skills and resources

- Active participation and involvement

- Communication

The Kaizen system is more focused on the development of the people and the company. It believes with a developed staff; the company will automatically start to grow and will lead to better results.

Kaizen and Innovation

Kaizen and innovation are often pitted against each other by many companies. Both these factors are essential but quite different than each other. Innovation can be defined as a huge leap in the strategy, while Kaizen is a smaller and gradual change in strategy. Japan and Japanese culture, believe more in the gradual changes while the West, especially America, believes in innovation i.e., huge leaps.

Innovation is a result of huge changes in technology and science. It is often a result of important breakthroughs. In organizations, innovation can also be present in the form of new management processes or new production strategies.

Compared to innovation, Kaizen is a lot slower and fairly subtle and less grand. The results of this philosophy are not immediately visible and may take a lot of time to show. Another major difference between innovation and Kaizen is that Kaizen is a continuous process. In contrast, innovation is a one-shot procedure, and a crucial difference between these two is based on their priorities. Kaizen prioritizes people and their development while the priority of innovation is always technology and money.

Kaizen and TPS or Toyota Production System

One of the best examples of Kaizen and its efficiency and effectiveness can be seen in the example of TPS or the Toyota Production System. Toyota uses this system, and it forms the focus of its business policy. All business schools feature the story of Kaizen and Toyota as an example of how companies can change their future.

Toyota follows all the guidelines of Kaizen strictly. In fact, it is one of very few companies in the world where any employee can stop the assembly line abruptly to either correct an error, to solve a problem, or even to recommend the supervisors a new and better way to do something, which can bring down waste and increase efficiency significantly.

According to the story, a lot of managers and Auto-experts visited one of the many factories of Toyota in Japan to see how the workers were able to produce such a large amount of good quality cars with extremely low errors and little to no waste. They found that all this was a result of the Kaizen principles.

Compared to Japanese companies, the American companies, too, were fulfilling their production quota, but they were also committing a lot of mistakes and errors. These errors brought in severe problems such as badly soldered doors, wrong steering wheels, problematic bolts, and nuts, etc. These problems continued to plague the model right up to the last stage of the production. These errors could only be checked and identified in the last stage i.e., QC or quality check. The nature of error then decides whether the car needs to be dismantled again or not. This dissembling and reassembling leads to loss of time, efforts, money, and various other resources. This loss could have been avoided if the mistakes were identified and rectified in the initial stages. Things could have been even better if the mistakes were avoided in the first place itself.

The American experts were able to see the production values and process of Toyota and were shocked to see how efficient and effective it was (and still is.) A common worker cannot stop the production line without the explicit permission of a manager in American companies. Similarly, the concept of rewarding a worker for identifying and correcting an error does not fit in the working culture of the United States of America. The biggest rule that all companies and employees of the companies follow is that the production line should never stop for anything. The show must go on all the time, constantly and continuously. Seeing how the Toyota method was working wonders, the American experts went back and started using similar methods in different companies. They, too, started to reward people who would bring out errors and provide high quality work all the time.

All these principles may sound to be preposterous, but they are a part of the Kaizen philosophy. This theory can really help you achieve great results and can significantly enhance your productivity. For Kaizen, quality is always more important than quantity. Kaizen asks you to find time to identify problems and work on them as soon as possible.

Always remember that Kaizen can really change your life if you are patient enough and try to understand its philosophy carefully.

Chapter Four

Kaizen and Personal Life

Kaizen is easy to understand the philosophy that is focused on one simple aspect 'little things matter a lot'. Kaizen believes that slow and steady wins the race. It believes that with small, gradual, but consistent steps, you can change the world and make it better as compared to rigorous and selective steps that promise immediate change. It is like losing weight; if you try to lose a lot of weight in a little time, you will get sick, but if you do so gradually by taking small steps, you will do it healthily.

The above-stated principle makes Kaizen an easy to follow and apply the method for everyone. It is easy to apply and us in personal life too. In personal life, every person strives hard to improve constantly, and Kaizen can help you do this with a lot of efficiencies. Kaizen can be used for a variety of purposes, including improving health, career, knowledge, relationships, and skills. It is possible to achieve all your goals with the help of Kaizen; you just need to remember to take gradual and small steps. These steps will bring in small changes in your life every day.

As stated in the previous chapter, Kaizen is generally used in the corporate and business world because it can decrease waste and can increase efficiency. But this does not mean that Kaizen cannot be used anywhere else. It is still a highly relevant concept for people who want to achieve their goals and also create good habits that will stay with them forever. Many people around the world have and still use Kaizen for personal growth and development. The Japanese were the pioneers of using Kaizen for personal growth. They used and still use Kaizen to improve their personal lives and grow significantly.

Kaizen is a brilliant way of changing and improving your personal life. According to research, it has been found that almost everyone tries to avoid sudden change. This is natural and has evolutionary relevance. Human beings feel threatened when they are exposed to abrupt changes. They feel mental as well as physical stress due to sudden change. They feel like they want to come back to their original setting as soon as possible. Many times their fight or flight response may get activated too.

While there exist many different methods of utilizing extreme changes to change personal life, these changes need to be studied and planned well. They require a lot of research, discipline, and support. If these ideas do not back them, the changes that take place will be momentary only. A common example of this is people who try extreme diets for quick fat loss. Almost 97% of people who try extreme diets for weight loss fail soon and gain back double the weight again.

This is why Kaizen is so effective as compared to any other management related activities. It can allow you to reorganize processes, people, organizations, etc. It helps you to make slow but steady and smart changes that serve you better in the long-term as compared to haphazard and hasty changes that often lead to more problems.

Kaizen and Perfection

Many people believe that Kaizen is a perfect strategy and that it can work in almost all kinds of scenarios. While it is true that Kaizen has a lot of use in a variety of scenarios and is great for managing organizations and companies, it is still not perfect. A fine line exists in Kaizen when it is used for personal growth. Organizational processes are 'abiotic,' which means they are not affected by emotions. This problem persists with humans, though. They are often influenced by emotions that make practical and simple decisions difficult.

Emotions make us human, but they often lead to other problems too. We like to find comfort when situations get too stressful or troublesome. We like to stay in such situations because they affect us mentally as well as physically. Many times we come across situations that we solve with almost no problem because we are full of ambition, energy, and positivity. When a person is full of these feelings, he can solve even the most difficult situations with ease. If a person lacks these things, then they will find even the most basic of tasks extremely difficult. This is because human beings tend to experience trauma, feel depressed, and often fall prey to diseases as well. These aspects of human life often prevent us from achieving things that we are normally capable of.

We are composed of Yin and Yang, i.e., all of us have our weaknesses and strengths. While we do have some sort of control over ourselves, our strengths and weaknesses, we do not rule them all the time. You may get over your phobia for a while in extreme conditions, but getting rid of it forever is a difficult task.

It is necessary to understand that taking small steps is much better than taking hasty and risky big steps. You may indeed face some problems in the beginning while taking small steps. You may even see problems while taking the small steps, but these small steps will surely provide you with a good result in the long-term. As long as you persevere and continue to improve yourself, you will surely be able to achieve great success in your life.

One of the best examples of how little changes and things matter a lot is related to muscle memory. Weightlifters and similar professionals often get injured due to a lot of different factors. When they are injured, they have to stop their regular workout. As soon as they stop working out, they start to lose a lot of muscles. This may seem to be quite a drastic thing, but these professionals gain all their muscles back as soon as they start working out again. This is because their body, especially their muscles, form memories of their own thanks to the years of training. They become so accustomed and well adapted to the workout regimen that the body recovers them swiftly. It is the same with habits, which is why people say old habits never die. Habits rarely change because our brain memorizes them efficiently. They are hammered down on the brain little by little, which makes them fix and unremovable.

Like habits, Kaizen is hammered into the brain little by little, which is why it is considered to be one of the best ways of developing one's personality. This is a great philosophy because it can bring down negative types and can enhance good habits. It is said that it takes three weeks or 21 days to form a habit. All good habits need to be developed with time, while all the bad ones need to be discarded over time. You cannot give up habits in a couple of days. Your brain is not like an on-off switch. It needs time and patience to change habits and other factors. This is why it is recommended to use Kaizen to change things around.

It is necessary to remember that changing oneself is not a cakewalk. You need to be dedicated and bold. You also need to be ready for all the challenges that you may or may not have to face. Many times, people tend to fail or go back while trying to change their habits. This is normal and is bound to happen. Each little step that you take will make a significant difference. The habits that you will develop by making small and gradual changes in your life will stick with you. Whenever you feel that you are a failure or you find yourself backtracking, relax, and think about the achievements that you gained, thanks to these simple changes. Keep pushing and keep on hanging in there; Kaizen will surely bring you all the success that you have always wanted to have.

Kaizen and Difficulties of Day to Day Life

As stated earlier, Kaizen is one of the best and ideal strategies to gain long-term success and development. Hasty and haphazard decisions and changes can lead to various problems, such as negative development. Negative progress is a fact in life that everyone has to come across at least once. If you cannot avoid negative progress, you should try to see how to handle it efficiently so that you do not lose all your positive progress too. Another problem that is commonly associated with negative progress is the feeling of disappointment and dejection. This disappointment can even make some people give up. Giving up is never an option in the Kaizen philosophy. To avoid giving up, the best method is to find short-term support.

For instance, many people try to cut down on junk food or sugar but find it impossible to do. This is a normal problem that a lot of people have to face. Many people fail to follow through their resolution. It is possible to avoid these problems and avoid eating junk food or sugar successfully. Whenever you feel the cravings for junk food or sugar, drink a diet soda instead. Yes, diet soda, a lot of harmful additives too, but with the time you will notice that your desire to eat sugar has gone down. You will see that your habit of eating sugar or junk food frequently will go down. When you see the habits changing, change the diet soda to some other food such as low-sugar sweeteners or low-fat alternatives of popular snacks. You will soon be able to change to green tea, albeit gradually. This shows that taking slow and gradual steps will take time, but the results achieved from this method will last long and will not vanish in a day or two.

This shows how Kaizen can really help you quit bad habits. You can improve your habits forever by taking small, gradual, and deliberate steps. If you try to cut sugar from your diet abruptly, your body and brain will not be able to adjust and will force you to eat sugar or junk food as soon as possible. Most of the people go on a sugar-free diet start eating it after a week or so. In fact, such people start to binge on sugar thanks to the haphazard decisions. This is why it is necessary to be realistic about your goals and start slow. You need to understand that while diet soda is unhealthy, it is still better than eating sugar or junk food all the time. It is all about choosing the lesser evil whenever possible. Just remember to stay dedicated and disciplined. You will surely be able to tackle all the problems that come towards you with willpower.

Not a lot of people can stay away from junk food or sugar for a long time, especially if the decision was made hastily. If you really want to get rid of these things from your body and life, you need to have some sort of temporary support. Diet soda can act as temporary support in this scenario. It can help you bring down your sugar intake by a significant amount.

Always remember that short-term goals and support can help you in the long-term. They can help you achieve great things, albeit gradually. While doing this, they also change most of the habits for good. These habits will stay with you for a long time, and you will continue to grow and improve as well.

Kaizen and Long-Term Improvement

While kaizen is the best method and tool for everyone who wants to have a long-term change in their life, it has a few problems too. For instance, it's a utility in personal settings. It is reduced as compared to in a professional setting. This is because human beings need to deal with emotions, which companies do not have. This is why it is necessary to understand the limits of the human mind and avoid caving into or getting trapped in certain traps. Understanding the concepts of Kaizen with complete clarity will help you avoid any problems that may arise later. This will also help you develop good habits that will help you achieve your goals with complete passion and strength.

Chapter Five

Using Kaizen to Improve Personal Workflow

Kaizen, as stated in the first chapter, is focused on the growth and development of the people. It is a process-oriented theory that is focused on people and not the end results. It believes in the power of smart work as compared to hard work. Kaizen tries to form the best practices all the time so that people do not have to waste a lot of time later on decision making. While Kaizen is mostly used in the corporate world, it has a lot of use in the individual world as well. It can change the world and life of individuals if used properly. In this chapter, let us have a look at how the Kaizen method and techniques can be used to improve the personal workflow.

Personal Kaizen

Kaizen is a subjective concept that is closely dependent on various inside and outside factors, including the atmosphere, situation, mental and physical condition, etc. This is why each person tends to have a different definition and understanding of Kaizen. Finding your own Kaizen is a journey in itself. This journey needs to be made carefully if you want to follow it successfully.

To find your Kaizen, sit down and relax for a while. Then take a pen and paper and list down all the things and areas in your life that you want to improve. This can include anything from your personal life to your professional life. If you are not sure on which days you want to be more efficient, you can start with a sample day and then adjust accordingly. While making a list of these things, you will soon find out how much time you waste every day on things that are useless or do not help you to develop at all. These things have little to no contribution to your personal improvement. You may find out how much time you are wasting on writing random reports, talking on the phone, replying to random emails, etc.

Sending replies to emails does not sound like a huge job, but you will be surprised to find how much time it takes when you note it down on your list. It often leads to disorganization and a loss of a lot of time. Each email requires at least seven minutes to respond to- one or two minutes to read and understand it and the remaining minutes to think, write, and send the reply. These seemingly inconsequential minutes add up, and you end up wasting a lot of time on things that don't even matter.

Dealing with emails or phone calls becomes an even bigger nuisance when you do it while working. Constant interruptions will damage your focus, and you will not be able to do your work with complete sincerity. To avoid this, the best way is to compartmentalize things. This means that if you have a couple of tasks in front of you, you should do them one by one instead of doing them all at once. So, in the above example, you should get done with the emails first and then go back to whatever else that you were doing. An important principle in the Kaizen theory is to finish the easy tasks first. In this scenario, answering emails is the easier task of the two. Doing the easiest task first allows you to feel elated and provides you with a sense of euphoria that makes you more confident about future challenges. This sense of confidence can help you tackle the more difficult and challenging tasks with ease.

To make the 'emails task' simpler, you can use tabs or folders option available in almost all email clients nowadays. Sort the emails carefully according to the need, urgency, and requirement. Put the emails that need to be replied right away in the 'Important' folder. Emails that are not urgent can be put into the 'Normal' folder. The emails that are not at all important should be trashed right away to save space and declutter your inbox.

To save even more time, you can answer your emails while doing other tasks. For instance, many people tend to answer the most important emails while having coffee in the morning. Later, set 10-15 minutes aside before your lunch and use the time to reply to some more emails. Similarly, before you log-off, reply to the remaining emails for another ten minutes. With the help of this strategy, you will be able to keep your inbox clean and uncluttered so that you will be able to check the new emails as soon as they arrive. This is a simple method that follows the Kaizen principle. Try it out, and you will soon start to see the difference.

While making a list, try to keep things minimal, or it will confuse you.

How to Remove Waste Using Kaizen

One of the most important factors related to Kaizen is that it tries to remove the 'waste' from processes. In the case of factories and assembly lines, waste stands for efforts and resources that go waste. Kaizen in the corporate world promotes proper management of the production process so that the waste can be reduced and ultimately eliminated step by step. The same can be done in your personal life. Reducing and then eliminating waste from your personal life can help you enhance your productivity and maximize your development. It does not need a lot of effort either, so you will not feel tired. Once you get used to this method, you will end up with a lot of extra energy and free time to dedicate toward other important things in your life.

In corporations, waste often includes tasks that are unimportant and lead to a lot of distractions. These tasks include using too much social media, chatting about random things with your colleagues and friends, and thinking about (not replying) emails. These interruptions don't take a lot of time each day, but at the end of the week, they add up to a large amount of time. All of this time is considered to be waste, which can be avoided with the help of Kaizen principles.

An important practice used in the Kaizen process is standardization. In Kaizen, it is necessary to identify problems, solve them, and then standardize the solutions. With the help of this process, you can concentrate on things that are the best for you. You will also be able to plan good things in advance and will be able to follow the plans through. You need to try and learn how to internalize these practices in such a way that they become second nature for you. These practices can save your life when things get too tough and impossible. Just take little steps and change your life gradually. Gradual changes are bound to last forever. You will surely feel grateful to the Kaizen method.

Kaizen to Make Your Life Simple

Kaizen is a system that is focused on improvements, as it believes that results follow improvements automatically. If you want to improve your life and want to make it easy and beautiful, you just need to learn how to apply the system to your life. You can use the Kaizen system to find more time for your favorite activities. It can surely make your life easier if given a chance to do so.

While Kaizen can be used for a variety of purposes, its main function will always be to avoid any kind of overwork. It is a philosophy that helps people relax and work in their own space, taking one step at a time.

Kaizen is a simple organization related system that you can incorporate in your personal life to avoid any significant problems. It is excellent for people who cannot maintain deadlines. You are supposed to make simple and gradual changes, and you will soon start to see how your life is changing for good.

Many times, your daily schedule will be full of activities and tasks, and you often find it difficult or downright impossible to add a new task on your list. Even if you do manage to get the task on the list, it does not mean that you will be able to complete it successfully on time. No one likes to drag around their work and wants to stay free of stress.

If you really want to get over with your tasks as soon as possible, you need to learn how to prioritize things. Think about your duties and try to find which matter the most. This will help you solve your problems quickly, and you will not end up dragging yourself to work every day. This is not a difficult task, and anyone can do it with some proper management. The best way to do this is to perform a weekly review at the beginning of a new week or at the end of the week. This way, you will be able to see what things you spent your time on and whether the time spent was worthwhile or not. Let us now have a look at this method in deep.

Kaizen and Weekly Review
The weekly review is a brilliant method of keeping an eye on what you do with your time and whether you are wasting it or using it for something important.

To do a weekly review, you need to decide a day or time each week where you can sit down and contemplate. You do not need more than an hour or two for this. Just sit down and try to chalk out your next week. Try to focus on things carefully, and do not let anything slip.

This review time can help you understand a lot of things about your week and time. This review time can help you become the manager of your professional as well as personal life. It can help you review a list of people you are supposed to talk to or organize all your tasks, and set up priorities. And, as stated in the last section, setting up priorities matters a lot because it can help you decide what things need to be done first and what things you can ignore for a while.

Do not use this time to work. This is a period reserved only for contemplation and thinking. It is a period where you need to take a step back and reconnect with things. You are supposed to be an executive manager managing your life like a company. Like a regular manager, you need to check your priorities and settle them at the earliest. Do not try to micro-manage things as it will frustrate you.

The Kaizen Weekly review is great because it can provide a lot of benefits to the practitioner. Some of the benefits that this review can provide includes clarity, creativity, and focus. Let us have a look at these three, one by one.

Clarity and Kaizen

The weekly review system can help you achieve a lot of clarity in your personal and professional life. For instance, it can provide you enough time and incentive to clear your inbox and workspace and get rid of inconsequential things and ideas. Once you are done eliminating the waste, you can focus on other, more important projects with total attention. Always try to find out, as soon as possible, what things matter the most and what needs to be done in the next week. Arrange these things on your list according to urgency and priorities. Thus, when the week begins, you will know what you are supposed to do first, and you will not waste a lot of time every day thinking about what to do.

Presence

Always check your calendar from time to time. You may have important meetings in the next week that will bring in a lot of changes in the company, but thanks to the confusion, you forgot to call people for the meeting or clear some doubts regarding it. Here your first priority should always be to call people up and clear all the doubts, if any. Once you start your weekly reviews, you will notice that you do not forget important things anymore. You will also get enough time to think, contemplate, and research over things before important meetings. It will also provide you with ample time to make notes and meet appointments on time.

Creativity

Many times, people want to do something creative like writing a story or working on their blog, etc. but rarely do people find time for these activities. Thanks to the weekly review method, you can find ample time to work on your hobbies and let your creativity reign free. You can be more efficient and effective about including these things in your day-to-day schedule. It is all about managing things properly and prioritizing them carefully. As the manager of your life, you can cut down activities that are useless and do not help you in any way. Spend more and more time thinking and doing things that will lead you towards improvement. Do not wait for life to take a good turn; force it to do so.

Adding Weekly Reviews to the Calendar

Maintain a proper calendar as it can help you avoid a lot of activities that are unnecessary. It will also help you to keep a proper schedule and will allow you to pay proper attention to the important things.

Do consider adding the 'Weekly Review' to your calendar. Remember, you are the manager of your life, so choose a day that you find the best for you. It does not matter whether it is a weekday or a weekend. It can be any day as far as it is convenient for you. Add this day to your calendar as the weekly review day. Along with the weekly review day, keep on adding little tidbits throughout the week to keep yourself focused. If you wait for the weekly review day every time, you may start to lose focus. Always try to maintain your schedule as it can make or break your professional as well as personal life.

A lot of people choose Fridays as their weekly review day. You can choose any time for this review, but evenings are often the most suitable. You may find it difficult to follow the review day in the initial stages, but with the time, you will form a habit and will be able to manage your weeks with ease.

In the initial stages, you will need around a couple of hours to do your weekly reviews. This is because the brain is not used to thinking like this, especially in the case of personal life. With practice and patience, you will be able to finish the weekly review in 30 minutes after the first few weeks. Do not forget to do it regularly, and you will soon start to see the difference.

Kaizen and Pareto Principle
The Pareto Principle or the 80/20 Rule is a good strategy that can help you become happier and more productive. It is a technique based on the Kaizen philosophy. Many people around the world use this method for their improvement and development.

This principle was first introduced by Joseph Juran, a famous management theorist. This theory was inspired by the works of Vilfredo Pareto, the world-famous Italian economist. He was the first person to observe that almost 80% of the total profit in Italy goes to only 20% Italians. He observed that this phenomenon was highly common because a significant part of the results in any possible scenario can be decided by at least 20% of all the causes.

If statistics are considered, according to the 80/20 principle, 80% of the total results are a result of 20% of input. This rule is considered to be true, but in a lot of cases, the ratio is different and much higher. In reality, the ratio can be as high as 1/99.

It hardly matters which ratio you decide to use. You just need to understand that certain parts and activities of your life are more responsible and important as compared to any other, and they have the most significant effect on your life, your happiness, and the outputs of your life.

It does not matter which numbers you choose to follow or use; the biggest thing that you always need to remember is to be happy.

The 80/20 principle is applicable to almost all fields in a person's life, including the financial field as well. You can put in 20% efforts and activities and can steal reap a lot of benefits. A large number of activities that you do in a week can really shape your income.

Example of the 80/20 Rule
There are many commonplace examples available in day-to-day life that show how the 80/20 principle works. For instance, the

distribution of wealth and resources in today's world can be explained using this principle. It is estimated that only 20% of the total world population controls the biggest chunk of resources and wealth. Similarly, in a regular company, 20% of managers are in control of 80% of the employees. The 80% are responsible for the output that the company produces, but without the 20%, they cannot create anything. It should be noted that these are not hard and fast rules, and they can change according to the situation. The number is just a rough estimate. Not all companies are the same. Similarly, no two individuals or their lives are similar either. There exists no 'one size for all' principle that can be applied to every company, individual, or situation.

Even in personal life, you can find many different situations where the 80/20 principle works. Just look at your daily habits, and you will see how relevant the 80/20 principle is. For instance, while our phonebook is often full of contacts, we only call or contact a select few of them regularly. Similarly, we spend a lot of money on just a few things, such as food, mortgage, rent, etc. Even socializing can fall under this rule. While everyone knows a lot of people, they tend to socialize with only a select few regularly.

Living the Principle

Once you start looking at your life as elements/sections, you start to realize how omnipresent the 80/20 rule is. You can use this principle for your own benefit. You need to try hard and find out which factors are responsible for your happiness. Then, work on these factors in a cumulative way so that you do not end up wasting time or resources. Harmony is essential as it allows you to focus on multiple things together without any problem. Do not waste your 80% time of things that do not matter or provide little to no satisfaction.

The moral of the 80/20 principle is easy; you just need to focus on the activities that will help you grow and develop and will ultimately lead to your happiness and pleasure. This should be your motive in personal as well as professional life. For a lot of people 'what they like' and 'what they do for money' are two extremely distinct things that exist in two different planes. This is why many rich people end up feeling miserable because they do not enjoy what they do for money. If this is the case with you, you can use a combination of the Pareto Principle along with Kaizen to solve this problem step by step. Do not make any drastic decisions, or you may end up feeling even more miserable.

'Struggling artist' is one of the most commonly used tropes in TV, cinema, media, etc. but real-life 'struggling artists' exist too. These people are creative, who either act, paint, write, or create something. The only difference between established artists and struggling artists is that struggling artists are undiscovered. They often have to work long hours doing horrible jobs. They often work in retail and hospitality, waiting for their big break. This break does come for some people, but for others, it never does. The ratio of artists who become successful and known for their art can be explained using the Pareto Principle, which is why only a few handful artists succeed in breaking the wall while most of the others fail and stay miserable.

It is the same with entrepreneurs. Many talented businesspeople often get stuck in irritating, boring, and menial day jobs where they cannot explore their creativity. Most of these people are not passionate about these jobs, so they rarely put their 100% in them. Instead of these jobs, if these people had better opportunities to prove themselves, they could have changed the world. Yet, not everyone can escape this triviality of life. It is an unfortunate reality that a lot of people have to face. Thousands, perhaps millions of people are doing jobs that they do not like or are not interested in or are not passionate about. They spend the after-work hours dealing with the things that they enjoy. In most cases, the work is so consuming that they rarely find time to do things that they like. Only a small percentage of people can live and fulfill their dreams as per their wish. If you want to be one of these people or at least want to change your life for good, the Kaizen and Pareto Principle will surely help you.

Material Things vs. Passion

There exists a huge difference between material possessions and passion, but the one thing common about both of them is that not everyone has them. Not everyone can be a brilliant and world-renowned artist. Similarly, not everyone can become a wealthy person. This does not mean that you should give up and should not try for these goals. Instead of just focusing on these goals, you need to start working in a smart way so that you end up improving yourself. It will bring you great joy and satisfaction. This is the Pareto Principle method based on Kaizen principles. Improving one's life is important because improving one's life improves your opportunities. You get more chances of becoming an entrepreneur or a popular artist if you continue to grow. This happens because while developing yourself, you also develop your best qualities that reflect on your work.

The process of improving yourself is an easy one. Let us have a look at this process in detail.

The first thing that you need to learn about improving yourself is to find out what your true passion is. This is the first and perhaps the most difficult step of all, as it requires preciseness and contemplation. Many people think that they are passionate about a lot of things, but finding something that interests you the most can be quite difficult. If you are one of such people who have a lot of hobbies or interests but are not sure which one of them counts as a passion, then your first step needs to be to contemplate. Introspect and try to find what you don't like. Continue this, and with the help of the 'elimination' process, you will end up with a handful of choices. Continue doing this, and you will soon find out your passion.

Once you find your passion, you need to learn how to prioritize things. Here Kaizen is essential. Manage your week carefully and observe how much time your waste is doing menial jobs that can be done quickly. Prioritize such jobs and get done with them quickly. This will allow you a lot of time to follow your dreams. Remember, in Kaizen; it is always better to get done with difficult and boring jobs as soon as possible.

Kaizen and Busy Bee

Not everyone can find free time in his or her life. Kaizen can help you find a lot of free time in your day-to-day life in a practical way, but these principles ask you to find separate time from your work. This time is used to contemplate and think over matters that will help you develop and improve. In Kaizen, it is necessary always to remember the core values and principles even when you are working. You are not allowed to get too absorbed in work, as it can lead to sulking. You may even end up losing essential and vital things.

In Kaizen, you are supposed to observe things. For instance, if you see a leaking faucet or a report (done by someone else) full of mistakes, then instead of ignoring them, you should do something about them, even if it is not your job. Not everyone will be comfortable with this in the beginning, but the more you practice, the better results you will begin to see.

One of the biggest advantages of Kaizen is that it provides you with a sense of ownership and authority over your job/career. In Kaizen, it is believed that you should feel engaged and passionate about your work right from the initial stages. It also believes that people need to do everything in the realms of possibility to make their service or product the best. It does not matter what position you hold; you should always want your company to provide excellent service or create world-class products all the time. This way, not only will the company succeed, but you will continue to grow personally.

Thinking like this can be especially difficult in the initial stages if your job keeps you isolated or if you do not feel engaged in your work. In such cases, a sense and desire for reward will keep you working. It will enhance your motivation. If you do not feel motivated now, try to find ways that will help you feel motivated. If you still cannot find the motivation, then perhaps you are in the wrong career.

The second most important principle of Kaizen is to reduce the 'waste' as much as possible. Waste refers to a lot of things, including wasted resources, wasted energy, wasted time, etc. It also includes wasted effort. Waste comes in many forms, shapes, and sizes. For instance, writing random reports that no one will ever read, or holding meeting that has little to no use are some classic examples of waste. Instead of wasting time in such useless endeavors, you can use this time properly and focus on things that are actually important.

An employee should always work smart and try to find new and better ways to do his or her job. Meetings are unavoidable, but this does not mean that they need to be inconclusive and excessively stretched all the time. Similarly, status reports are a necessity. Still, if you find that it is possible to do away with a particular report or a meeting, it is recommended to avoid it. Try to find a way to offload or automate them. Or you can find another person who will do it for you.

If you get a lot of emails and managing your inbox takes at least half of your day, then you are in trouble. You are wasting a lot of precious time that could have been used for much better purposes. Try to look out for systems or software that will automate the process. This way, you will just need to observe the system from time to time and check out the essential only. This will save a lot of time and effort and reduce a lot of waste. Always keep an eye on the watch and see whether you are wasting your resources or are doing something worthwhile.

It is simple to do things as they come and fulfill your duties likewise. This may sound soothing and relaxing, but it does lead to a lot of waste. You should not think about passing the day; instead, think about utilizing it and growing. As stated above, you should always try to find better ways to do things and do your job. While looking for better ways to do your job, you should also try to learn new tips and skills. This way, you will continue to grow and will be able to achieve goals that will bring real change in your professional as well as personal life. The best thing about this will be that you will be able to save time and resources. With all the extra energy, time, and money, you will be able to do things that you have always been interested in.

You may find it difficult to follow Kaizen in the initial stages but continue to persevere, and you will surely see success.

In the next chapter, let us have a look at how you can achieve goals with the help of Kaizen.

Chapter Six

Goals – How to Achieve Them

As stated above, Kaizen is a people-oriented philosophy, as it believes that more you concentrate on people and improve the better results, you will get. This does not mean that you can't use this principle for personal growth and achieving your goals. The SMART method is one of the many ways of achieving goals. These same principles can be used in personal life to grow, develop, and prosper.

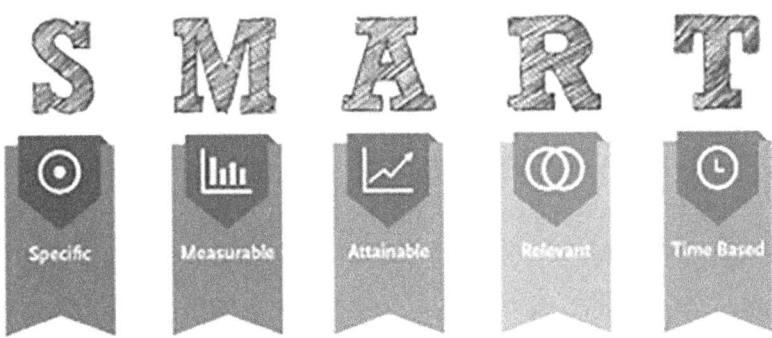

SMART Goals

How to Have Achievable Goals

Goals are important if you want to succeed in your life. You may spend your whole life looking for things and never achieving anything worth achieving if you do not set up goals.

People who do not have goals often feel like they work extremely hard, but still, nothing goes on in their life. They may often see some sort of improvement or development in their achievements, skills, and life, but nothing comes out of it. Such people often find it difficult to know what to do and how to fulfill their ambitions over time. All of this happens just because people do not have a proper goal.

A lot of people nowadays tend to spend their life going from one job to another and moving from places frequently. Some try to rush around all the time, but the amount of trouble and stress that they put in is too much compared to the results. These people do a lot of hard work but accomplish little to nothing. For such people, one of the major Kaizen techniques is the SMART goal technique. SMART goals are goals that are clear and allow you to use your resources and time productively. They allow you to focus on the efforts and thus enhance the chances of being successful and achieving what you want and why.

This chapter will focus on this methodology and will try to answer all the necessary and relevant questions related to this topic and will teach you how you can become a better person and achieve your colas using.

What Does SMART Mean?

SMART is an acronym that covers essential principles of goal setting and fulfillment. SMART stands for:

SPECIFIC (Sensible, simple, significant.)

Measurable (Motivating, Meaningful.)

Achievable (Attainable, Agreed)

Relevant (Realistic, reasonable, result-based, resourced)

Time-bound (Time-limited, time-based, timely, cost limited, time-sensitive)

It has been noted that the definition of SMART needs to change and should be adapted according to the needs and requirements of the situation. It needs constant updating according to the requirements of the individual. This updating can keep it efficient and worth using. Another thing that can be done is to make the acronym longer. For instance, certain researchers now use SMARTER, which includes Evaluated and Reviewed along with the traditional words.

How to Use SMART

The biggest challenge that people face while striving for success is an attitude problem. If you want to be successful, you need to feel 'successful.' Your attitude can help you become more confident, bold, and hardworking. It can influence your overall personality and can help you achieve goals that would have been otherwise difficult. Let us now have a look at each individual aspect of the SMART acronym. All these aspects are necessary, and they can help you achieve your goals with efficiency.

Specific

Your goals need to be specific and clear. This clarity is essential. If you are not clear about your own goals, you will not be able to focus on them. Similarly, you will not be able to focus on the process of achieving these goals. Being clear about your goals also makes you feel motivated and strong. When you are setting up a goal, do not forget to ask yourself these questions:

- Why is this goal crucial?

- What do I want to achieve from this goal?

- Where is this goal located?

- Who are the other people involved in this goal?

- Who is involved?

- Which resources or limits are involved?

Example

Picture it, you are a marketing supervisor, and you want to become the head of the department. Your goal, in this case, needs to be, "I want to gain the level of experience and skills that are required to become the head so that I can lead my team towards success and become successful in my career too."

Measurable

Many people confuse goals for dreams. Dreams can be unreal, but goals need to be realistic and measurable. This way, you will be able to track them and track your progress while achieving these goals. It is necessary to track your progress, as it will keep you motivated and focused. It will also allow you to meet your deadlines. The excitement of reaching close to your goal cannot be expressed in words and can only be experienced.

To check whether your goal is measurable or not, ask yourself the following questions:

1. How many?
2. How much?
3. How will I know whether I have accomplished it or not?

Example

Continuing with the last example, you can check to measure the progress by checking whether you have achieved enough skills or not. This can be checked by checking how many training courses you have done. Another aspect that can help you measure your progress in this example is the amount of your experience.

Achievable

Goals should always be attainable and realistic; otherwise, you will never be able to achieve them. Your goals should always stretch your abilities, but they should always be realistic. They cannot dwell in the realm of fantasy. Once you set an achievable goal, you will be able to see the opportunities that you once overlooked. Similarly, you will find resources that can bring you close to the goal.

You should ask the following questions to judge whether your goals are realistic or not:

- How realistic is the goal of financial, physical, and mental levels?
- How can I accomplish this goal?

Example

You need to question whether it is possible to develop your skills in such a way that you will be able to become the head of the department. You can ask questions such as whether you have ample time to finish your training. Do you have the resources to develop your skills? Are you financially stable to afford these things?

Tip

Sometimes we tend to set goals that are not under our control or power. For instance, one of the most commonly set goals is "Getting a promotion." This is a brilliant goal, but if you check the fine print, you will notice that others control it. Only your boss can promote you. Instead of setting a goal like this, you can word it like "Get training and experience that will make me suitable for the promotion." This framing will help you set up a goal that is under your control and attainable.

Relevant

Relevancy is an important factor while setting up a goal. Your current goal should be relevant to your life and your other goals too. Everyone needs some sort of assistance and support while attaining their goals, but do not forget that it is your goal, and it needs to be under your control all the time. Ask for help from others, but don't forget that you are supposed to be responsible for your goals, and only you should achieve them.

Questions for Relevant Goals:

- Is this goal/process worthwhile?
- Is this the right time for this?
- Does this goal match with other goals?
- Is it suitable for the current situation?
- Am I the correct person to achieve this goal?

Example

You will need to develop your skills to become the head of the department, but ask yourself whether it is the right time to do so and whether you will be able to undertake the training and responsibilities. Similarly, ask yourself whether you will be the right person for the position? If you are married or are with a partner, consider their goals too. While setting up goals, never think in a vacuum, or you may end up feeling miserable.

Time-Bound

Each goal needs to have a target date. This target date will provide you with a deadline that will keep you focused and attentive. This will allow you to focus on your task only. It is necessary to prioritize the task so that other everyday tasks do not take it over.

- Time-bound Goal Setup Questions:
- What can I achieve in the next six weeks?
- What can I achieve in the next six months?
- When?
- What can be achieved today?

Example

It takes a lot of practice, skills, dedication, and hard work to become the head of any department. Do you need to ask yourself how much time will require to achieve these skills? You also need to check whether you need further training so that you can become eligible for important exams and such. Be realistic about your goals, and realistically frame them as well. This will help you achieve small goals step by step so that you will be able to achieve your ultimate goal.

Benefits and Drawbacks

SMART is a great tool to achieve focus, clarity, and motivation. These factors are necessary if you want to achieve your goals. SMART also helps you to reach your goals by encouraging you and allowing you to set up a personal deadline and specifications of your objectives. SMART goals are easy to set up, and anyone can use them almost anywhere. You do not need any kind of special training or tools to do so. Along with many different pros of the system, there exist certain cons as well. For instance, there exist multiple variants and interpretations of the system. This means, if a person misunderstands the process, they may end up using a very ineffective and inefficient version of the method. Many people think that the SMART method does not work for long-term goals, as it does not have the flexibility that is required for such goals. Similarly, some people believe that the SMART method can hinder creativity. These beliefs can hinder the process of setting up a goal and achieving it.

Key Points

SMART is a well-renowned method of setting goals and planning things accordingly. It can surely help you achieve your goals with ease if you know how to set it up carefully. There exist many different variations of the acronym, but just remember to follow the five basic goals:

- Be specific

- Choose a measurable goal

- Choose an achievable goal

- Choose a relevant goal

- Keep it time-bound

Following these five goals to the T will help you set up meaningful, clear, and attainable goals with ease. You will be motivated and will be able to develop action plans without any problem.

Apply This to Your Life

All of us have certain dreams that we want in our lives but cannot achieve them thanks to a variety of problems. For instance, many people want to travel the world but cannot do it because they are busy with their duties or other multitudes of reasons. You often try to convince yourself that you will do it next year because you do not have time or money this year. This soon forms a cycle, which keeps on repeating itself endlessly.

Suppose you find yourself stuck in this cycle, set up SMART goals, and make your plans according to the five goals theory. You will soon realize the real reason why you avoid traveling is vague or even unrealistic. Think about your life and how you can readjust it to achieve your goals.

Everyone has dreams that they want to achieve, but many times it is difficult to achieve them due to a lot of constraints. Fulfilling these dreams require a plan that needs to be precise and accurate. You need to follow it carefully, and soon you will see a huge difference in your life. The best way to create a plan and follow it to achieve your goals is the SMART goals method.

As explained above, the popularity of the SMART goals method continues to grow every day. Many new and old companies now use the SMART method. Similarly, many individuals have started using this method to achieve great success in their personal as well as professional life. The SMART goal method can really change your life with the help of Kaizen.

What are SMART Goals?

As explained earlier, SMART goals are like stable targets that you plan to gain over a certain period of time. These goals can be drafted by anyone. In personal life, they are generally drafted by the person himself. These goals need to be followed carefully as they will help you achieve maximum success. SMART is an acronym that covers all the five important goals i.e., "specific," "measurable," "attainable," "relevant," and "time-bound." Whenever you create a SMART goal, it is necessary to remember to put in all the five characteristics in the goal. This way, you will stay focused, and you will surely be able to fulfill the goal. Writing a SMART goal may seem to be a difficult task in the beginning, but with practice and precision, you will be able to write proper goals with ease in no time. You just need to understand the basic theory of the method, and you will be good to go.

You can learn a lot of things about yourself and your life while setting up new goals according to the SMART method. These new lessons can help you become a better version of yourself, and they can make you a more happy, complex, and clear-minded person.

- How to Make a Smart Goal
- Always use proper and specific words
- Always aim for measurable goals

- Always try to keep your goals realistic

- Keep the goals relevant to your personal and professional life

- Make the goals time-bound so that you know when to finish them.

Mistakes of SMART Goals

Vagueness

One of the biggest mistakes associated with SMART goals is vagueness. The first principle of SMART Goals is specificity. When you keep your goals vague, they tend to be open-ended. Open-ended goals can be quite confusing, especially for team-oriented events. Instead of setting up goals such as "I will become a better reader this year," set up a goal like, "I will read at least 20 books this year." This removes the random vagueness from the goal and makes it much more concrete.

No KPIs

This is similar to vagueness. Success is often measured in qualitative terms and not in quantitative terms. It is difficult or almost impossible to measure and track progress using qualitative terms. To measure the progress, you need to use some sort of quantifiable KPI. This means instead of setting up goals like. Try to measure everything in percentages or numbers. This will help you understand your current position and will help you track it as well.

Unattainable Goals

It is always better to dream big, but this does not mean that you should set up goals that cannot be achieved or are too deep-set in fantasy. You should always strive to improve, but do not choose goals that are impossible to achieve; otherwise, you will never be able to reach your mission. Always choose realistic goals that can be attained within the stipulated time. Excessively difficult or downright impossible goals will only lead to frustration and sadness. Remember the principle of Kaizen - slow, small, and gradual steps will help you to achieve great success in life.

Losing Sight

Always keep a close eye on what you want to do and what your ultimate goal is. Do not lose sight, or else you may end up being stuck in a never-ending loop. Keep the focus on your target and continue to move in the direction carefully while taking small steps. Do not make any haphazard or hasty decisions as it may lead to a lot of problems later. It is better to stay calm and take gradual steps.

No Time Frame

When you decide to have a goal, you need to have a proper timeframe as well. Without a proper timeframe, it is impossible to focus on the goal. Without a timeframe, your goals will continue to shift, and you will find it difficult to stay on track. Keeping your priorities straight is important as it keeps you focused. Having a deadline will also keep you motivated, and you will continue to strive hard to achieve success.

SMART Goals - Example

In this section, let us have a look at some SMART goals that will give an idea on how to set up goals that will help you become 'smart.' Each of these goals is divided into SMART sections so that you will be able to understand the intricacies carefully.

Blog Traffic Goal

Specific: Be specific about increasing the traffic of your blog by increasing posts. You can publish around 5-8 posts per week. Each blogger and editor will increase his or her duty so that the blog grows well.

Measurable: A 7% increase in traffic.

- Attainable: The blog traffic needs to increase 5% by the end of the month. This is thanks to the increase in the frequency of publishing.

- Relevance: As soon as the blog traffic goes up, the awareness regarding the brand will go up as well. This, in turn, will increase the number of leads and will provide you with more opportunities for sale.

- Time-Bound: End of the month.

- SMART: By the end of the month, the blog needs to have a total of 7% growth in the traffic. This is done by increasing the frequency of posts.

Facebook Video Views Goal

Specific: You want to increase the number of views for your videos by focusing on only five topics instead of spreading yourself too thin.

Measurable: 20% in the traffic.

- Attainable: Once the number of topics is reduced, you will be able to focus on the remaining topics with more attention. This way, you will be able to create more relevant and interesting content that will surely get you traffic.

- Relevance: Increase in the number of vies on video will enhance your social media presence. It will help your brand grow and may invite many more new, potential customers.

- Time-Bound: In 4 months

- SMART: In 4 months, the Facebook page will grow and will attract 20% more viewers on the video. This will be done by cutting down the number of topics and focusing only on the main and relevant ones.

Email Subscription Goal

Specific: You want to increase the number of email subscribers by increasing the budget for Facebook advertising and creating ads regarding posts that have brought in a lot of subscribers in the past.

Measurable: A 45% increase.

- Attainable: Once this tactic begins, you will see a lot of growth in the number of email subscribers.

- Relevance: A growing number of email blog subscribers will bring in a lot of traffic towards the blog and will enhance brand awareness. It will bring in new leads and increase sales.

- Time-Bound: 3 months

- SMART: In three months, you will see a 45% increase in the number of email subscribers. This will be achieved by increasing the budget of Facebook Ads.

Webinar Sign-up Goal

Specific: You want to increase the number of subscribers for your webinar. This needs to be done by promoting the event using email, social media, and blogs.

Measurable: A 20% increase in the total number.

- Attainable: By promoting the webinar, you will be able to see at least a 10% growth in the number of subscribers and sign-ups.

- Relevance: More attendees mean more leads, and more leads mean more opportunities for sales.

- Time-Bound: By the day of the webinar.

- SMART Goal: By the day of the webinar, you plan to have a 20% increase in the number of subscribers. This will be achieved by promoting the event through blogs, social media, email, etc.

Landing Page Performance Goal

Specific: By switching the format of the blog to two columns from one column, you plan to get more leads.

Measurable: A 25% increase.

- Attainable: A new column design is bound to perform better as compared to a traditional one. You will surely see ample growth in your blog. You will be able to get more subscribers and leads when you change the format of your blog. It will be more peppy, relevant, and oriented towards the goal.

- Relevant: Getting more leads can increase the number of customers. It will also improve brand value.

- Time-bound: 12 months

- SMART: In 12 months, the landing page will start to create more leads. This is done by changing the format to two-column as compared to the traditional one column.

Link-Building Strategy Goal

Specific: You want to grow the traffic of your website organically with the help of a new link-building strategy through which other publishers will be able to link with the site. This will enhance SEO results and will create more organic traffic.

Measurable: 30 Backlinks

- Attainable: There are many low-quality links that direct to the homepage of the website. These links do bring in a lot of organic visitors to the website. This can be increased significantly if the website is linked to better websites. This way, you will be able to get more and more organic visitors every day.

- Relevance: Organic traffic is one of the best ways to get good leads. Backlinking is a good way of generating organic traffic. With the help of backlinking, you will be able to improve your presence in the search result of various reputed search engines such as Google, Yahoo, etc. Backlinking can become even more effective when the links are present on good and high-quality websites.

- Time-Bound: 4-6 months

- SMART: Over the next six months, you will get new backlinks that will be linked to the homepage of the website. To achieve this, the PR team will talk about collaborations with these websites to formulate a good and efficient strategy that will bring good fortune to all the parties involved.

Tips and Tricks

There exist many different methods of establishing SMART goals. Many people generally only establish three goals at a time, one for the mind, one for the body, and one for the lifestyle. Even though people establish only three goals, they still tend to fail. This is because people tend to set extremely visionary goals that are difficult and sometimes even impossible to achieve.

The main thing that you need to remember while setting up goals is that they need to be realistic and attainable. Do not go around setting goals that you cannot achieve. Always have a proper direction and take slow steps towards it. Concentrate on one goal at a time. Remember, Kaizen is all about smart work and not hard work. You will soon start to notice a difference within a couple of weeks. You will be able to notice a positive change happening in your overall lifestyle. By focusing on one goal, you can stay motivated and keep the distractions away. Even if you manage to get distracted, you will always be able to go back to the original goal in no time.

Your personal Kaizen plays a big role in this process. Remember that Kaizen is all about personal growth and daily development. You need to focus on these things so that you will continue to grow and develop every day. Even if you feel tired or burnt out, you will still be able to stick to the goals thanks to your personal Kaizen. Just continue to be dedicated and stay focused on your habits; you will surely continue to grow.

Once you have established a proper SMART method, you can start using the Kaizen principle to keep yourself focused and motivated. Work hard every day and rest at night with full satisfaction. As you already know what you are supposed to do on a particular day, you will be able to put in a lot of effort into it. This will help you stay motivated. You will feel proud of your work. Contentment is a necessary feeling that instills confidence in you. Remember to be dedicated, and it will surely keep you happy.

After a few months, you will be able to see how much you have achieved in the past few days. It will surely help you stay focused.

Kaizen and Perfectionists

Perfectionist people may find it difficult to stick to the Kaizen routine. Perfectionist people may face certain barriers that may stop them from achieving their goals. Perfectionist people find it extremely difficult to do anything if they cannot do it perfectly. Perfectionist people often tend to set up goals that are extremely difficult to achieve. These people are too ambitious, which is why they often suffer while following the Kaizen regime.

While many perfectionists find it difficult to follow the Kaizen regime, it is still the most perfect and best tool for them. Instead of setting down unattainable goals, perfectionists should set up simple goals that can be achieved with ease. They can also break down a large goal into multiple pieces and set a lot of smaller goals instead. If you are used to making annual goals, set up monthly goals instead. Similarly, if you are more accustomed to setting monthly goals, set up weekly goals instead. Keep a clear picture in your mind and only focus on the things that you want to do in the stipulated time.

For instance, if your goal is to lose weight in a few months, chalk out how many hours do you want to spend for it in the stipulated time. Then create a schedule and try to follow it carefully. Track your progress regularly using a tracker or a notepad. Tracking your goals and progress will help you stay focused and motivated. Divide your goal into multiple smaller goals and achieve them one by one.

If you want to get rid of debt, you should plan your months accordingly. Focus on the payment and try to reduce your spending as much as possible. Pinch your pocket, and do not be a spendthrift. Monitor your expenses carefully and note them down in a notepad. Do this for a couple of weeks until you form a habit. Do remember the SMART method and follow it to the T.

Perfectionists tend to give up on things when they realize that they cannot be perfect about something. Do not give up if you ever feel like giving up. Seeking perfection is a good trait, but if this search is hindering your progress, then it is better to get rid of it. Everyone fails, and everyone commits mistakes. You cannot avoid it. In fact, you should try to learn from your mistakes and try not to repeat them again. Making mistakes is a perfectly natural part of being a human being, but what Kaizen can do for you is that it can help you avoid gigantic and costly mistakes. It can save you from a lot of trouble by keeping you away from haphazard decisions.

Chapter Seven

Habits and Kaizen

Everything goes back to its original state once its work is done. Ice melts to form water again. Water evaporates to form a vapor, the vapor condenses to form water etc. Everything in nature has a tendency to go back to its original state soon. This fact includes human beings, as well. We tend to start things with great pomp, but soon return to the status quo. This includes diets, exercise routines, new hobbies, etc. The beginning of these things is highly celebrated, but once we realize that we are not able to meet the personal goals, we fail. This is because most of the goals set up by people are too ambitious and are difficult to achieve.

While it is true that people fail a lot of time while setting up goals, it does not mean that you should stop setting goals at all. There are many different methods that can be used to set up goals that will help you to stay put the goals and feel confident about them. Setting up goals is a skill that is necessary for everyone. Everyone must learn how to set up goals as they can help you to become a self-reliant and self-sufficient person. If you do not know how to set up goals properly, you can always learn it. It is a skill that develops over time with practice and patience. Keep practicing, and you will surely be able to set up goals that you will be able to follow through.

Many people establish goals all the time, but they are scared because they do not know whether they will be able to fulfill them or not. This sense of self-doubt often leads to the development of problems such as lack of confidence, low self-esteem, and lack of judgment. All these factors come together and break your spirit. Once you lose your spirit, you end up failing miserably at your goal. When you set up a goal, you need to consider the risks involved. You should feel scared about the risks and should be able to face them with full confidence. When you lose your confidence, you come back to the original position, and you start doubting yourself once again. You get scared of whether you will be able to achieve your goal or not or whether the goal itself is doable or not.

Kaizen can prove to be quite beneficial to you in such situations. Kaizen principles can help you to stay focused on the task that you choose to do. It can also help you to stay attentive towards your goal. As the Kaizen method allows you to divide your bigger goal into many smaller ones, it helps you to simplify the otherwise complicated-looking problem. It allows you to take continuous steps one by one and achieve your goal gradually.

Let us now have a look at how you can change your habits using the Kaizen principles.

Examples of Kaizen in Personal Life and Habits

Social Media

Let us assume that you want to reduce your social media presence and reduce the time that you spend browsing on websites such as Facebook and Twitter. It needs to be noted that being on Facebook or similar social sites is not inherently wrong, and in fact, it can have a lot of benefits too. It allows you to connect to your friends and family and allows you to meet new people too. It can also keep you updated about current events happening in the world.

Another common benefit of such social media platforms is that they allow you to express yourself. The only thing bad about social media is that too much of it can take away a lot of important time from your busy schedule. You should never spend hours together browsing through the newsfeed. People tend to waste a lot of hours browsing on Facebook and wasting their time when they can utilize this time on something more momentous. Wasting time on Facebook does not improve your life. Similarly, it does nothing for your development and growth. You may find and read interesting articles on Facebook, but if they do not benefit you personally or do not lead to any kind of development or improvement, they are practically useless. Such reading then ends up being a wastage of time, which is a strict 'no' in Kaizen. So, how to avoid this?

Some people believe taking drastic measures can help you avoid wasting time on Facebook and other platforms. Such people decide to delete their account once and for all and try to enjoy the freedom. Deleting your social media account abruptly may seem like a great decision in the beginning, but you will soon realize that it is not. You start to feel excessively miserable. You tend to miss social media and its adaptability. You may even feel slight anxiety attacks because you will feel that you are missing out on fun and important events in the world. This will leave you feeling sad, and you will soon open another account to get back on social media. Once again, you will start to browse social media for hours together, except this time, this browsing will be accompanied by anxiety and misery. You will feel dejected because you will take this as a failure. Some people may not decide to wallow in the sadness and instead will try to convince themselves hard that they did nothing wrong, and this was the best decision they could make because they were losing on important updates.

If you really want to reduce your social media presence or get away from it forever, the best method for you will be Kaizen. Kaizen believes in taking slow and steady steps. These steps will surely help you to keep focused and will allow you to take a break from social media. Break down your ultimate goal into smaller, easy to take steps. For instance, instead of deleting your account right away, reduce the time you spend on social media by 5-10 minutes every day. This way, you will not have to convince yourself of giving up the whole deal. It will also remove any doubt that you have in your mind about giving up on social media.

Instead of picking up a random, excessive goal, a smaller goal is always better because it is easily achievable. Once you are done with this goal, you can move on to the next goal. For instance, you can bring down the time spent on social media further. Slowly you will be able to wean yourself off the platform and will have a lot more free time to utilize on various developmental and growth-related activities.

Reading Books

Another example where you can use Kaizen in your life is reading. Many people desire to read a lot. Some of them used to read a lot when they were young, but now they don't have the time. Brilliant and attractive books sit on their shelves and bedside tables, collecting dust by the hour. Many people do not even have a significant goal; they just want to read one book per month, which is a simple enough goal. Still, it may remain only a dream for many. Hectic schedule, busy life, etc. are various reasons why people cannot find time to do something worthwhile. In such cases, Kaizen can be your saving grace. Think of reading as a task. Break down your book into multiple sections (if it's not already divided into sections) and read the sections one by one. Do not try to read the whole book in a couple of days; instead, try to read at least ten to fifteen pages every day. If you are a new reader, you may bring down the number even further. Your mind will tell you that reading ten pages a day is nothing, and it will not help you in any way possible. Do not listen to your mind; it is trying to confuse you. Even ten pages a day will help you a lot and will help you change significantly.

You may feel like reading just one book in a month is not a lot, but you will soon realize that even these baby steps will help you significantly at the end of the month. Continue to persevere, and you will soon be able to read more and more books in a few months.

Vacations

Vacations have become commonplace now, and all families try to go on at least one vacations per year. Planning for vacations is not an easy job. It takes a lot of precision and attention to detail, especially if you plan to travel with children. If you find yourself in a lurch while planning for a vacation, use the Kaizen method. Divide the plan into multiple sections and deal with them one by one. For instance, you may divide the vacation in- finance, locations, travel, shopping, eating, etc.

The first thing that you need to focus on is the money. You need to plan how to pay for the trip. Start small, and start saving money week by week for the whole year. This way, you will be able to save a lot of money and will be able to have a decent holiday. Talk to your bank to find out if they have any scheme where a specified amount gets cut from your account automatically to be saved for later. This method can be really beneficial as you would not have to think about it, and the money will be saved automatically. This way, you will be free to do other things and focus on the other parts of the plan.

Whatever your habit may, you need to follow certain Kaizen principles that can surely change your life. These principles are essential and can help you implement and use Kaizen in almost all walks of your life. Let us have a look at these principles one by one.

Break Down the Goals

Always break down your goals into manageable pieces and do not try to tackle the goal as a whole. Breaking down the goal into manageable pieces has a lot of benefits. You can be much more subtle and focus on the details when you break down a goal into pieces. Fulfilling each little chunk will help you feel confident and bold. It will allow you to persevere and focus more. You will not have to spend a lot of energy to fulfill the goals and will be able to finish off the main goal soon enough.

The only problem people tend to associate with this method is that it is slow and takes a lot of time. This is half true. This method does take time, but it also works every time. The results achieved from this method are oftentimes a lot better than jumping into the game right away. Jumping into something in a haphazard manner can lead to a lot of problems. You may lose confidence soon and end up feeling absolutely miserable. Ultimately, you will fail. To avoid this, it is better to take steady, albeit slow steps, which will ensure your success.

Give It Some Time
Many people are not ready to set some ties aside for Kaizen. Time is the biggest resource that anyone of us has, but it is a limited resource as well. It can also cause a lot of hindrances in achieving one's goals if not used correctly. Having a couple of minutes extra can turn your loss into a win. Let us go back to the reading example. Nowadays, many people tend to commute daily for work. If you spend an hour on the train every day, why not use it for something productive instead of staring away at the window or browsing social media? You can use this time to read and improve yourself. Not only will you end up doing something productive, but you will also end up finishing your goal of reading one book a month with ease.

Be Persistent and Think About the Present

Kaizen is not a goal-oriented method; it is a change-oriented principle. It focuses on change and believes that the goal will follow automatically. Kaizen is not an event; it is a process that deals with change. Never focus on the goal while getting into Kaizen, focus on the process instead. You are supposed to build your brain in such a way that it will be receptive to change and can accept it all the time. To do this, you always need to think of the present and not the future. Be persistent while concentrating on your goals. Do not try to focus on random ideas and try not to lose your priorities. Your first goal should always be your development; everything else can follow later.

Believe in Your Vision

The power of the human 'vision' is unlimited. Kaizen has been devised in such a way that it allows you to believe in your vision and teaches you how to achieve your goals by focusing on them. Visualization can help you change the process significantly and can allow you to learn a lot. It can also help you to become a better, bolder, and more confident person.

Remember what you want to achieve in your life with the help of Kaizen. Kaizen is all about creativity. It forces you to look at things from a creative point of view and allows you to look for solutions that may not be visible to people otherwise. Always be constant and consistent about things.

It is necessary to train your brain about achieving your goal. You need to teach it that your goal is attainable, and you can achieve it without failure. In fact, your brain needs to understand that you can't fail, and you are bound to succeed when trying hard along with the steps of Kaizen. Teach your brain that along with the goal, the progress that you gain while moving towards the goal is important as it can help you a lot in your future life.

You will be surprised to see the level of growth that you can achieve just by breaking down your habits in smaller pieces. You will be able to see the changes in your body and mindset quite soon.

Chapter Eight

Kaizen Events

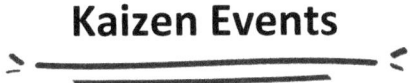

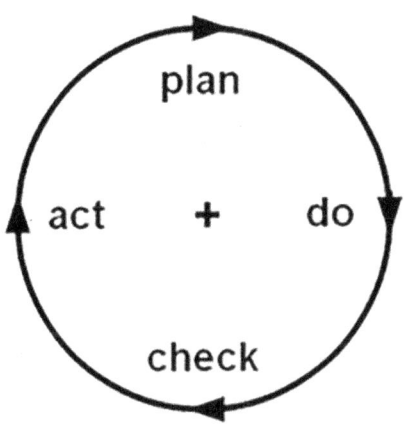

One of the most renowned things related to Kaizen is Kaizen events. These events take place all the time and now have become a staple of many companies. These events are supposed to be short-duration improvement projects that are mainly focused on improvement only. They are generally a week or two long and are led by a person known as a facilitator. The implementation team consists mostly of members from the area in which the Kaizen event is going to happen. Often a few members from event management and other related support area participate in these events too.

These are often seen as one-off events, but they need to become an integral part of all the companies as they teach the most important principle of Kaizen, which is continuous improvement. Only with continuous improvement can a company develop, grow, become successful, and achieve satisfactory results. Many times such events are held at places where Kaizen is not readily accepted, understood, or even supported. In such places to the events provide a lot of help, but as the help is not understood, all the benefits go away in no time, and people once again go back to their original self.

Types of Kaizen Events

Kaizen events are known with a variety of names nowadays, for instance:

- Kaizen Burst
- Kaizen Blitz
- Accelerated improvement events
- Kaizen Workshops
- Focused Improvement Workshops
- Rapid process improvement workshops
- Continuous Improvement workshops etc.

Kaizen events also have targeted workshops, for instances some companies events that target tools like:

- 5S Kaizen

- Setup Reduction Kaizen (SMED)

- TPM Kaizen

- Supply Chain Kaizen

- Value Stream Mapping or Flow Kaizen

Kaizen events may have a lot of different names, but all of them have the same or similar events. They are often structured similarly, too, because they focus on the creativity and ideas of the workforce they work with. These events can serve as the first of many steps towards improvement for you and your business.

A Kaizen event can never succeed unless it is planned properly and is led by a good leader. If any one of these things is missing, the event may prove to be a huge failure. In a failed event, the whole team of participants just stand around together, looking at each other, extremely confused, as they do not understand what they are supposed to do and what this workshop is supposed to do too.

In contrast to this, a successful and properly implemented Kaizen event can help you achieve a lot of growth and improvement in your company. A successful Kaizen event can bring in anywhere between 20% to even 100% improvement in areas including quality, efficiency, and delivery performance. It is recommended to use Kaizen events in various other departments instead of just the production one. This way you can create a lot of savings as well as improvements in many different areas of your company, including the service areas, the management, the manufacturing, etc.

Kaizen events are nothing but small brainstorming and implementation events based on the principles of Kaizen. They are used to improve any current process of procedure that the employees and the employers find outdated or not productive enough. In these events, everyone, including managers, employees, and C level owners, all come together and chalk out the current process and then sit down and discuss how these processes can be worked upon and improved. They try to see what things can be done and what things will be plausible to do.

As stated above, Kaizen events are often marketed as one-time events or one-time solutions for all your ailments. This is a myth. To address these myths, let us have a look at when and how you should use Kaizen events:

Kaizen Events

There exist many different versions of Kaizen, but all of them can be classified into two rough qualities- daily or short-term Kaizen and long-term Kaizen. It is necessary to keep improving your ultimate goal, and improvement can only be achieved with the help of a continuous process. If you continue to grow every day, you will be able to sustain the growth and improvement achieved thanks to the principles of Kaizen. All the Kaizen improvements and methods already implemented need to be revisited from time to time. To do this, short-term Kaizen is necessary. Short-term Kaizen or daily Kaizen is closely related to 'Kaizen culture.' Nowadays, many companies run on a Kaizen culture, which means that they follow the Kaizen principles and employees, managers, etc. all have made these principles a part of their personal and professional life.

Not all changes can happen overnight, and some require a lot more focused and long-term approach. For instance, if you want to have a proper long-term Kaizen event in your company, you need to invest a lot of resources, including employee and manager time. Kaizen events generally run for 3-5 days, where they focus on one targeted process. Normally, a long-term Kaizen event may include the following steps:

- Training
- Define the goals or the problems
- Have a look at the current scenario and document it
- Brainstorming session for development
- Implementing the suggestions
- Creating a follow-up plan
- Displaying the results
- Celebrations

Not all problems require a long-term or a short-term Kaizen event. However, there are certain problems where these methods can serve as the best tool to get rid of the waste and improve the satisfaction of not only the customers but the employers and the employees as well. It thus becomes necessary to check when you need to invest your and your employees' and your organization's time in any Kaizen event.

Many times your company may run into an urgent problem for which a quick and swift decision or fix is required. In such a case, a 'firefighting' mechanism needs to be used. This mechanism consists of quick fixes that can solve the problems instantly. Urgent problems often happen due to the production of defective products, failure in inspection, and a lot of complaints from the users. Such problems require an immediate solution, or they may end up tarnishing the name of the company.

When to Use Kaizen Events

When You Want to Fulfill the Target Goals

Many times your team may become slow and cannot hit the target goals, KPIs, or the strategic goals. This can be especially frustrating when you want to hit the issue quickly. In such cases, a Kaizen event can help you push your team towards the goals and, thus, towards success. This is done by documenting the current process and then comparing it with the new one that you will brainstorm.

When You Have Little to No Daily Improvement

Kaizen events can help you quite a bit when your team gets stuck in the lethargic day-to-day processes that are often uneventful and useless. It is necessary to get your company and team into daily Kaizen events so that you can create a 'Kaizen culture' mindset. This can be done by including them in the process and asking them to change their daily routines for better. Instead of changing the daily routines out of the blue, it should be done step by step. Remember, Kaizen is all about incremental changes that happen gradually over time. These changes will allow them to observe how they are a huge part of the company, and their stake is bigger than what they used to think or believe. This will increase their level of satisfaction. Satisfied employees are better employees.

When You Want to Work with Other Teams
Many times the biggest problem that leads to a lot of dysfunction and confusion is when teams are supposed to work together in collaboration. Every team or department has its own method of working, leadership, and has its own priorities as well. When two or more teams are mixed to work together, it may lead to a lot of confusion and hurt egos. To avoid this, arranging a Kaizen event beforehand with all the teams involved can work wonders. In a Kaizen event, all the involved teams get a well-defined and structured environment with different scenarios where all the team members can put their heads together and brainstorm. They can think over how they can collaborate well and can work towards a common goal with total efficiency. In a company, the production team needs to be on the same page as the shipping and receiving team; otherwise, it may lead to a lot of confusion and missed orders.

When it Has Been Too Long
If you have not had a Kaizen event in a long time, you need to have one immediately. It is quite commonsensical to have frequent Kaizen events, but many companies treat it as a one-time solution, which is why they do it once and then never does it again. This goes against

the basic principle of Kaizen, which is 'continuous improvement.' If you want your Kaizen event to be successful, you need to do it regularly. You need to hone your collaboration skills and sharpen your problem-solving methodologies from time to time. It is recommended to do a Kaizen event whenever you welcome a new member to your team. This will present them with an opportunity to meet everyone, but it will introduce the employee to Kaizen tools and techniques.

How to Use Kaizen Events

There exist no correct way to implement a Kaizen event. There are many techniques and tools that may work the best for your team, but most of these events generally utilize a philosophy and an action plane. Kaizen can be divided into these two categories, Kaizen as an action plan and Kaizen as a philosophy.

Kaizen as an Action Plan

Under this type, a focused event is organized that concentrates on one or more than one specific and targeted areas that the company or organization wants to improve.

Kaizen as a Philosophy

This type is closely related to the 'Kaizen culture' aspect of Kaizen. Instead of just focusing on targeted spots, this method focuses on engaging employees and asking them to suggest, implement, and bring forth new improvements and ideas from time to time. It focuses on creating a 'culture' of Kaizen that is sustainable and will last a long time.

Where to begin then? There are many different ways of how to introduce a Kaizen event. Generally, they are planned with the help of value stream mapping to focus on the areas that are in need of improvements. There are various problems that can be solved with the help of Kaizen events; some of them are given below. It is recommended to crosscheck your problems with these problems to see whether you need a Kaizen event of not. This is not an exhaustive list, and it is possible to have these events for other reasons too.

Why you Should Choose Kaizen

Reducing Changeover time for a process or equipment: With the help of Kaizen, you can bring down the time required for changeover of a process or a piece of equipment. You can improve this time with the help of various Kaizen tools.

- Organize the workplace with the help of 5S.

- Create a Pull System

- Create a one-piece flow work cell

- Enhance the manufacturability of the design of a product

- Improve the development process of a product

- Improve the reliability of equipment with the help of Total Productive Maintenance or TPM

- Improve all other administrative procedures, including the processing of orders, engineering change, procurement, and all other information processing activities and/or paperwork.

Planning a Kaizen Event

It is necessary to check out and define what and where you want to gain from the Kaizen event. This will allow you to understand whether your Kaizen event will be successful or not. Here is a list of some common steps that are frequently used in almost all kinds of Kaizen events. These steps overlap all the time, which is why you need to plan the whole event carefully. Use common sense when you add the details in the plan of your Kaizen event.

Hire or Train Your Facilitator

You cannot have a great and highly successful Kaizen event if you do not have anyone who will lead it with full efficiency. You need to have a good leader or a facilitator who will facilitate the event, and along with a facilitator, you need a team leader or an area manager who will lead these aspects. The leader of the event needs to have proper experience related to lean techniques and related philosophy. They should be experienced and qualified enough to run these events with full efficiency.

The role of a facilitator is crucial as a good facilitator can help the team to stay on track all the time and can enable the team members to move in the right direction, thus achieving the best results possible.

If you do not choose a good facilitator, the Kaizen event will fail as well. You will achieve nothing out of these events. The attendees will be quite confused, and they may even get disheartened with the whole event and may stop participating at all. If you have decided to bring in a new consultant as a facilitator, ask for references and check whether they are really good or not.

Seek Commitment From the Management

You may plan a great Kaizen event, but it will prove to be useless if you do not get the senior management team involved in it. The team needs to support you with a full heart and needs to be involved as well. If the team is not committed to the cause, you will have a very disappointing event with little to no results. In fact, whatever results you achieve will soon slip back once again.

Define the Boundaries of the Event

Kaizen is such an interesting and intriguing philosophy that it is possible to go overboard and try to exceed your expectations. It is necessary to set up boundaries when you decide to have a Kaizen event. This will allow all the participants, departments, and areas to know what they are supposed to focus on. They will know what they are involved in and what their duties are. These boundaries need to be set right in the initial stages of the planning and need to be hammered down throughout the event frequently.

Understand What You Want to Improve

There are many reasons why a company can have a Kaizen event. You must check your reasons and know the purpose of your event. Having a well-defined purpose is like having a well-defined goal. A well-defined goal allows you to focus on things carefully, and you stick to it until it is done. Having a clear idea of what you desire from the event before you even begin, it will keep you, and all the participants motivated. It is necessary to have defined the purpose in at least some basic or general terms. Once that is done, you can then focus on providing more clarity to these goals.

Communication

Everyone in the company should be aware of what you are planning to do and what you are going to do. This is not supposed to be a surprise event. Let the people know and understand what you are going to do and why it's important. If all the crucial details of the event are not shared with the participants, random rumors may start to spread, which may be impossible to control later.

Create Your Team

Kaizen events are supposed to be team events, and without a team, it will be impossible for you to run one successfully. Choose your team wisely. Normally, the team leader is supposed to be the supervisor of the team (exceptions exist according to the structure of the company). It is necessary to check that the team leader is an optimistic and positive person and understands why it is necessary to make improvements. They should not feel threatened because of the improvements and should welcome them with open arms. If they feel threatened, then you perhaps need to find a better leader.

A team should consist of people who work in the area that you plan to improve. Along with these employees, you should add some other employees from departments such as administration, maintenance, and sales. It is also recommended to add a few people from the next planned area for Kaizen so that they will understand the workings of

Kaizen, especially if you have never done Kaizen in your company. They will gain some experience with the Kaizen principles and will be able to share it with their colleagues so that they will be prepared when they come for their Kaizen.

Define and Implement Measures of Performance

It is necessary to be more specific about what kind of improvements you want to have and make so that you will be able to compare them with the current performance levels. This means that if you plan to improve efficiency, you need to collect data about your current performance so that you will be able to compare both the 'before and after' once you are done with the event. This will allow you to see your progress. Some commonly used measures include:

- Space Used
- Output per person/hour
- Lead time
- Travel Distance
- Reject Levels
- Inventory
- Work in Progress

You should also try to shoot some videos or click photographs so that you will be able to compare the before and after properly.

A word of caution: If you want to improve efficiency, you will have to bring down the required manpower too. This might lead to a commotion as your employees may start to believe that they are being laid off. Let them know that they won't be laid off; rather, their duties will be changed. No one will be at risk of losing their jobs. All the persons who are free of certain duties will be used elsewhere or will be provided training for other duties.

Pre-Event Training

Before the event begins, the team needs to be made aware of the seven Mudas or the seven wastes of lean. They should be able to identify these wastes instantaneously.

In this section, let us have a look at these seven Mudas one by one.

The Seven Wastes or Seven Mudas

It is necessary to get rid of the seven Mudas or the seven wastes with the help of the principles of Kaizen, but what are these seven wastes? Before moving on to the description of waste itself, let us first have a look at how you can remember the name of these seven.

There is a simple mnemonic device that you can use to remember all the seven Mudas. Just ask yourself, 'Who is TIM WOOD?' In the above sentence, TIM WOOD stands for

- Transport
- Inventory
- Motion
- Waiting

- Over-Processing
- Over-Production
- Defects

All seven of these are Muda or wastes. It is one of the easiest ways to remember all the wastes. Another acronym that you can use these seven Muda is WORMPIT

- Waiting
- Over-Production
- Rejects
- Motion
- Processing
- Inventory
- Transport

Just use any of these two acronyms, and you will be able to remember all the seven Muda efficiently. These acronyms are especially useful for beginners and teachers who are training beginners. Just write them down on the board and ask them to remember them.

What is Waste?
As stated above, waste is something useless of something that is unimportant and adds little or no value. Customers will never be

happy to pay for something that has no value or add no value to something. Customers know what they want and selling them something that has no value and adds no value either.

For instance, a customer would never want to pay a bill for food he never ordered or consisted of bad ingredients. Customers never pay for errors caused by the service or the company. They would argue and demand a new bill. Similarly, they would never buy a product that has unexplainable costs.

There is a lot of waste of resources that goes on when products are produced. This waste inflates the price of the products, but as customers would never pay these extra costs, the company has to bear them, thus reducing the profit of the company quite significantly.

Why Remove Waste?

A company receives profit by selling products; thus, the selling price of the products is directly responsible for its profit. Many people think that the company can decide their own selling price and can sell products for whatever price they want. This might be true in the case of some luxury brands, but for most companies, this absolutely false. The market and not the company decide the selling price of the products. Too much and too little, both are bad. For instance, if you charge your customers too much, they may find it obnoxious, and they will just pick up a cheaper alternative. Similarly, if the cost is too low, the customers will think that there is something wrong with the product, and they will once again go elsewhere. Ultimately, there exists only one way of improving your profits, reduce your production costs. There are many ways of reducing your production cost, but there are only a few handfuls of ways that reduce production costs without reducing the production value. You cannot expect your customers to buy subpar products at a large price. Ultimately the only way to improve your profits is by reducing the wastage.

Waste is extremely bad for your profits, but it is also bad for the satisfaction of the customers. If you reduce waste, your products will be manufactured in no time. This way, you will be able to save a lot of money on delivery, quality, and for the right price too. This is why it is necessary to get rid of these wastes and make your processes better.

Let us now have a look at these wastes one by one.

The Waste of Transport
Transportation costs you a lot of money and is a waste.

Transport means the movement of materials from one place to another place. Many people feel this is a necessary evil, but it is not, it is a waste that does not add anything to your product. No one should pay anything for an operation that has no value or adds no value to the product.

Transport does not add any value to the product. As a company, you pay people to move material from one place to another, which only costs you money but does not provide you anything in return. This is an excessive waste that can lead to a lot of high costs, which can turn your profit into a loss. This is because you require a lot of people to operate and maintain the transport-related machinery and equipment. The movement is quite expensive and, thus, should be avoided.

The Waste of Inventory

Inventory can keep problems hidden.

Inventory is not free; it costs you a lot of money. Each piece of product that you manufacture has a lot of hidden costs, including raw material, storage, etc. In fact, all the manufactured and non-manufactured goods cost you a lot of money because you need space to store them. Until the product is sold, it costs. This is a pure inventory cost. Along with this, the inventory can have other costs and can lead to the development of other wastes too.

Inventory requires space, and it is necessary to store it. It requires packaging and needs to be moved around i.e., transported. Transport is not always the safest option, and the inventory may get damaged. Damaged goods lose all their value, and they are good for nothing. Thus the waste of inventory has many other wastes hidden deep inside it.

The Waste of Motion

Over or excessive movement or motion of machines and people both are a waste.

Excessive, unnecessary, and too many movements or motions of machines or men are bad and can waste a lot of resources. These motions include feeders being situated the level of feet instead of the waist, etc. If a worker has to bend down constantly to pick things off the ground and then get back and feed the machine, they end up making a lot of unnecessary movements. These are not only bad for the health of the person but also bad for the company because it takes a lot of time to do so. If the feeder and the equipment both are at the waist level of the employee, it will reduce a lot of stress and time, and the process will become a lot more efficient as well.

Similarly, if the workers have to move workstations a lot or the machine has to move too much, it also counts as a waste of motion.

All these motion-related wastes can lead to loss of resources such as money and time, and they can also put a lot of stress on the health of your employees and machines. This will increase the costs for health problems and maintenance of the machine.

The Waste of Waiting
If you can get rid of the waste of waiting, the whole process will become a lot smoother.

Life is all about waiting. We spend months in our lives waiting for answers, people, replies, etc. Even in companies, you have to wait for answers from other departments in the same organization, wait for deliveries from suppliers, or servicemen to fix machines, etc. A huge chunk of our working and personal life is wasted in waiting.

This waste is bad for a multitude of reasons. It leads to the loss of resources such as money and time. It also causes problems with the flow of the work. As the process of the flow of the work is an integral part of Kaizen, this waste is considered one of the most problematic and dreaded of all the other seven wastes.

The Waste of Overproduction

Excessively producing things that the customer does not need immediately is a waste.

This is considered to be the most severe of all the wastes because it can bring down even the biggest of companies. The waste of overproduction means making too much too early. This generally happens when you work with oversize batches. Other reasons for this waste include poor communication with the supplier, long lead times, and many other minor as well as major reasons. Overproduction leads to over-saturation of inventory, which in turn can bring up a host of other problems in your company.

There are two principles that companies tend to follow, the JIT or the JUST IN TIME principle and the JIC or the JUST IN CASE principle. Most of the companies tend to follow 'Just in Case' because they feel it is better to be ready with the products. This may sound like a great strategy, but it is not. It is recommended to follow the 'Just in time' principle instead. The ultimate aim of any company is profit and the 'Just in time' principle will help you to achieve a lot of profit. Your goal should be only to make what is required and WHEN it is required.

The Waste of Over-Processing

Do not do more than what the customer wants as it will cost you extra money.

This is another severe waste. It happens when companies use oversize equipment, improper or inappropriate techniques, etc. It may also be observed when the companies tend to use processes that are not necessary or not required by the customer or when working to tolerances is extremely tight. All of these things are not free, and they cost us money as well as time.

Nowadays, many companies tend to use a 'huge mega-machine' that can do the job of all the machines combined together. On paper, this sounds excellent, but in practice, it is a train-wreck. Such machines require a lot of resources and a lot of maintenance as well. Each of the process flow has to be carefully carried through without any scheduling complications. If complications occur, it may lead to a lot of delays or waste products.

Kaizen is focusing on small and gradual things. It believes that instead of taking large, haphazard steps, it is better to stick to simple ones. Similarly, instead of using big and heavy machinery, Kaizen promotes the use of small machines that are easy to handle and do not break the flow of the process.

The Waste of Defects
Like inventory, defects too hide a lot of problems and can lead to a lot of wastes as well.

This is the most obvious one of all the other wastes but is often quite difficult to detect. Many times the defects in the products are detected when they reach the customers. There are a lot of quality errors that may lead to a lot of defects. These defects can often drive you into a lot of loss if they are not rectified or handled immediately. Each defective item needs to be either reworked, repaired, or even replaced. This not only wastes essential resources such as time and money, but it also wastes materials. You also need to create a lot of work. You may even lose a lot of your customers thanks to this.

It is necessary to avoid this waste as much as possible because it is better to prevent it instead of repairing things later. There are various methods of doing so, but the strict QC remains the best method.

Additional Wastes

Along with the wastes stated above, there exists a variety of other wastes too. Let us have a look at some of these wastes one by one:

Waste of Talent

Not using the talent of the people in your workforce to their full extent is a highly common issue in almost all companies and fields, but only a few people dare to address it. Especially in the West, companies run by following strict rules, and their environment does not allow the talent of the people to grow. Employees receive little to no attention, and often what they say is ignored immediately.

It should be noted that for any company, their employees are their best assets. They can help a company to come out of many severe problems with ease if they are provided the opportunity to do so. Understand the psyche of the employees and allow them to speak. You will be surprised to see how much talent stays hidden thanks to the archaic rules.

Waste of Resources

This is a highly common waste that is seen in almost all companies. Resources like electricity, water, gas, etc. are costly. They should always be used with ample efficiency.

Human beings do not own resources, they are communal property, and when you waste a resource, every human being suffers. To avoid this, it is necessary to use resources efficiently.

Wasted Materials

Some material is bound to go waste in the process of production, but if you see that a large amount of material is not being utilized properly, it is necessary to check your manufacturing process.

You should also consider recycling and reusing. Most of the material can be reused in other departments. One of the best examples of this is a detergent factory. The process of making soap and detergent produces a lot of NaCl or common salt as a by-product. Instead of wasting it and throwing it away, most soap companies sell the salt as a manufactured product.

Eliminating the Seven Wastes

It is possible to get rid of all the wastes with the help of Kaizen and various other lean tools, but it should not be your sole focus. Reduction or removal of waste is a result of the process. You need to concentrate on how to improve the company and how to attract more and more customers. You need to add value to your product so that it can become popular. When you concentrate on improvement, various processes continue to grow and become more efficient.

Efficiency kills waste automatically. So, let your focus be on improvement and enhanced efficiency all the time.

All employees should be made aware of basic lean principles. Learning the 5S is absolutely necessary, as they will allow you to learn a lot about improvements. 5S can also help you make proper choices and select the correct version of the training. You will find out more about the 5S in the next chapter.

Pre-Event Planning

No event can be successful if you do not plan it properly. This is why it is necessary to have a rough outline of your Kaizen event. A good and well-experienced facilitator can help you make an outline as they will know what to do, expect, and change. Plan out everything carefully and follow it.

Have a rough timeline of your event. An example timeline will look like this:

Day 1: Training, gathering data, analyzing data

Day 2: Modeling and analyzing

Day 3: Change layout

Day 4: Refine layout, standardize instructions

Day 5: Refinement, presentation of the team, a small celebration

If you plan to change the physical layout of your office or production room, you will require electricians, movers, moving equipment, and various similar manpower. Pre-arrange it to avoid any confusion. Make a list of all the equipment and material that you need for the event and buy it a couple of days before the actual event.

Remember, it is always better to have a plan and then have everything in order instead of rambling around in a shambles. Check the specificities of your team and the requirements to keep everything happy and satiated. This way, you will be able to avoid any unnecessary tension, stress, and confusion.

The Kaizen Event

It is necessary to create at least a rough schedule or outline of a schedule in the initial stages of your Kaizen event planning. It should serve as a map of what you plan to achieve from your event.

Your facilitator is responsible for providing support and training to the team. They should also change the pace from time to time so that the team does not get bored. The team must be enthusiastic about things. Their enthusiasm should be maintained throughout the project. They need to feel involved all the time. If they begin to feel that they are not involved, then the whole event may start to collapse on its own.

Many times leaders have a vision for which they choose to have a Kaizen event for their team. However, many times, the team vision is different as compared to their leader's. This should not come as a surprise or a shock; it is perfectly normal. If this happens, it is recommended to go with the decision of the team because they are more aware of how things are and how they work. They are the experts in their areas, and they know what changes will make their job easier. Do not try to pull them towards your vision. Allow your facilitator to assist them in creating their vision. The ideas that the teams come up with are often more profitable and sustainable than the ones that are forced down their throats.

Always remember to click before and after photos and videos, as they will help you keep track of things in the long-term.

Presentation

The team needs to make a presentation to the rest of the workforce and management at the end of the project. This is a great chance to display what all the members have achieved together as a team. Many Kaizen experts swear that these events lead to a lot of advancements, which can come as a surprise to a lot of people. When the team presents these advancements, they will feel motivated, and their success to inspire others.

Ask the team to display their before and after pictures in the presentation and ask them to show what benefits they received by doing the Kaizen event. If the data is available, display the data too. These presentations can prove to be good for all the workforce, as they will feel more energized and excited about their own events.

Congratulations

This is a non-existent in the west; when we succeed in doing something well, we do not celebrate it often. It is necessary to celebrate even the littlest of things, as it will keep people happy and motivated. Celebrations do not need to be lavish, try to keep things simple. In fact, simple celebrations like a small pizza party allow the employees to connect with each other further, and everyone feels even more comfortable working together.

Review and Improve

Kaizen is all about taking small steps and making small changes that lead to small improvement continuously. It is necessary to monitor these changes and check out the performance from time to time. You should also come with more and more improvements, as it will help you in the long-term.

You need to motivate your team from time to time to improve. Improvement does not happen right away; it takes a lot of time and hard work. You need to allow your team some time to improve. If you try to hurry the process, all the gains that you received in the past will disappear, and you will have start anew.

Rinse and Repeat

As stated earlier, Kaizen events are supposed to be run area wise. They are targeted at specific areas, and they should stay well within the boundaries. Once you are done with the Kaizen event in one particular area, you rinse and repeat it in a different area. Kaizen events are not supposed to be solutions for immediate crises; they are supposed to serve as tools that can improve the overall work culture and ethics. They will provide you continuous improvement. This is why it is necessary to have a Kaizen event at least once in a couple of months (depends on the size of your company). Each event should be focused on a different area or department. It is also necessary to revisit the area from time to time to see whether Kaizen is working properly or not and whether the change is continuous.

Conduct Your Kaizen Event Before the Time Runs Out

Kaizen, along with various other lean tools, is essential, and they are supposed to form an integral part of your work culture. They are constant and continuous. You need to practice them constantly and become perfect in them. They are used to seek perfection all the time, and are not supposed to be quick fixes or 'one-time-solutions' for crises or problems. They form an essential part of a philosophy. Many times when a company runs into a huge problem, people approach Kaizen experts to have a Kaizen event in the company to solve the problem. These problems are so difficult they can even threaten the business to the core and can bring down the viability of the business itself. This is impossible. Kaizen is not a last-minute resort that will save you from your ultimate doom.

Kaizen may prove to be efficient for such companies for a couple of days, but if the company has already entered the stage of decay, it will collapse sooner or later. No one can save it. Kaizen too can only delay what is imminent. So, instead of waiting for the right opportunity for Kaizen, do it right away. Allow it to become a part of your daily work schedule. Let it become an essential part of your office culture. This way, you will be able to keep your company safe and your customers, managers, and employees, all happy.

Chapter Nine

Basics of 5S

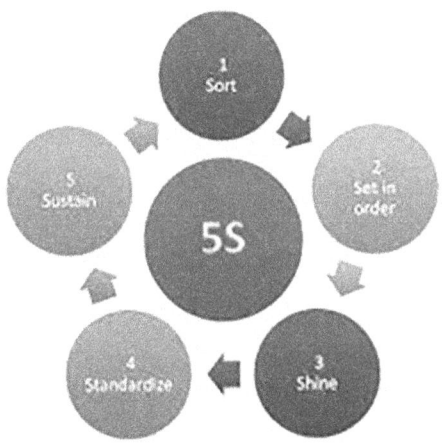

What is 5S?

5s can be considered as one of the most useful and powerful of all the lean manufacturing tools and thus hold an important connection to the Kaizen methods. If you can employ the 5s principles carefully, you will be able to help your business grow and prosper significantly. 5S stands for 5 steps, which are as follows: Seiri, Seiton, Seiso, Seiketsu, and Shitsuke. These five steps can help you achieve your goals.

This is an easy to use tool that is used to manage and organize your workplace. It can make your work very efficient, clean, and safe. It can improve your productivity levels and can help you to standardize your work. It also helps you in visual management and can increase efficiency.

Most of the definitions on the Internet regarding 5S are related to aesthetics, how it is possible to become more efficient and bold with the help of the 5S method, but there is a lot more to the method than just this. In the truest sense, 5S is a tool that can help you standardize procedures and practices that make things repeatable, efficient, and safe.

Along with this, 5S can also help you make improvements and developments in other departments of your company. This can be done by incorporating various lean tools along with Kaizen in the 5S system. The best thing about the 5S method is that it can help you see problems instantly. Thanks to this immediateness, it is possible to diagnose and solve the problems as soon as possible. It can prevent future, more severe accidents.

S5 is a team-building and running process that is to be done by the members present in the team. It is recommended to apply for the program in chunks; otherwise, you're the whole stay become confused and start losing focus immediately. An efficient and effective 5S session can help even new employees to work in a department about which he has little to no experience. It is a tool that can be applied into an area without the knowledge and cooperation of the people within it.

Origins of 5S

The history of 5S is quite interesting as it traces history and past to the TPM and the TPS system, i.e., the Total Productive Maintenance and Toyota Production System. This does not mean that it is of secondary importance, in fact, the 5S system combines the best things of both the systems and thanks to many practitioners over the years, and 5S has become a system that can bring a lot of efficiencies, ergonomic, and excellence to any workspace. These workspaces and places include big offices to comparatively less popular jobs. It can help you physically, mentally, officially, and emotionally too.

Let us now have a look at the concept of 5S in brief.

The Concept of 5S

5S can be called a pristine and methodical way that is used to manage and organize the working practices and workplace. It is not just a 'tool'; rather, it is a philosophy that you need to understand and incorporate in your day to day life, personal as well as professional. 5S refers to five steps or five phases in which the process is divided. Each of these processes starts with the letter 'S,' which explains the nomenclature of the tool. These five processes are Seiri, Seiton, Seiso, Seiketsu, and Shitsuke.

Let us have a close look at these steps one by one. Understanding the basics of these steps will allow you to understand the 5S system with ease. Understanding these five principles does not take a lot of time or effort; you can do it almost instantaneously.

Steps of 5S

(5S) Seiri: Seiri means classification or clearing things. It also stands for 'to sort' or sorting.

(5S) Seiton: Seiton in Japanese means to simplify things and set them in perfect order. It also stands for configuration and straightening things up so that they look good and presentable. The biggest role of the step is to reduce chaos.

(5S) Seiso: This means to clean, scrub, sweep, or shine.

(5S) Seiketsu: This stands for conformity and stabilization. It is used to standardize things.

(5S) Shitsuke: This stands for sustainability, customs, practice, and self-discipline.

Some companies and organizations also like to add a sixth step or level to the above formula, which is 'Safety.' Certain other companies believe that safety is an integral part of the original 5S anyway and should be incorporated in each step with total efficiency.

5C and CANDO

Certain companies find the use of Japanese terms and words uncomfortable. This is why many Western companies and organizations now use the 'CANDO' method instead of the 5S method. The core value of both the tools remain the same, except instead of using Japanese words like 5S, the CANDO method uses English words instead. Different companies use different words and names for the method; however, their core remains the same, and all of them follow the same principle.

In certain circles and companies, the 5S method is known as the 5C method. In this each Japanese word starting with an S is replaced by an English word starting with a C. So, the 5C stands for:

- Clearing
- Configuration
- Check and Clean
- Conformity
- Custom
- Some people also prefer to use the CANDO method in which the following words are used:
- Cleanup
- Arrange
- Neatness
- Discipline
- Ongoing Improvement
- 5S Definitions

In this section, let us have a look at the brief definitions of each of the five steps of the 5S method one by one.

5S Seiri or Sort

The first step of the 5S method is known as Seiri, which stands for sorting. In this, the clutter of a lot of items, especially in the workspace, is sorted out and cleaned carefully. In this step, you need to take away or discard all the products, objects, and items that do not belong in the working area and are useless there. Only the items that are explicitly necessary or needed in the workspace should be present there.

5S Seiton or Straighten

Once you have sorted everything and have discarded the useless items, you need to move on to the second step- Seiton. In this step, you are supposed to arrange all the remaining, useful things in an efficient manner with the help of certain ergonomic methodology. In this step, each item should have its individual place, and everything should be in order.

5S Seiso or Sweep

Once you have arranged all the items carefully, you should move on to the third step, i.e., Seiso or clean. In this step, you are supposed to clean everything efficiently. This includes tools, the area, all the equipment, and machines as well. Anything that does not conform to the standards should be cleaned or removed. Clean all the oil leaks or dust from machines and keep everything fresh and clean.

5S Seiketsu or Standardize

The fourth step of the 5S method is Seiketsu. This method stands for the standardization procedure. It is used to make a standardized process of the first three steps so that you can create proper and common standards that can be reflected in the way of your work. Standardization is one of the most crucial steps in the Kaizen and lean tools world as it helps you to form a schedule and have some order in your professional life.

5S Shitsuke or Sustain

The last step of the 5S method is Shitsuke, which means to sustain. In these steps, it is ensured that the company continues to improve constantly with the help of the first four steps. This is done with the help of continuous audits, housekeeping, maintenance, and various other methods. If you want your company to succeed magnificently, it is necessary to make the 5S method a part of your company culture. This will improve the overall condition of your company and provide everyone with a sense of responsibility for their work.

Chapter Ten

How to Lead a Kaizen Event

Leading a Kaizen event may sound to be difficult, but it really is not. You just need to understand the basics of the whole thing and work carefully using the principles efficiently; you will be able to lead the event with ease. Here are some tips that will help you lead your Kaizen event and make everyone comfortable.

- Make the opening extremely welcoming and happy. The members should remember it forever.

- Have some small but memorable gifts ready for all the members. The gifts should be personalized with tags.

- Document everything both in the form of texts and videos and pictures. This will not only help you keep memories of the event, but these documents will also help you to compare your results and track the progress.

- Click pictures of the members and post them around the main event area with their nametags.

- In the contact information, add the names of support staff and their pictures.

- Make the event comfortable by having water, coffee, snacks, and soda available all the time.

- Always keep an eye on the supplies. If possible, to frequent supply runs and keep supply requests forms/lists ready.

- Ask members to bring their favorite stationery items such as clipboard, pencil, and stopwatch.

- If possible, make a digital or a video camera available for all the team members. Teach the members how to use the cameras and provide them with ample instructions.

- Assigns various hosts for questions, what-ifs, and regular check-ins.

- Keep one evening free, and enjoy yourself with all the team members.

- To make everything comfortable and arrive on time, take a cab, shuttle, or any other form of transportation available for all the members.

- Begin the event only then when all the staff is present in the house. Not all members will be able to reach the same time because of planes, automobiles, or trains delay.

- Always see things through the perspective of the guests.

- Have a printer and WIFI available in the event venue.

- Keep all the necessary forms ready and bundled. Document each day carefully so that you have everything ready.

- Keep the files that you want the teams to use ready all the time.

- One of the top observation forms adds 'rules that are being used.'

- Always add dates and names on all the forms.

- Add easel boards, tape measures, rulers, post-its, tape, etc. all a part of the stock kit. Provide these kits to all the members.

- Post notices everywhere explaining the event so that no one gets surprised.

- Keep all employees present in the facility in the loop and informed all the time.

- Send all the necessary and relevant forms in the form of an email way ahead of time. This should include all the necessary study guides and visual identification tools too.

- Always instruct the members about aspiring, first aid kits, band-aids, tweezers, etc. Keep extra stock handy.

- Have frequent lunches with people who are not members of the event. This will help you bring in the much-needed flavor and communication to your team events.

- Add non-event members to the event. They can act as observers. These observers should be allowed to view the event for half a day or more. They can provide a lot of lean exposure to the team.

- Try to keep the teams on time and make them follow the schedule. Note down the people who do not follow the schedule. Do not allow stragglers to participate.

- Have multiple plug-in coolers available around the event space. Keep people hydrated.

- If there is some sort of language barrier, please check the options that can be used to overcome this problem. Try to find out more about the background of the participants and check how you can use their background for their development.

- Have extra trashcans around the event area. Similarly, ask the cleaning crew to clean the place more than often.

- Provide the teams with binder supplies. These should contain all the papers related to work. These papers should be filled up carefully.

- Provide all the team members with team rosters. This should include the title, location, and everything else related to the participants.

- Ask the team to suggest resources that are not available or visible.

- Remind the team members to practice their 5S skills all the time. If you really want them to practice the skills, led by example.

- Always have some downtime activities planned.

- Post progress reports around the event place; this way, new teams can check how old teams grew and developed.

- It is necessary to meet host employees outside of the vent. This will improve your communication with them.

- Get rid of all the responsibilities of the host team members for the time of the event. They will not be able to fulfill their routine jobs thanks to the event. Allow them to do so.

- Write and build your report-out books at the end of the day. Keep all the indices, clear sheets, and labels ready and fill them at the end of each day. It should be a part of your daily report-out methodology.

- If you plan to use cloud storage for all your data, keep all the locations safe and check out what your team needs every day.

- All the team members need to contribute to the final presentation. To keep everyone in the loop, keep all the instructions and documentation ready. Add examples whenever and wherever they are necessary.

- Try to maintain a level of balance. You should have people experienced in organizational methodology and technical fields to maintain optimum balance.

- Have a sensei ready. Sensei or consultant will help you stay focused. Ideally, you should have a sensei for each changeover team. These sensei will help you maintain a proper direction and will provide you with ample support.

- People who have already attended Kaizen events before this or are used to other forms of Kaizen should take the lead and help others understand the basics.

Conclusion

I hope this book was able to help you understand the principles of Kaizen in not only your private life but your professional life as well. I hope you will be able to use the principles given in this book to make your and your friends' life easy and more meaningful.

This book is like a stepping-stone, which can throw open doors to unlimited possibilities and chances. It can surely change your life for good if you follow the principles carefully.

The next step for you is to stick to the newly established habits and continue working towards your personal and professional goals. This will keep you focused.

Kaizen is a broad term, which has applications in a variety of fields. This makes it one of the most relevant and relatable methods of organization and management. It is flexible and can be adjusted according to your needs and requirements. This makes it a great way to change your life around.

Kaizen is a philosophy that teaches you the importance of slow and gradual steps. It allows you to focus on the minor details and problems that, in turn, can solve the largest of the problems. It enables you to move step by step and get rid of problematic issues.

Follow the tips given in this book and use the methods to arrange great Kaizen events.

References

7 Kaizen tools to reduce waste and improve Lean Process. (2019, August 9). Retrieved from upKaizen website: https://upkaizen.com/en/2019/08/09/7-kaizen-tools-to-reduce-waste-and-improve-lean-process/

A Brief History of Kaizen: The Key Players. (n.d.). Retrieved from Creative Safety Supply website: https://www.creativesafetysupply.com/articles/a-brief-history-of-kaizen-the-key-players/

Chi, C. (n.d.). 5 Dos and Don'ts When Making a SMART Goal [Examples]. Retrieved from https://blog.hubspot.com/marketing/smart-goal-examples

DeShaw, J. (2017, June 2). Kaizen for Healthy Lifestyle Changes. Retrieved from ZUM Fitness website: https://zumfitness.com/kaizen-healthy-lifestyle-changes/

Dolcemascolo, D., & Trout, J. (n.d.). Kaizen Events: When and How to Use Them. Retrieved from www.reliableplant.com website: https://www.reliableplant.com/Read/8904/kaizen-events

Hargrave, M. (2019). Kaizen. Retrieved from Investopedia website: https://www.investopedia.com/terms/k/kaizen.asp

How to read more using the Japanese method of Kaizen. (n.d.). Retrieved from Pan Macmillan website: https://www.panmacmillan.com/blogs/lifestyle-wellbeing/how-to-break-a-habit-kaizen

Howard, A. (2019, September 24). Kaizen Events 101 - Before, During and After. Retrieved from Kaufman Global website: https://www.kaufmanglobal.com/kaizen-events-101

KaizenGaining the Benefits of Continuous Improvement. (2009). Retrieved from Mindtools.com website: https://www.mindtools.com/pages/article/newSTR_97.htm

Kaizen – Lean Manufacturing and Six Sigma Definitions. (2019). Retrieved from Leansixsigmadefinition.com website: http://www.leansixsigmadefinition.com/glossary/kaizen/

Kaizen Creates a Culture of Continuous Improvement | Lean Production. (2011). Retrieved from Leanproduction.com website: https://www.leanproduction.com/kaizen.html

Lin, A. (2018, October 18). Kaizen Events: A Complete Guide to Planning & Holding a Kaizen Blitz. Retrieved from Tulip website: https://tulip.co/blog/lean-manufacturing/a-practical-guide-to-kaizen-events/

Oppong, T. (2020, February 12). 7 Modern Life Habits That Can Be Incredibly Bad For Your Brain Health. Retrieved from Medium website: https://medium.com/kaizen-habits/7-modern-life-habits-doing-the-most-damage-to-your-brain-e392c9cfee42

Planning and running Kaizen Events. (2012). Retrieved from Lean Manufacturing Tools website: https://leanmanufacturingtools.org/625/planning-and-running-kaizen-events/

Roussel, J. (2017, October 18). Kaizen Event Planning in 7 Simple Steps. Retrieved from blog.kainexus.com website: https://blog.kainexus.com/improvement-disciplines/kaizen/kaizen-event/kaizen-event-planning-in-7-simple-steps

Sirk, C. (2020, April 2). The History of Kaizen. Retrieved from CRM.org website: https://crm.org/articles/the-history-of-kaizen

Sherman, P. (2018). Understanding Kaizen Events | APICS Magazine. Retrieved from www.apics.org website: http://www.apics.org/apics-for-individuals/apics-magazine-home/magazine-detail-page/2018/10/10/understanding-kaizen-events

Thakur, S. (2010, December 23). Seven Best Kaizen Tools. Retrieved November 19, 2019, from Bright Hub PM website: https://www.brighthubpm.com/project-planning/100412-a-survey-of-kaizen-tools/

The Seven Wastes | 7 Mudas. (2011). Retrieved from Lean Manufacturing Tools website: https://leanmanufacturingtools.org/77/the-seven-wastes-7-mudas/

What is 5S; Seiri, Seiton, Seiso, Seiketsu, Shitsuke. (n.d.). Retrieved from Lean Manufacturing Tools website: https://leanmanufacturingtools.org/192/what-is-5s-seiri-seiton-seiso-seiketsu-shitsuke/

What is Kaizen ? - Five S of Kaizen. (2015). Retrieved from Managementstudyguide.com website: https://www.managementstudyguide.com/what-is-kaizen.htm

What is KAIZENTM. (2019). Retrieved from Kaizen.com website: https://www.kaizen.com/what-is-kaizen.html

Wilding, M. (2018, January 22). The Japanese philosophy of Kaizen can reinvent your daily routine. Retrieved from Quartz at Work website: https://qz.com/work/1183536/the-japanese-philosophy-of-kaizen-can-reinvent-your-daily-routine/

KAIZEN

Japanese Tips, Tricks and Strategies Using Kaizen and Ikigai Theories and Principles

ROBERT MILLER

Introduction

Japan has always been at the forefront of applying philosophy to business. The purpose of this was to push people to start seeing business as not just a corporate venture to make money but as an important aspect of our society. Kaizen as philosophy became famous in the 1980s when multiple Japanese corporations started to use it to make incremental gains that eventually lead to them dominating the whole world in terms of production, profits, and employee happiness.

Kaizen is a holistic approach that teaches us how to focus on the small things in life and pay attention to them. It eradicates the need to have huge objectives and goals; instead, it focuses on the importance of gradual improvement that can be carried out daily.

It is a never-ending process because it argues that perfection simply cannot be achieved – everything can be improved and, therefore, must be improved. It is this zeal that is intrinsic to the nature of Kaizen. It motivates workers and pushes the management to make better policies, find areas of improvement, and revolutionize how the company works.

Kaizen's exclusivity lies in the fact that it involves every aspect of the company – it doesn't believe that the upper management and the workers are different from each other. Instead, it focuses on the importance of every aspect of work, and there is a reason behind this. It's the workers who do all the labor, and they are the ones who work with the machinery. Kaizen pushes the management to take into consideration the suggestions of workers so their expertise and knowledge can be used to find areas of improvement.

In this book, we're going to talk about the different strategies that constitute the Kaizen system, such as the 5S, the TPS (Toyota Production System), the 5M's, the Lean Production System, and so on. We're also going to talk about how you can incorporate Kaizen into your business by conducting Kaizen events and Kaizen training. There is also a section that specifically focuses on the application of Kaizen to startups. Lastly, we will focus on what applications Kaizen has beyond just the corporate world and how it can benefit you in your personal life.

Other than Kaizen, there are other Japanese philosophies as well that can help guide you in your life, like Ikigai, which pushes people to search for their purpose. We will also discuss this theory and its principles in detail.

Chapter One

Basics of Kaizen

To learn about Kaizen, we must start from its history to trace how it originated and why it has been successful. As a business philosophy, Kaizen was made popular by Masaaki Imai about three decades ago. He published a book introducing the term and the philosophy into the canon of business management and as a social practice within the larger mainstream culture. It is a term that is mostly rooted in business practices, but it can also be implemented in your daily life to improve your habits.

It is a Japanese word that, when divided, yields its meaning. The word Kai means "change," and the word Zen means "to improve for better." When these words are combined, it can be simply interpreted as "improvement."

Kaizen's historic origin might be in Japan, but it was only in America that its manufacturing and business potential was able to truly take hold. During World War II, American manufacturers did not have the time or money to carry out radical changes to increase production, and so they had to depend on making small changes in their everyday working space to get better results. These small changes eventually led to new changes happening every day, and as the workers got used to this, they started to function better and adapt to the changes. This technique was then formalized and now is a part of almost every organization.

What popularized Kaizen was the company Toyota that published a book on its manufacturing ideals in 2001 that highlighted the importance of incremental change in its work process.

So, what is Kaizen? It's a method that focuses not only on the larger goal and the eventual revolutionizing of business and our daily habits but instead talks about the importance of daily growth. According to

Kaizen, we have to improve every day if we want to be successful – this approach believes that larger goals would be automatically fulfilled if every day, incremental changes are carried out.

The psychology behind this is interesting because when you set a goal for yourself, you always tend to think beyond what is realistically possible. We all like to set goals and objectives that are as large as they can be and that can negatively affect your mind because you are constantly thinking of how you are going to achieve it. This makes us not want to work because the task we have set for ourselves is so huge that it would take extraordinary effort to complete it. This is why only a few people can take on such tasks and complete them, while others just end up giving up completely.

Kaizen is different because it asks you to enjoy the journey and not focus on the goal. If your goal was just completed in one second as most people imagine it will once they have daydreamed about it, it wouldn't be any fun at all, and you would learn nothing. By breaking the task into smaller sections that are achievable, you're not only going to be motivated to complete your tasks but will also see improvement within yourself too.. This kind of improvement is priceless because it is a change that takes place over every day, so you can study it and learn from it. Kaizen also changes how we look at achieving goals; instead of just accepting that change can only happen through hard work and taking giant steps, it teaches us that it's in those small steps that life is made.

When he takes small steps every day, a man will eventually reach the summit of a peak, but he can only do this if he doesn't rush it and end up exhausted. Climbing a mountain is not about just staring at the peak, hoping you will reach it and crying out in pain when you realize it's still far away. You are much more likely to reach the peak if you forget about it and focus on every step that you're taking. You will soon realize that each step can be enjoyable, and once you start to focus on those small things, work will seem much more manageable and enjoyable.

Imagine a worker who has been told by his team that he must complete a certain task no matter what by the end of the year. He has the directions he needs to do this. Once he takes his first step to complete his goal, he is going to start thinking about all the other work he must do to reach the goal and how difficult it is to reach that goal. This will only demotivate him from working on the task at hand. Not only that, but the stress of the larger task will reduce his productivity and focus, leading to deterioration in the quality of the work as well. If he only focused on the task that was in front of him without worrying about larger goals, he would have been happy to put all his attention and willpower into the task leading to better results for the organization.

Our brain also pushes us to be motivated by looking at what has been done and reveling in the fact that at least some part of the goal has been completed. But, when we only care about the larger objective, our brain will simply never be satisfied, and instead of the small steps we take motivating us to work harder, they end up demotivating us because we are constantly reminded of the smallness of the task we just completed when compared to the herculean task that is still left to be completed. Kaizen tells you to see the small task as the entire goal itself. By doing this, your brain remains motivated because every small task is seen as a great achievement. Replicate this every day and your self-esteem will be boosted significantly.

Kaizen also ensures that, every day, you have a goal to reach and that you can end every day knowing you have improved just a little. The success of any business is dependent on its workers; it's only when the workers improve day by day that the business will as well. The total effect of this is that Kaizen helps you focus on what is in front of you. It helps you feel confident as well as motivated, which eventually leads to a rise in productivity and the achievement of the larger goal.

Core of Kaizen

Five main principles form the core of Kaizen:

- Know your customer
- Let it flow
- Go to Gemba
- Empower people
- Be transparent.

All five of these principles, when followed in unison every day, allow for continuous improvement to take place within the organization.

Know your Customer

Everything about Kaizen starts with the customer. If you know how to capture the imagination of your customer and produce exactly what they need, you will be successful. The purpose of any organization is to find out what their customers want and ensuring that they enhance their experience by providing them with fulfilling products. Improvement in the business through Kaizen can easily be judged by how well the company is creating value for the customer.

Let it Flow

Kaizen also focuses on creating zero waste within the organization. It sees everything as valuable and wastes as the reason for the organization's failure. When daily tasks are set under the Kaizen system, the biggest goal every day is to ensure that nothing is being wasted and the maximum value is being extracted from all possible sources.

Go to Gemba

Gemba is the place where all actions happen, generally considered as the household. This is a directive that all managers must follow at the end of the day. You must be connected to where labor is creating value and see what is going on for yourself.

Empower People

Kaizen cannot work unless everyone knows what steps they have to take. Without proper communication within the team, not everyone will be able to do what is required and will just focus on the larger, end goal instead of the smaller steps. An empowered organization is one where everyone trusts each other and communication is free-flowing so that everyone knows what they have to do.

Be Transparent

Kaizen cannot work unless people see for themselves the larger goals that are achieved at the end of the year. You can't just keep on making random improvements without checking to see how the results are impacting the larger productivity of the organization. So, management must ensure that they have the right data and they publish it regularly for everyone to see.

PDCA Cycle

Kaizen is achieved when the PDCA cycle is continuously repeated. It means the Plan-Do-Check-Act Cycle, which is also known as the Deming cycle. This cycle ensures that every person who is working has an attitude that pushes them to strive for higher levels of productivity. This cycle ensures that there is continuous improvement in the quality and quantity of the work while at the same time reducing costs at every step. It essentially means that larger improvement in the organization can only happen when every day we check the cycle of work to better the quality, reduce the waste, and extract more value from the resources we do have. Kaizen eventually, when combined with this cycle, leads to everyone working together harmoniously in a way that all processes of production go through scrutiny so that productivity can be enhanced as much as possible.

Plan

The first step in the whole process is to plan everything properly. You have to decide what the production theme of the company is – what you are producing and how you are producing it. This theme is important because it tells your workers how work should flow and what they are expected to do. It also allows everyone to understand the production process and to look out for problems. After this, study the financial and material status of the company and come up with new ways to do tasks. Decide what these tasks should be, identify the problem areas, work on the analysis of these problem areas to ensure that you know what the root cause of all the mayhem is and start working on solutions to fix the problems.

Do

Once you have done all the analysis, the next task is to identify what should be done. Then draw up a checklist of measures that must be implemented throughout the organization for an increase in productivity.

Check

Once you have set some standard measures that must be carried out through the organization, this step is all about checking that implementation is perfect and being followed.

Act

In this step, you have to standardize the measures so that work can happen in a continuous stream. Revise all the measures based on which ones have worked and review everything within the organization.

After the PDCA Cycle is completed, you must move on to the SDCA Cycle. While the first one is concerned only with the improvement of everything within the organization, the second one is all about maintenance. Once you have recognized all the flaws within the workspace, you have to standardize what should be done so that you have some measures based on which you can determine the success of all the tasks being performed. The S in the latter stands for standardization as well as the idea of support because this cycle can be seen as the pillar, which supports the everyday functioning of the business.

Standardization is key to the success of an organization because it gives you a way to measure the effectiveness of the production cycle. You won't know how well you're doing unless there are some set measures to judge by. It also allows your workers to know how they have to do their job and what the easiest way to complete the task is. Furthermore, when new employees come into the organization, it will be easier to train them because you will have a solid base that you can just ask them to follow. Standards also ensure that there isn't too much variance in work – everyone knows what they should do and how so that all tasks are completed similarly. This will prevent errors from happening because deviation would be easy to spot and fix.

History of Kaizen

The word Kaizen itself got worldwide applause through Masaaki Imai's works. Masaaki Imai (born 1930) is a Japanese managerial scholar and the board expert, specifically on Kaizen, recognized for his research on quality control. The Kaizen Institute Consulting Group (KICG) was founded in 1985 to allow western institutions to understand Kaizen's ideas and how they can be implemented across different cultures.

Kaizen was founded in various Japanese companies that had, in some way or another, acquired some leadership methods and competencies from the United States and even from Europe. These strategies were developed under the direction of a few influential companies, which are responsible for fostering efficiency and increasing productivity.

The starting of Kaizen goes back to World War II when Japanese companies first carried out effective production cycles using this method, becoming the first to integrate the philosophy into their manufacturing. This had been influenced to some degree by American educators in business and quality management who visited the country. In the 1950s, this revolutionary concept turned out to be highly popular in Japan, and now all modern companies follow this method because of its effectiveness.

Following World War II, during the time of economic reconstruction, Japan's goods were considered relatively inexpensive but of rather inferior quality. To reverse this kind of bad publicity, the drive to boost quality and efficiency began, and one of the organizations that played an important role in that movie was the Union of Japanese Scientists and Engineers (JUSE). They performed several educational workshops on statistical management methods and even quality assurance for big corporations, as well as executives from time to time. Through these initiatives, companies started to understand the value of quality management and also began to make efforts at prepping world-class manufacturing facilities. In each phase of development, voluntary organizations were formed to carry out a range of workplace improvement activities, some of which were waste disposal (Muda-Dori), cost efficiency, industrial safety management, reduction of defects, 5S (which we will discuss later) and formation of quality circles. A quality circle is a group of workers doing the same or similar roles, who meet periodically to understand, analyze, and take ownership over work-related issues. A quality circle is the same as the PDCA Cycle but carried out by workers rather than the management.

In 1955, the JPC (Japan Productivity Center) was founded by groups representing labor unions, academics, and businesses. JPC served as a leader of the campaign for growth while succeeding in becoming a national group. Since 1955, the JPC has sent several missions for industrial tours to numerous modern manufacturing facilities in developed countries, including the U.S., to study their efficiency and development techniques. The results obtained were exchanged at feedback sessions held across the country, and were also collected for dissemination to interested firms. This approach helped to facilitate the increase in quality and efficiency in Japanese firms overall.

By working extremely hard on the quality of their goods from the combined point of view of manufacturing, producing and sustaining good products and services, a large number of Japanese companies launched several initiatives to help boost efficiency and performance as a form of effective business strategy. The TQC (Total Quality Control) was born at this stage. Several high-ranking companies in Japan, such as Yamaha, Sony, Honda, Canon, Nissan, Panasonic, Toyota, and Suzuki constantly pushed for the universal application of Total Quality Control. That is what has allowed them to become world leaders in effective development and manufacturing.

Many public and private sectors institutionalized these measures and expanded their scope. Soon these measures were not limited to the manufacturing sector alone but were also applied to boost customer loyalty. The Kaizen modification drew the focus of some American and European corporate executives, academics, and engineers who came to Japan to research the essential factors of Japanese companies' power to improve their businesses. After that, several businesses then imported Japan's production and manufacturing management skills and knowledge and reorganized them to suit the American and European business climate.

As stated earlier, the quality and manufacturing methods were first introduced from the U.S. to Japan and were changed as time went by and also refined by Japanese producers based on their various sizes, markets, the climate of production, and other related factors.

TPS

TPS (Toyota Production System) is a widely recognized, established management system. TPS is based on two main concepts - the Jidoka, and the Just-In-Time. The Jidoka is for instantly halting a malfunctioning system to avoid the manufacturing of faulty goods. On the other hand, the Just-In-Time method is based on producing only as many goods as is necessary to avoid producing excess goods. While at the same time, ensuring that enough raw materials are in storage to ensure a smooth manufacturing process.

To further elaborate, these are the key principles on which TPS is based:

Jidoka

Jidoka is about illustrating and visualizing issues so that they are not repressed, but everyone can see them ensuring that issues are quickly fixed. It's based on the idea that the value of a product and the whole company depends on how manufacturing takes place. For example, if a faulty component is found or some machinery malfunctions, the damaged unit will immediately stop running, thus forcing the operators to halt manufacturing and requiring them to respond to and fix the problem.

What does it mean? This means the system stops until normal operations can be resumed. This also ensures that if an equipment issue occurs or there is a service issue, the machines stop on their own and identify the problem, and then, only the goods that follow the company's quality requirements can proceed to be manufactured. Because the system automatically stops when a problem occurs, it is conveyed on the visual notice boards (ondon). This helps operators to continue researching other systems and to quickly detect something that could have triggered the issue to avoid their recurrence.

This means that multiple operators will be in charge of as many machines as there are in the business, resulting in better efficiency and, at the same time allowing for constant limitless changes, leading to greater production power.

Just-in-Time

This method applies to quality growth. It allows the manufacturing of only those products that are deemed necessary and in the quantities required. All parts manufactured and supplied must follow the appropriate quality requirements already set by the manufacturer, and this is done through Jidoka. The development of quality goods in this particular method is effective because by removing waste altogether, unrealistic conditions on the manufacturing line, and even inconsistencies, better profits can be generated. For example, if a customer is to receive their new car when they want it, the car must be manufactured effectively as and when required. This means that manufacturing has to be so effective and efficient that it can happen within a limited amount of time.

Masaki Imai has made it clear that Kaizen is an overarching philosophy that promotes the continuous development of an organization's activities. It is often said that the task of change is never over in any business because their current system is always under question, at every second.

How did this strategy become famous? It became popular after Toyota used it to become the ruler of the world of cars. Instead of only pursuing large ventures, Toyota's employees were motivated to recognize the company's challenges, no matter how small they might sound. They were allowed to map the origins of the issues and find the best answers for them as well.

The Japanese industrial business typically uses two strategies. These are – the empirical method, focused on data processing, and the bottom-up approach, led by a community group under the Quality Control Process. The purpose of this is to first make sure that no knowledge about the organization is hidden. All problems must come to light and be resolved as quickly as possible. The bottom-up approach ensures that the workers are invested in what they're doing, which makes them do their job with care rather than mindlessness that can lead to faults in manufacturing. This is the biggest reason for the success of Japanese firms – they treat their employees with respect, pay them enough and give them a good reason for being invested in their work. The whole organization consists of people and not machinery.

As a result of the extensive quality and efficiency enhancement programs pursued by a significant number of Japanese firms, their production levels have changed from poor to outstanding, making Japan the "nation of world quality."

Let's look at an example: in 1990, an MIT (Massachusetts Institute of Technology) study team researched the Toyota Production Process to identify sources of competitive advantage for Japanese car industries and then published a book called "The Machine Changing the World." In this book, TPS was expanded on, reorganized, and eventually dubbed the "Lean Manufacturing System." This system was further critiqued by these researchers, who believed that a top-down approach is better than a bottom-up approach.

Eventually, General Electric (GE) Company improved it further. The Kaizen system has now been extended to the whole production system to ensure an improvement in all processes. The "Six Sigma" and the lean manufacturing method, which were later merged to form "Lean and Six Sigma," have been integrated with Kaizen and become examples of western efficiency and product development in this present era.

Kaizen's core is that individuals doing all roles in the business are the ones most informed about the job, so by expressing trust in their skills, managing the project is improved to a greater degree than was originally possible. This unique collaborative project encourages creativity and transition as well, and both of these include every tier of workers. For more efficient progress to occur, every wall has to start vanishing. Kaizen is a philosophy for all and not merely an approach to manufacturing sector profitability. That is because everybody is invested in change. Through dissecting problems, analyzing each part, and making changes where appropriate, Kaizen helps make the job easier for every person. Kaizen cannot just involve one person but has to include everybody in the company because everybody is a member, and therefore, they all play a role. To every person, Kaizen must become an approach of constant enhancement, both to them and the company.

There are three major Kaizen pillars, according to Masaki Imai. He claimed that an organization's management and staff must be capable of working together to satisfy the core standards. He positions three main considerations that need to be taken into account for the effectiveness of this, and these are the visual administration, the role of the leader within the organization, and the development of a business that relies on education and experience.

Kaizen's Pillars

Housekeeping

The place of work is known as Gemba in Japanese. This method is mostly focused on the transformative process of handling the workplace. The Gemba was established as a location where value is added to the good itself and the service it provides before they are moved on to the next production cycle. To this end, a technical framework was used. They are known as the 5S.

This was taken from the Japanese words' first characters that correspond to the 5 words. It is a list of five standards for a safe and healthy work environment. The 5S are Seiri (organization), Seiso (purity), Shitsuke (discipline), Seiketsu (cleanliness), and Seiton (tidiness).

Their English translation can be summed up as to arrange, straighten out, sweep the workplace, sanitize it, and maintain it. The 5S helps provide information into how organized a working environment is. Particular standards must be followed by manufacturing and non-manufacturing organizations: cleanliness, health, and ergonomics. The Five S involves analyzing employee input about a company's manufacturing area, the whole firm itself, and even one another. This has now become an integral resource for any manufacturing organization. The 5S strategy allows manufacturing companies to reach a world-class level.

The 5S
The 5S are:

Seiri

Seiri means finding out what is not required from what is. Use the red tag method to tag things that you do not find to be important for this. Everybody should also be allowed to determine whether the products are needed or not until they are discarded. Any object that has been red-tagged should be sold, given away, sold to employees, trashed, or given to scrap dealers.

Seiton

Seiton is meant to highlight the objects that need to be preserved and must be protected. The purpose of this is to make those things visible. Materials should be labeled and outlined for easy identification through their location. It is based on the law that everything has its place, and workers should envision to find these appropriate spaces.

Seiso

Seiso means scrubbing whatever is left. Ensuring they are clean and, if possible, painting them to give a more eye-catching and eye-pleasing look.

Seiketsu

Seiketsu has to do with daily dissemination and testing. When there is a change in some of the company's chosen Kaizen areas, everyone wants to be educated about it too. You should give them the training that they require and ensure that everyone has access to the necessary information concerning such changes.

Shitsuke

Shitsuke is about standardization and self-discipline. Firstly, set a relatively smooth schedule and make sure you use your downtime to clean up and straighten your area of work.

There are other benefits of the 5S, those being:

- Creation of healthy, friendly and safe working environments for employees

- It revitalizes the workforce and also increases employee productivity and morale within the company.

- Reduces wastage of time by eliminating the need to search for instruments. This makes the operators' job very straightforward.

- It helps to reduce exhausting work while also freeing up the workspace.

- It creates a sense of belonging in the workplace, and solidarity is shared among the workers, which makes them feel like they are part of a caring community.

Waste Disposal

Waste is called Muda in Japanese. Wastes are things that do not add value to the place of work. Work is said to be a series of activities that add value to the product. There are multiple things ranging from parts of the finished product or even raw materials that don't add value, but rather create more problems. Below are some examples of a company's waste:

• Overproduction, faulty parts, surplus inventory, components that are unnecessarily transported, and inspections that delay production.

• Routing documents, unnecessary paperwork, and signing certificates, workers getting a lot of papers and files that bury them, unnecessary data, and transmission of error-filled work are all considered office waste.

The Seven Deadly Wastes

Overproduction

This develops when machine failure, staff absenteeism, and rejection occur. At other times, trying to be ahead of production can cause tremendous waste. It also causes wasteful input of utilities and human resources, increased interest burdens, consumption of raw materials before they are needed, high administrative and transportation costs, more space than required to store excess inventory, etc.

Motion

Any form of staff movement that does not add value to production is considered a waste. The staff needs to avoid lifting or carrying items that require great force and exertion because it is dangerous, difficult, and is a reflection of non-value - adding activities. Rearranging the workplace would be of great help to eliminate unnecessary human movement.

Deficiencies

Manufacturing stoppage, rejection of products, and their subsequent reproduction are perfect examples of duplication of time and money. These rejections can require additional time spent on repair, more time spent on inspection, requiring employees to always be on standby to stop the machines when ordered to do so and also increases paperwork.

Waiting

This happens in case the operators are idle. This is called waiting because an operator's job is put on hold either because of missing small parts, or downtime, and it results in a waste of time. Lead time, during manufacturing, starts when the company pays for the raw materials required to manufacture the item and finishes when the company collects payment from the consumers for the given product. Lead Time applies to cash turnover. If there is a shorter lead time, it means that resources are being used efficiently, there is an outstanding degree of flexibility in fulfilling customer demands, and a relatively small amount spent on operations. Waste disposal is a very significant tool under Kaizen. Other forms of waste in this category are things, products, documents, and information that lie dormant and add no value to the production process while at the same time costing the company in maintenance.

Inventory

Inventory waste is semi-finished items, end goods, and component materials that are retained in the inventory but do not add value to the business or to the item's production; rather, it just costs money.

In merely occupying space, they add more to the running costs; they require additional equipment and facilities such as forklifts, computerized conveyor systems, and storage units. If these products are kept for a long time, they begin to deteriorate in quality, and as market demand increases, consumers build a preference for new goods. As and when new products are launched, these old products become obsolete. The storage units also require additional operational administration and manpower. They are also vulnerable to disaster and destruction by fire. To solve this dilemma, the Just-In-Time development method that was mentioned earlier should be implemented and initialized.

Processing

There are several ways that waste can form during processing. An example is; all processes struggle to synchronize. It can be avoided by requiring assembly line redesign, which would reduce input consumption to generate the same amount of output needed.

Types of input are materials, equipment, and energy, while the output is the customer-requested goods, services to be rendered, added value, and yield. Redesigning the assembly line means reducing the number of workers on the line because less the employees, the fewer errors that can be made. This will minimize quality issues because only highly trained employees are left on the line. This doesn't automatically have to cause other workers to be fired. They can be allocated to other output areas. As productivity increases, there will be a cost reduction. Additional employees would be needed in the manufacturing sector when there is a long production line, so this would also mean additional work-in-process so longer lead-time.

The possibility of making more mistakes increases when there are more workers, and this leads to an increase in quality problems. In short, longer lead-time, inefficient equipment, more staff, and newly recruited employees with little to no training whatsoever will result in higher production costs, reducing profits.

Transportation

Transportation requires the use of forklifts, trucks, and conveyors in the manufacturing industry. This is also a very important part of manufacturing, but the movement of materials does not add value to the product. Plus, there is always space for damage during transportation, so any area of the processing line, which seems distant from the mainline should be relocated closer to the mainline to avoid waste.

Chapter Two

Kaizen and Business

Another major objective you can utilize Kaizen for is to start and expand your own company. Rome wasn't founded in a day, and a business doesn't spring into being instant. And even after your company is already underway, you'll always need incremental enhancement — to set up a brand and keep on rising. This is why Kaizen's all about "gradual progression" – it is built to ensure that companies last.

Ever dreamed of opening a company? What stopped you from doing just that? Is it because your time is tied up in your current family commitments, day jobs, or other activities in your life? Not everyone is meant to be a businessman. But if you believe this path could be for you, then what steps should you follow to make it happen?

Consider this: Choose a suitable moment each day to sit down and envision what your business looks like. Now, pause a second to picture yourself as a businessman. Ask yourself the following questions: what is it that you will produce? Where will you sell it? How many people would you have to hire? Where will you come across suppliers?

The exercise is going to do two things:

- You'll be more focused now on starting your envisioned business.

- Your imagination will begin to search for the answers to gather the resources that are required.

Note that our goal with Kaizen is to introduce you slowly to this revolutionary approach: a little bit every day can lead to larger changes. So, think of the most realistic action or measures possible, one that could make your vision come true:

- Maybe begin by granting yourself an hour a day — to explore the sector you are contemplating.

- Try to interview one individual a day who already operates in your sector, who might be able to assist you in setting up your company.

- Meet other businessmen who are sympathetic to your business idea and make inquiries about what they think about it and how they were able to become successful.

There is no need to quit your current job before you're prepared to jump-start your own business. Even if at this stage you continue to work professionally somewhere else, small acts are still perfectly doable. In the end, the intricacies of your financial strategy will determine how fast you are able to succeed. Remember that with Kaizen, all concepts are divisible into smaller concepts. And this is, of course, the main reason why it's a successful philosophy – to make little gradual progress (weekly or monthly) towards your goal, allows you to take everything at a stride rather than at a run. It's this regular continuity that will ultimately contribute to your organization's growth, no matter what kind of speed you wish to grow at.

Expanding your Company

If you already run a company (or work in a supervisory position), then a Kaizen attitude to things certainly pays off. This is perfect if you can bring the Kaizen theory into practice in your household and work life. But your employees should also be on-board with Kaizen to completely incorporate it into your company. Here are a few ideas to create a "Kaizen working environment":

Look at the Key Business Practices

Start by identifying business areas that are essential for the success of your organization. Such activities may include manufacturing, procurement, sales, and helping clients. Then, every month, try to get the staff to focus on one big target for each of the company's branches. It may be something like: "This quarter, we're going to expand our client base by at least 10 percent." This goal could include improvements to your manufacturing capability, customer service, and marketing needs. Finally, you should build an annual target to develop your company, one that involves every department.

Find Daily Activities

Then find three daily activities that your sales team should regularly execute to accomplish this goal. For example, you can tell them that to boost the company's market share, they should:

- Reach out to five happy current customers every day, and ask if they might suggest anyone else who may be interested in our product.

- Give the current subscribers an email update and notify them about the latest updates that we can give them this quarter.

- Post on the company website one new blog update per day to let folks understand and become aware of our service innovations.

Of course, the acts you select rely on your own business. But the idea is to have the entire organization regularly working on the most important projects, and achieving the monthly targets. These routine gradual measures inspired by Kaizen help to keep the staff on track every morning and prevent them from losing track of what is important to a successful work shift.

Using Kaizen to Create a Team Spirit
When the team feels motivated, it improves its efficiency. An employee, who becomes involved in the business processes, is more likely to accept new ideas that work for the business. Team spirit is the sense of unity that employees feel – it allows them to feel connected to their job, company, peers, and work. When people feel like they're part of something greater than them, it allows them to feel fulfilled. When people feel fulfilled, they're likely to work better. It also makes them selfless, as they start to help others out with their work or take on extra work just to see the company rise.

If you want dedicated employees, you have to start building team spirit. However, you can't just build team spirit by taking all your employees out to lunch every few days. You have to make them think they're all alike and think similarly. To create this sense of unity, get some matching t-shirts, cups, and other things that remind them that they're part of the team. Things represent our feelings, and we form meaning through them; by giving people things that remind them of the team they're a part of, you'll keep their team spirit alive.

You can't manage your employees, and you have to accept that. All you can do is tell them what to do, give them the means to do it, and hope that they succeed. When you try to dictate what your employees should do all the time, it can lead to frustration, anger, and demotivation. When you let them do what they wish to do, employees start to feel like they have your trust. The best motivator for most people is to allow them to challenge themselves. If you showcase your trust in their abilities and leave them alone, they're far more likely to push themselves to prove that they deserve your trust.

Three Kaizen acts you can use to inspire the team are:

- Assign tasks (which must be performed by each team member) on a regular, monthly, or weekly basis: Allow each worker to inquire, and answer honestly, "why" they have been assigned their respective duties. It should make them feel respected and empowered to be doing those duties.

- Do not delegate accountability automatically without any kind of preparation at all. Organize proper preparation and training for members of your group and your employees. Even a tiny, regular training period will effectively prepare the workers for their obligations.

- The final step is the most significant one. A gradual change in the productivity of workers is an assured guarantee only when you correlate the positive behavior you want to a reward system. Know that you are not firing underperforming workers. You are just inspiring your workers to do better and rewarding those who perform brilliantly.

There should not be a financial benefit, though. Research work sponsored by the Federal Reserve found that monetary incentives unexpectedly decrease the efficiency of the employees because they start to see their work only in terms of money. Instead, use other methods to fulfill the emotional needs of employees. The best motivational technique is appreciation and reward. Most people don't believe in themselves, and they need external validation to make them feel like they matter. Many people crave such validation from figures of power and authority whose word matters far more in their eyes than their own. By appreciating and rewarding people, you will create an incentive system that will push people to work harder. Both of these things also add a hint of competition in the mix between employees. As long as this competition remains healthy, it will act as a great motivation for your employees.

You should reward good and exceptional work with tokens of appreciation, such as medals, certifications, or even perks. When you do give such memorabilia to people, remember to mention the specific act, their name, and everything else that personalizes the achievement for them. They should feel seen and heard; also, make sure that you don't just distribute such things to everyone because it has to be a rare commodity to make people work for it.

Make sure that you acknowledge and reward good work within the working community by celebrating all successes as a team together. Highlight work anniversaries, individual milestones, and even personal events like birthdays, etc., to ensure that the team is satisfied and that they feel respected and humane.

Kaizen Event

A Kaizen event is carried out by a company with the sole purpose of improvement. It's a short event and typically only lasts a few days. It's called an event because the whole company is required to participate in it and learn about Kaizen. It not only teaches the company workers about Kaizen and how they can implement it but also is a sort of survey that looks into the functioning of the business to find areas of improvement. While Kaizen itself emphasizes on taking gradual steps every day, the purpose of a Kaizen event is to set the base for the rest of the year. Once a Kaizen event takes place, it teaches everyone what they have to do and what they have to focus on, while at the same time clarifying any potential queries. This way, Kaizen can be incorporated into the working of the company, and every day after the event, small gradual steps can be taken to improve the productivity of the company.

It is mostly carried out by trained Kaizen experts that a company is supposed to hire. It's a collaborative effort, which is why the company is also required to set up a Kaizen team that is then trained by outside consultants. Once the event is over, this Kaizen team can then take over the proceedings to ensure that everyone is implementing what they have been taught during the event itself.

Once a Kaizen event is conducted, most companies tend to forget about it and not care anymore. This is a bad strategy because the gains that are made during the event will stop right there and not be carried forward into the rest of the year. If you want the benefits you can receive from Kaizen to be sustainable, you need to ensure that your team takes Kaizen seriously. If the workers go back to their original way of doing things, then the gains can be reversed in no time, which means that you just wasted a great opportunity.

The event itself can lead to great improvement in efficiency and productivity by teaching the workers about the various programs that come under Kaizen. For example, by teaching workers how to reduce waste, the event itself can boost your profit margins by almost thirty to forty percent. But, what this requires from you is to ensure that the workforce is willing to listen and is receptive to the changes they're being asked to make because otherwise, they will just listen to the advice from the Kaizen trainers and forget about it. A Kaizen event should also focus on areas other than just manufacturing – you can even have your sales team and service team take a few sessions with Kaizen trainers so they can learn to tackle their problems using the Kaizen approach of dividing everything into smaller components.

Here are the steps you have to follow to conduct a Kaizen event:

Hire or Train Kaizen Leaders

You need a person who can take charge of the event for it to be successful. Kaizen is like any other management technique; it requires the trainer to be someone who can sell the Kaizen ideology to the workers. It also needs to be someone who knows what they are doing. Find a person who is aware of the lean philosophy and understand how Kaizen works. If you don't have the money to hire someone, just start doing your research and conduct the Kaizen event yourself.

Gain the Trust of the Senior Management

If you want to ensure that the changes you are making to the company structure are successful, you have to ensure that your top management is on board. This means that you have to make them understand the importance of Kaizen and why it's something they should commit themselves to as well.

Come up with a Game Plan

You need to first set the boundaries of the event. You have to be clear about what areas of your work do you want to apply to Kaizen. Is it just the manufacturing area, or does it include the office as well? Do you want the secretaries to learn about Kaizen as well? The boundaries of the event will depend upon your needs. If you think that there's an area that has been unprofitable and unruly, then you should include that within the fold of the Kaizen event. More importantly, you need to ensure that everyone participates in each Kaizen workshop. The top management needs to know what the manufacturing workers are being told because this way, they know how Kaizen can help increase profits and what specific policies need to be followed to achieve this result.

You need to also set the purpose statement for the event. What is it that you want to apply to your company? Do you want to teach your workers about the 5S technique? Or do you just want them to find areas of improvement every day? You need to communicate well with your team when it comes to institutionalizing Kaizen into the workspace. You have to remember that most of your workers might not have ever heard about Kaizen, to begin with, and if you confuse them even more, they're not going to be particularly enthusiastic about doing the tasks you want them to.

A Kaizen event is only successful if everyone is excited by the prospect of this new philosophy. You want your workers to start implementing Kaizen even outside of work. The purpose of Kaizen has always been to teach people how they can deal with any obstacle as long as they divide it into smaller parts.

Kaizen Training

Kaizen Training involves teaching the entire organization about the system and preparing them for the incremental changes they will be required to carry out every day. It starts from the top managers of the company – they have to learn why Kaizen is important and how it envisions their role within the company to comprehend its meaning. Kaizen is eventually a philosophy, and it can only be successfully carried out if everyone is motivated by its potential.

Top Management Training

Top Management Attitude

The main elements of the upper executives are required to be deeply committed to the Kaizen cause and to be great leaders for the progress of Kaizen operations. Demanding outcomes right after implementing Kaizen without really taking part in any of its operations will not improve employee morale, and instead, horrible results will be produced, which will lead to even more problems. The top managers need to be able to highlight the core points through their behavior for the successful implementation of Kaizen. The core points they should teach the whole workforce are: What is Kaizen? What separates creativity from Kaizen? What advantages does Kaizen have? What techniques are necessary for measuring Kaizen outcomes? What processes and techniques are available for implementing and tracking Kaizen activities?

Actions which the top executives need to take to demonstrate dedication to Kaizen

- Starting Meeting: It marks the official announcement to each company employee of the official commencement of Kaizen operations by the top executives. This indicates the deep dedication of the top executives to Kaizen, which will lead to a rise in employee motivation because they will see that their managers are trying to expand the company's operations and productivity.

- Selecting and Supporting Kaizen Leaders: Assistance can be carried out in the form of quick selection and confirmation of

Kaizen leaders, authorization to carry out other Kaizen activities within the work time, and other implicit support that can be given. This will allow the whole organization to witness the importance of Kaizen.

- On-site patrol: This includes visiting shop floors to collect details on workplace climates as well as the servicing of equipment. Top managers need to know how everything is functioning and, more importantly, need to show their readiness to check at any time so that employees are always on their toes.

- Enthusiasm for Kaizen meetings: Participation will demonstrate clearly how deeply the top managers are dedicated to Kaizen related reforms. The employees should witness all this and become motivated through it.

- The investment needed for Kaizen: one of the key features of Kaizen is to make use of existing resources within the organization without pushing the company to make major investments. Kaizen typically needs relatively little effort in terms of large purchases and incurring more costs. Rather, it reduces costs.

- Diagnosis by top managers: Top managers need to periodically receive updates from the QCC (Quality Control) team and then determine the condition of the Kaizen activities. It is also a great opportunity to let the staff hear what the views of the top executives are. It is an important juncture to bridge the gap between management and workers.

- Incentive system: Any reward given to a person or a team is provided because they have generated amazing outcomes that helped in achieving the stability of Kaizen execution. This reward can be anything from peer recognition, acknowledgment, gift card, or cash. Everyone wants to be recognized in different ways, some people like to be celebrated, and other people just want an email. It's important to change your recognition system based on the individual needs of the employees.

It is necessary to implement an education system before trying to undertake training specifically for Kaizen leaders to ensure that the top executives are aware of the activities mentioned above. This not only allows them to get a better grasp of Kaizen, but it also gives them the ability to share valuable knowledge and discuss problems with other companies' top managers. It can eventually lead to a collaborative environment where results and statistics can be shared to holistically develop better Kaizen techniques.

Creating and Training Kaizen Leaders

The Role of Kaizen Leaders

Kaizen leaders take the lead in Kaizen activities, including enforcing the advice provided by both Advanced Trainers and Basic Trainers. Leadership and dedication are among the key factors that determine the effectiveness of Kaizen operations. Kaizen leaders are required to do the following:

Kaizen leaders should serve as the ones to carry out Kaizen practices under the direction of a Kaizen Trainer(s). Some of the things that they can do are:

- Project QCC: A quality control circle is a group of workers led by a Kaizen leader that ensures that Kaizen practices such as zero waste, incremental change, and removing manufacturing faults are implemented regularly.

- Guidance during QCC leadership selection

- Supporting QCC teams or individual members with slow or lagging activities.

Another function they have to carry out is to establish event strategies, yearly project plans, instructional plans, technological plans, spending plans, produce internal posters, prepare badges and brochures, etc. This is required for the development of Kaizen activities and also to obtain prior approval from top managers for Kaizen related tasks. They have also to collect progress reports and submit them to the top managers of all Kaizen operations. As well, they must be involved in planning presentations, delivering and checking data, and even taking leadership at conferences or meetings that are about Kaizen.

Training of Kaizen Leaders

The ability and expertise of Kaizen leaders can be developed through the activities mentioned below:

- Sharing their knowledge of the issues faced during Kaizen training in open community discussions. This will help the whole organization because the issues they face are likely to be also faced by the staff of the whole organization. By addressing these problems as early as possible, they can be sorted, and dilemmas can be clarified.

- Introducing Kaizen-related activities

- Mentoring and training led by Basic Trainers, Intermediate Trainers, or Kaizen Experts.

- Making presentations at conferences and workshops on Kaizen.

Total Quality Management (TQM)

Kaizen is a term that incorporates practices and programs such as recommendation by workers, and TQM. What exactly does TQM mean? It is a trend-focused on enhancing organizational efficiency at all levels of the company. Total Quality Management includes health, quality control, employee engagement, cost management, increased efficiency, and performance improvement. People are critical to the success of the TQM cycle, and it is highly emphasized because it's the part of Kaizen where everyone plays a role. Common practices under TQM include things such as preparation, coordination, opportunity creation, and collective participation in the job.

The TQM process deals with the organization's cross-functional leadership, the organization's growth, and also the organization's efficiency increment. TQM is used as a resource and philosophy for enhancing the individuals' potential and success within the company.

TQM combines current development programs, common management strategies, and innovative methods in a structured approach focused on the organization's quality improvement. Ultimately, these efforts are directed towards ensuring an increase in customer satisfaction. What needs to be emphasized is that the technological aspects of change can be either innovation-related or mechanical. Change has very little to do with individuals and is only related to the relationship they have with such technology. This means that changing people does nothing to foster innovation; it's only when how they work and relate to the machines is changed that growth occurs.

To achieve profitability, and to increase efficiency and quality, an organization needs to harness the potential lying dormant in the workforce by encouraging each employee to do their job correctly right from the start. This will also allow the top managers to show each worker in the company that every one of them needs to show dedication and carry out constant efforts to enhance the efficiency of the whole organization. Once the workers understand this, they will become more motivated because they'll realize how important they are for the success of the organization.

The organization must have an atmosphere in which each employee works willingly to attain the organization's objectives. When employees are forced to work, they end up not caring about what they're doing, which harms production. This also allows the management to consider any ideas that come from employees who want to contribute and are able to contribute to the company's success. The top management is just streaming orders and priorities downwards to the workers and then allowing ideas to float upwards. This serves as a self-checking mechanism because as orders go down, they meet workers who float the probable issues with the order back upwards so that the top management can solve them.

TQM's methodology helps by offering detailed ways to enhance the efficiency of the company. It does so by analyzing the way work is performed from an organized, structured, consistent, and operational viewpoint. The main goal of the Total Quality Management method is to:

- Satisfy all domestic and foreign consumer needs.

- Involve every operational entity within the organization and leave no one out of the zone of consideration.

- Understanding the impact of heterogeneity on the TQM processes and the possible ways of improving those processes.

- Highlight the continued development of Kaizen.

- Employee engagement and encouragement to become the key motivating force behind increasing the organization's profitability and efficiency.

When there is no tolerance and patience during the TQM cycle, the outcome will always be dissatisfaction and disappointment. Respect and teamwork are key to the success and development of the organization. It is quite clear that employee engagement and process-oriented strategies of manufacturing are significant factors and, therefore, the foundational pillars of TQM. The team's structure and practices are the fundamental aspects for nurturing the individual members and improving the capacity of the company to follow these processes throughout the Kaizen session.

TQM that drives organizational enhancement is similar to the Kaizen approach. The features and different components of both are mutually cooperative and may require a single organizational framework. Integrating them both is the best strategy for organizational success.

Quality, Cost, and Delivery (QCD)

It is well recognized that consumers are kings in a market economy. Therefore, the ultimate aim of any company is to meet consumer standards for services and goods in terms of QCD. The main goal of Kaizen and its operations is to enhance QCD. That makes QCD a top priority for a firm's survival.

Value of a good is determined by its quality, which is created, maintained, and sustained through different processes, from buying raw materials to creating, developing, manufacturing, distributing, supplying, and even servicing the goods or services during the entire cycle. Imai said that the work of creating new goods or services, or of designing new engineered ones, begins with sketches and documentation. Rather than being discovered later, malfunctions can be quickly detected and rectified, which would be very costly to fix if found later. To achieve this mission, the management of Japanese firms used the Quality Function Deployment (QFD) or otherwise known as the Quality Assurance Process Diagram, as a tool.

Cost-efficiency comes right after the quality, and it applies to the total expense of designing, manufacturing the product, marketing to consumers, and even providing the product or service offered by the organization. Reducing costs isn't cost-cutting; it's about cost control. The management team that handles expenses should supervise the production, marketing, and sale of high-quality goods or services while maintaining a low price. The way a commodity is developed, produced, and marketed will decide if there will be an immense waste of resources or not. At the same time, improving efficiency while reducing prices is the best survival choice.

Cost management involves a wide variety of practices, such as overall cost control, by reducing duplication and expense planning to increase the difference between revenue and expenditure. Cost reduction through waste disposal will occur only when the methods of waste disposal that were described earlier are followed properly. Reducing costs by restructuring, negotiating harshly with vendors, and dismissing workers will interrupt the cycle of production, and this often results in quality degradation. Effective administration to decrease costs and increase quality includes other tasks such as standardization, regulation implementation, training, and education. Presently, when it comes to instructing workers, most businesses continue to put too much focus on teaching skills. In Kaizen, great emphasis is put on strengthening the organization's fundamental values that are enforced continuously by the community through learning and teaching programs. These ideals that everyone should inhabit within the organization are self-discipline, good judgment, shared culture, and justice.

Chapter Three

Kaizen's Benefits

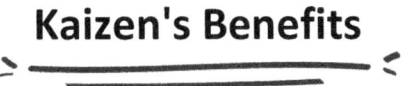

Kaizen has multiple benefits that it can provide your organization, and in this section, we're going to take a look at how Kaizen helps businesses, people, and the entirety of our society.

Motivation

Motivation can be engendered by displaying respect, taming, or firing people who do not fit into the fold of the organization and also inspiring workers to take the same small steps that produce incremental change and find solutions to their problems. For example, the management knows their employees' morale is poor. To solve this, they then recruit people to fix this problem that costs more money and eat into the companies' profits. They promise that they will enhance employee happiness, which includes workplace breaks; this ends up eating into the productivity of the business as well. Instead, if the company had maintained good levels of morale, the employees would have worked even when they were allowed to take a break, saving the company a substantial sum of money.

Building motivation is important, and it can only occur when you pay people properly for the job they have done. All people want is to feel valued for the effort they put into their jobs. Employees appreciate small gestures that thank them for what they have done too. Employees can become dissatisfied because of things like recent layoffs, freezing on pay increases, and discontinuing benefits offered to them. Most workers seem to recognize that at any given moment, the company's financial problems are not the responsibility of the management but a reflection of the economic environment. As mentioned earlier, incremental steps are required to build sustainable success within the organization. Morale can be improved by allowing employees to build solidarity through "holding each other" tasks that can be performed for five minutes a day. This doesn't mean they have to hold each other literally but simply show appreciation for the work everyone does so that nobody feels like they're not part of the team.

When this is done, you can go about your daily business. When staff thank bosses for being excellent communicators, it's not a reflection of their extroverted personalities or their oratory abilities. The explanation is that the leaders did what they were supposed to do and took advantage of the tiny moments they have to communicate with their workers. They saw their workers as people who are smart and know what they're doing and talked them to them instead of barking orders.

Try to remember the employees' names so that you can ask questions directly to them. Make sure that you wait for answers and also display gratitude by saying thank you. You need to set the right emotional tone in the workplace by emphasizing small interactions if you want high morale. Low morale is one of the biggest global corporate challenges, but it can be solved by being kind to your employees for just a few minutes every day.

Talk to your employees from the beginning – you can get a good team together, but they won't be able to work well if they're disconnected from each other. Motivation isn't an attribute that comes from our need to make profits in a business; it comes from our personal needs. Even wanting to make a profit is attached to your ambitions, experiences, and emotions. So, your employees will only be motivated if they feel connected to you and others in the team.

It will also help you to motivate people as the leader because you will have the opportunity to know their personalities and needs. This way, you can put them in the right roles and tweak your behavior to match theirs, so they feel some sort of connection, and you can use their desires to motivate them into working harder. You don't have to be so covert about all of this either – by forming personal connections, you can have more open conversations with your employees. This will facilitate a relationship where you'll be able to know what is impacting them, and you can give them the right advice to help them find their motivation for work.

Kaizen helps with building motivation by pushing the focus of the top executives towards small tasks like having a personal conversation with their employees that they tend to skip over. When the whole organization is integrated into Kaizen philosophy, it'll become second nature for everyone to thank each other for the smallest of tasks because everyone will start to see why these small tasks matter so much.

Cost Reduction

The Kaizen cost management strategy is one that requires workers to shed any mechanism that does not lead to product and service efficiency and quality enhancement. In no way does Kaizen impair employee well-being in any organization. Employees in Kaizen companies are supposed to stay alert about wastage of essential capital. If workers try out a method that destroys the consistency of products or deteriorates value, the company eliminates the method from the list of allowed and encouraged activities. This makes cost management powerful and reliable.

It might just seem unproductive to rely on employees to control costs, but if they are asked to take small steps to save money for the company, then they will help manage costs for the company.

Employees appreciate being given a purpose – it makes them feel connected to the company, and they take up the initiative.

It does not, however, grant the management the right to put responsibility for cutting costs on the employees' shoulders and leaving them to it. First of all, this would generate a form of fear amongst the employees that would be detrimental for progress to happen. What needs to be done is to influence the employees' attitude towards their day-to-day work in the company, so they can spot opportunities where costs can be saved. Once you give them the freedom to think for themselves and start valuing their inputs, they're going to be your best resource.

As the manager, you should help them circumvent their fear of making idiotic and stupid suggestions and help them conquer their fear of your judgment. Allow your workers to think creatively and appreciate their unconventional ideas.

Employee recommendation programs appear to be reliably effective in Japan, but the opposite is the case in the United States. According to a study, the United States provides cash bonuses that are equal to the amount of money saved by the company because of the employee's recommendation. This encourages the workers to find places to save money because that money, in turn, goes into their pocket.

Unlike Japan, either there are small cash incentives, or there are no incentives at all. Psychological experiments have shown how complex human motivation can be. There are two forms of motivation: external and internal. The inspiration that is intrinsic to us comes from our emotional needs. We want to participate in teamwork, engage in constructive projects, and also take pride in our jobs. People want to be given tasks they can rise up to and be proud of what they are doing. They have an inner desire to go about creating important things that have an impact beyond themselves. The extrinsic needs are found outside of a person. Some of the external attributes are drivers, such as money and fame. The external motives push people to keep working at jobs that might stress them out. The trick to minimizing expenses is keeping the incentives as low as possible. People feel more motivated when their inner desires are fulfilled; when you just offer them money, they stop caring as much. This is why giving cash bonuses as a reward has a reverse impact.

While some managers seek to ensure quality performance from their staff, they are very rigid in their strategies, and this causes setbacks. Managers who are strict and push their employees to end up causing more harm. Using such methods will not result in things being done as easily and efficiently as you would like them to be, rather it would make the employee feel humiliated and uncomfortable in your presence. They will be so scared of you that they will give be ambiguous and never answer your questions with conviction. An example of a question that paralyzes all employees is: "how can the company save money and make millions in profits?" This kind of question will dumbfound the brain of even the smartest manager and will leave all the employees silent. What you need to do is to use a softer approach by saying, "Do you think the company can save a bit of money here and there?" You should push the employee to think about things that they don't think should be thought about while working. Kaizen presents you with unlimited possibilities to institutionalize change, and one of them is simply pushing employees to think.

You can also put up notice boards where people can put up their suggestions. Make sure that those boards are emptied every day, and you read all the suggestions because it will tell employees that their voices are being heard.

Employees are also hesitant to make recommendations because they don't want to make you mad. They leave any cost-saving idea they have in their mind only unless their feedback is strongly focused on, and they are encouraged to speak. Once Kaizen is implemented, workers will be given tasks to find out about potential areas of cost-cutting. This does not mean that you're not in control as a manager and won't be allowed to do anything. What you are responsible for is reviewing ideas that have already been given and to determine their efficacy. You should set up suggestion-management procedures so that this task can be standardized. Take every suggestion seriously when sorting the recommendations provided.

Remember that sometimes the suggestions will seem stupid, but if you look beyond that, you might find a great idea. The most immature idea can often hold the secret to creativity. Do not neglect to thank the workers whose recommendations brought about the desired improvement in the company.

Better Accountability

You should try to enhance your ability to spot minor errors. At first, such errors may seem very irritating and frivolous, but if they are not handled early on, they may turn into problems of quality control. Kaizen asks us to discover and correct mistakes when they are still small. It might be tempting to ignore these problems before they turn into catastrophes. Many companies prefer to disregard minor errors as long as the organization puts on impressive displays every day.

If a company succeeds, it continues to honor the things that lead to its success, which are the individuals and the administrative procedures. If something doesn't work properly in a company, it's impossible to bring it to light. Instead, most people just gloss over the errors, and with that, they lose their chance to become better and compete effectively. Whenever you ask your workers if there are things that need to be addressed, and they respond that there's none, mark their assurance as a red flag. The idea that people are going to make mistakes is a fundamental assumption within Kaizen.

Keep in mind that each person is accountable for an organization. So, do not shy away from accountability and teach your employees to do the same. Develop the ability to find these little mistakes, declare that you want everyone in the business to see them too, and give them the solutions needed to fix these issues. Kaizen maintains that accountability for efficiency and profitability rests with everyone in the business, no matter what level they work on. The management also must make it easy for feedback and suggestions to move from the lower workers to the top executives.

Innovation

There is a common myth that the small steps we take under Kaizen end up producing little results only. In reality, these little steps we take the lead to great innovations that change the world over a span of time. Innovation occurs through creativity – when we start paying attention to those little moments of life that otherwise might seem insignificant. Creativity in business begins by questioning because by asking what is not there and what might be wrong, we can bridge the gap between reality and imagination. Imagination leads to productive programs, development of new products and modifications. Although innovation can be exercised at any time, there are some moments when it can truly shine through and make an impact. These moments occur when actual work is being done; it's only when we invested in our work completely that we can also find the radical potential that imagination gives us to make it better. Other moments of innovation are:

- Wastefulness: If something is out of alignment, time is lost, or something ends up breaking, composure is lost, and that will either make us reorganize our schedule or fix the object that has been broken. You should behave with curiosity at such moments because wherever there is wastefulness, there is also the potential for change.

- Shame: Often, it's shame that triggers curiosity because there is a gap between what has been done and what should have been done. This feeling is an awkward one, of course, and it's instinctive to try not to feel it by simply attempting to conceal the error from those who may not have learned about it yet. Many people may own up to their mistakes and may even laugh at the fact that they made them and move ahead with their lives as quickly as possible. Within that condition, ingenuity can come in the form of attempting to cover up the mistake.

After all, what you'll understand is that imagination doesn't require any such unique talent. It just calls for us to focus on what we are doing. You must exercise discipline in order to always be concentrated and curious. The steps in Kaizen will help maintain the attentiveness and also give you the excitement you need. Another Kaizen technique is to attend to the errors made if you want to bolster your imagination. It is a paradox that mistakes need to be made because creativity is triggered only by a trial and error approach, but at the same time, nobody wants to make mistakes. Therefore, the best way to address this paradox is to build small pilot projects and also to promote mistakes that enable learning while at the same time reducing costs. When you enjoy the advantages of innovation, you will remember that it was persistence that gave birth to such creativity. Therefore, patience is an important resource that yields long term benefits.

Better Sales

Sales are frightening, no matter how you try to understand it. Sales are an act of manipulation that encourages other people to trade money for products and services, with the implicit goal of paying the money being support for the company's ideas. A salesman's job is to sell the goods and services they are required to for money, while also selling themselves and their company. But often, they don't seem like generous people to the world. Many people react to them with rudeness and dismissal, but the salesman is still required to keep pressing until their job is completed, that is, whatever they are required to sell is sold.

Many people are frightened by the act of making a sales call, and for such people, there is Kaizen. Most salesmen don't like the fear that comes to their heads when they think about the turnover rate they are required to achieve. Kaizen is an excellent resource for recruiting and retraining sales workers. Kaizen is a great device, especially for scary scenarios. A lot of us are conditioned to mentally shut down if we find ourselves in difficult circumstances. Now that does not make anyone a bad salesperson. It is simply a physiological reaction that a person can't help. For starters, the amygdala in the brain senses a sort of threat to our survival when presented with obstacles that seem extreme.

It's smarter than you should choose those as salesmen whose brains instinctively appreciate the excitement that comes with sales, but such people tend to burn out quickly and easily. Training can be very costly for a salesperson, and dropouts are unreliable and very costly too. The question that needs to be asked is why most management companies don't teach Kaizen techniques to handle stress and fear in their sales department. The fear management technique is a Kaizen method of pushing beyond the anxiety to think while focusing on one move at a time. Rather than forcing the workers to change their way of doing things, empower them to make small adjustments in the way they think.

Taking small steps towards the main objective will keep your mind at ease and drive you to keep moving. Often an action may seem daunting or scary, or you may feel emotionally stressed if it seems that it is difficult to take such huge measures. In such a scenario, what can be done? This is where sculpting of the mind comes in. One of the many basic Kaizen devices is mind-sculpting. It's a way of removing the emotional resistance that we all possess. Mind sculpting was built out of a technique known as directed imagery. The goal was to help patients develop a specific physical skill without actually doing the act. For instance, if a patient wants to develop their vocal capacity, they would cover their eyes and breathe deeply. Once in a comfortable state, the psychologist then encouraged the person to visualize being in a dark cinema hall, sitting very peacefully in front of a blank screen. During that point, the patient is expected to see a voice presenting a demonstration on the screen.

Mind sculpture aims to draw upon what other psychologists have learned from the method of guided imaging. It is an imagined sensory experience, but it is a complete one. Instead of pretending to be in a movie theatre, you can imagine that you are doing any task. If you are a salesperson, you can just imagine the sales call over and over again. Athletes used this sculpturing mentality to train when injuries make it impossible for them to train. Once they return to the field, their success is better than ever before. Musicians use mind modeling, too. It is just a way of training the brain by imaging possible scenarios and training it to respond to them.

For example, if you seem to react to your anxiety by either speaking too quickly or emotionally withdrawing, put yourself mentally in a stressful sales situation. Imagine addressing the situation in a way that you won't be able to in real life. Imagine that every part of your body lets the stress out. Now, slowly start to make the other person in this situation real too. Imagine asking the right questions, answering the customers' expectations, and seeking to understand their needs with real interest. You need to slowly make your voice more confident and clearer.

Conduct this mind sculpting exercises for thirty seconds or less every day. When the time spent every day doing these tasks starts to seem effortless and even routine, try to increase the time you spend practicing. The pace at which you become better at performing the exercise of mind sculpting is dictated by how much you enjoy the exercise. You should not increase the time unless the whole exercise starts to seem effortless.

Increase the time spent on continuous mind sculpting until you have accomplished one of two potential outcomes. The first step is setting the foundations for improvement. You need to start feeling relaxed throughout the practice session. You need to feel ready to carry out the activity even if you still prefer to take it one tiny move at a time. You may also want someone to practice sales with, preferably a friend you are comfortable with. If you feel like challenging yourself, you can also pick someone you are intimidated by. The second possibility is that with little or no additional deliberate effort on your part, your brain will automatically become good at the task and even create new patterns that you might not have even practiced. You might be in a sales call, and suddenly, new lines might popup in your head that you didn't even think of.

Eventually, you will know when mind sculpting worked perfectly when you're in a tough sales situation and see yourself using words as easily as you've been practicing. You will know that you had mastered selling when what made you feel uncomfortable and forget your words, now comes intuitively, and that which seemed unachievable would become normal to you.

By just practicing a few minutes a day, or even less, mind sculpting can be very useful for instilling new behaviors. It is the brain using repetition to store new abilities in the neural pathways and cells. That's why advertisements are constantly pushed throughout the day because the advertiser knows it's the only way to truly reach your brain.

Healthy Workers

Back in the day, nobody would have thought that executives would feel responsible for their workers' good health. Yet, they do now because health insurance has become a huge expense for businesses. Companies are now required to ensure their workers against health risks. This is beneficial for businesses because if a worker keeps on getting sick and missing work, it's eventually going to cost the company a lot of money. A worker with stable health is one that saves money for the company by ensuring that the labor they produce and the rate at which it is produced is stable. Companies care so much about their employees' health now that they have events such as marathons to emphasize how important staying fit is. The business is not just concerned with your ability to come to work, but now also cares about what you're doing outside of it, what you're eating and if you are taking good care of yourself or not. Most companies now understand that people are resources, and good workers are not easily replaceable. It costs less for companies to maintain the health of an efficient worker than just hiring a new worker when they get sick.

Many companies try to maintain the health of their workers by offering rewards to them for losing weight. They incentivize its employees by engendering competition between departments whereby whichever department collectively loses the most weight is given a day off. Such rewards might work in the short-term, but in the long-run, they fail because the employees go back to their old routines once the program is over. What managers need to realize is that losing weight is the toughest thing in the world for a person to achieve because it requires a complete overhaul of the lifestyle they have built. This includes changing how they think, caring about their health more, and being motivated enough to do better. This kind of self-discipline is not easily achievable, and why is that so?

The biggest reason behind this is fear. Kaizen assumes that all change frightens people because they are set in their practices, and people like being structured. Too many changes end up, making them feel anxious. Kaizen is effective in such situations because by breaking down complex changes into small incremental steps, the fear factor that comes with lifestyle change vanishes. Once fear goes away, people tend to think clearly and are able to appreciate the rewards that come with a healthier lifestyle.

But, how do you teach your employees that Kaizen is effective in dealing with their health issues? All you have to do is explain to them the importance of applying Kaizen to their everyday life. By breaking every task into smaller components, everything is going to start to seem easier. Kaizen is a philosophy; it's not just about business; once you accept Kaizen as a way of life, you will start to see the world differently. This is why Kaizen, once integrated into the workforce, completely creates so many added advantages that you might never have thought of. The amount of money you spend on maintaining the health of your workforce is going to be reduced because people will start living healthier lives leading to fewer health issues. Kaizen is an overarching idea, and it has an impact on everything within and outside the organization.

Chapter Four

Kaizen and Startups

For your new startup venture, you have loads of options to introduce Kaizen to achieve a strategic advantage right from the start now that you understand what the theory is about. Every founder of a startup thinks of hitting it big with his goods or service. Not everybody can achieve their vision through. It is only one in every three thousand entrepreneurs that will be able to pave their way to victory and development so their startup can skyrocket. This isn't a matter of pure fate or chance. It is a product of carefully taken judgments and building an environment that continuously develops and grows! Things only happen when there are an optimal learning and development environment.

Startups should first ensure that workers are prepared for potential shifts, challenges, and innovations to get a lead over other companies. The significant thing is educating the existing workforce so that they, in turn, can train the potential workers that might come in. For every company, a learning culture brings about change and ongoing progress as well as enhancement.

This is the secret to building an atmosphere where innovations, feedback, and ideas are discussed freely. Every employee will feel like a company stakeholder when they are part of the process, and decision-making includes everyone. Train your workers not to simply obey orders, but more significantly, to be judgment makers, if you want your company to grow into an institutional force that can compete with the other companies.

Applying Kaizen

If you want to apply Kaizen to your startup, these are the areas and principles you should focus on:

Building a Team

Creating strong teams is at the heart of the Japanese Kaizen theory, as we discussed in the earlier chapter. In accordance with the Kaizen tradition, the team will include experts as well as workers who are willing to question positions of authority. If you want to push for meaningful and systematic changes, there has to be a shift in the status quo. It goes against Kaizen's ideology to adhere to a static status quo. Transformation and constant improvement are crucial to implementing the Kaizen theory effectively.

Enhancement

How does one in a startup develop or drive quality improvement? You should start focusing on brainstorming, devising, establishing an open-door policy for feedback, developing a less hierarchical organizational structure, etc. That's where data gathering comes into the frame. Start from day one by gathering information about your company. Use this knowledge to recognize what works and does not work in favor of the company. Although dropping systems that are unsuccessful at the very start, when it comes to startups, is pretty risky because you might not have complete information since the system hasn't been functioning for too long. A compilation of information over a span of time will help you make relatively reliable judgments and drop unsuccessful systems over the long run. You may not have such extensive records as a businessman or company founder. However, they are critical for long-term decision-making and decommissioning of unsuccessful programs. Collect data, evaluate it, and figure out what adjustments need to be made for the company to perform successfully in the long run.

Implementing Changes

The greatest enemy of development is the inability of a company to reconfigure its processes, strategies, and structures to adapt to modern, cheaper, and more successful ways of doing things. Assess the impact of those changes on the company's growth. Begin by measuring the effect of the changes over a month. Then, turn to evaluate the impact of administrative, procedural, or other improvements over a one-year period to ensure that the changes are successful. It will also help you envision what the company will look like and will prove to be an important guiding pillar.

Contextualizing Kaizen to Startup Culture

Kaizen is all about teamwork at its heart, which means you have to include all of your staff entirely in the policies and procedures. They should be allowed to share their thoughts, logical deductions, insights, and business feedback as if they were their own. The ideas and recommendations will include improving business operations, increasing the efficiency of the job, saving money, and enhancing the criterion used to measure quality and safety.

Employees need to get the motivation that is essential to engage in their thoughts and ideas and understand them actively. Startups do not have the resources to recruit an expert at Kaizen. Through holding Kaizen workshops, you can resolve this by recognizing the finer aspects of this Japanese revolutionary ideology and start using it to achieve your managerial and business goals. Employees will be motivated to get a rating in six sigma business practices. There are also other training methods you should encourage, like project management, which can help increase their overall performance by reducing mistakes and optimizing the working structure of the manufacturing process.

Tips and Tricks

Kaizen involves more than simply including the workers in the change and growth process. Below are some of Kaizen's theory tips and tricks which will teach you what to do and what to avoid when it comes to applying it in your company:

1. Do not rely on your experience alone, or have undue confidence in your skill over and above that of others. If you want to develop a profitable and innovative business, seek the talents, insights, knowledge, and expertise of other people in the team. Following strict structures and procedures will hamper your performance, allowing rivals to make more improvements in the game.

2. Do not wait for perfection to happen suddenly. Even with a forty percent chance, you can reinvent a company and continue to develop and make improvements along the way. If you wait until all is in the right place, you will just be driven into a condition of stagnation.

3. Do not neglect the issues and challenges. Resolve them as soon as you know about them, rather than ignoring them or

hoping for the right time to fix them. The best time to learn is on the go. The more you ignore your startup's tiny, every day constantly nagging problems, the larger they develop into and cause significant damage to the startup's overall profitability, performance, and progress.

4. If it comes to telling others about something you don't understand and asking for some help, do not hesitate. Do not encourage confusion and ambiguity to build up just because things aren't obvious to you. In the beginning, especially, it is vital to discuss and debate rather than allowing for confusion to take ahold and an incomplete interpretation of processes, procedures, and technologies to be developed over time.

5. One of the biggest errors many startups make is not relying on facts and figures and instead just obeying opinions. Everyone wants to give their two cents because it's a new venture. It is not an efficient strategy, though, when it comes to productivity and performance. Take on all suggestions and proposals, by all means. However, ensure that the facts back them up whenever it possible to get them. Keep in mind that decisions are not made in the meeting room over cups of coffee, which means that most decision making is just thirty percent debate, and seventy percent instinctively made decisions that occur during daily functional activities.

6. Always believe you do not have it in good order, and you need to change everything. You have to aim for quality growth, transformation, and enhancement. This is

particularly true in a startup where various structures, both organizational and operational, are continuously being tested to evaluate and determine what works best for the entire company.

Guide to Instilling Kaizen Changes

Start your Kaizen journey by determining which business activities are essential.

Although conventionally, Kaizen methods are related to the production and manufacturing industry, just like Six Sigma — it is now used in all kinds of trade and other different sectors. Identify procedures that can be used daily, weekly, and monthly for your startup. It will help you to focus on enhancing the procedures. It is critical to have some cash reserves ready to handle and streamline the cash flow. Manage urgent cash shortage conditions by having a company credit card and other credit lines ready. When the procedures are not already in place (which is the case for a lot of startups), it is the best time to put in place documents that can easily guide all aspects of the company. Do not depend on only one person's knowledge and expertise. Some of the greatest mistakes startups make is that they rely heavily on the founders' knowledge and not proper paper trails. This means that whenever a problem occurs, the employees must seek the expertise of the founder rather than looking up what to do in a structured procedural guide. This is not a healthy way to carry out Kaizen. A successful Kaizen practice includes recording all consistency processes and giving the whole team a chance to revisit procedures whenever they want to. This is the way you will be able to build better produces and more effective processes. You may find certain old procedures that can be removed, changed, or revamped — leading to tremendous savings.

Which are the areas that push or drive the company forward, and are completely necessary for the organization's functioning? Carry out our regular training and evaluations, and use the input to improve. When recording procedures, it's easier to identify ways to build on them by spotting problems.

Your startup will eventually expand, and the market climate will change tremendously as the startup continues to grow. You will have to adapt to these developments and adjust to new policies and procedures. This will be key to your startup's success.

Consider these aspects to integrate Kaizen into your startup: What is it that you are doing? How can you make things better? Is it possible to change what you are doing at the moment, even if it is only a marginal change? Perhaps adjust the way you treat your invoices, so that, rather than spending a few hours per day managing them, handle them all collectively on a Saturday or Sunday to streamline the invoice payment procedure. There are many such questions that you can ask yourself, which will point you to the right path when you're applying the Kaizen theory to boost your company's performance.

Encourage the Workforce to Make Steady Changes
Is the company a healthy and welcoming environment for employees who want to submit innovative ideas or helpful advice? If that is not yet the case, then your company will need a Kaizen solution. As a

startup, engendering motivation and getting innovative new concepts from employees is even more critical. It would help them feel part of the start-up and will improve overall engagement, which will lead to more ethical behavior from your workers. Think about it, every time an employee is allowed to come up with a suggestion within your newly launched company, and their recommendation is implemented, they feel valuable, respected and motivated, which leads them to come up with yet more ideas for change and development. Allow the workers the freedom to fix or overcome issues they find. Ideally, a manager or a similarly competent person will be in charge of the operation and decision-making within the company. They should, therefore, have the creative control to fix problems and develop processes to make their tasks more effectively. Those processes will be shared with the team once they are identified.

Nevertheless, it is also essential for workers to believe they have the power to make things better anywhere they experience problems. Encourage and inspire the staff to come up with creative, imaginative, and resourceful ways to enhance their job processes and assignments. Inspire them to find opportunities to do things differently, and exchange them with others. Start celebrating small successes to build a constant and consistent enhancement community. All workers at your company should feel encouraged to make decisions or take an active role in decision making. It is important for small companies because you are at a stage where the position of each employee is critical. They are all part of the founding or early team, making them feel like they are a crucial part of the growth, culture, and story of the organization. You can help them feel even more deeply about their position in the company when you encourage these already essential employees to make decisions. It's not unusual for a single individual to embody the entire organization in a small company or startup, which is why transparent communication is crucial.

Whenever an employee speaks to you, take suggestions, reviews, and seriously study what they say. They can give you ground-level perspectives about something that your eye has probably overlooked. Your workers are the ones who do hands-on work on different procedures and programs, and they learn better. Encourage them to explore what works well and what does not. Understand that they are specialists in their unique processes, and they should closely analyze how those processes operate. This is precisely why they should be trusted, and you should run after them for their knowledge.

When applying the Kaizen philosophy inside your company, you will realize that no information is too big or too small. It's all essential and has meaning. Any chance to show just the tiniest inkling of progress should be appreciated. Small changes will add points, which will gradually become big improvements over a period of time. This extends to all aspects of the business and not just expenditures. Waste can be found in different ways - anything that occupies the time of an employee or even the physical and virtual storage space should be researched and checked as a potential implementation field for Kaizen.

Understand that the end result of the journey is not progress or enhancement. This is not the finish line but rather a belief that one must continue to follow the discovery and progress arising from the discovery. Kaizen's not about going somewhere; it's about always being on the journey and never stopping. It aims at gradual progress, one step at a time. Continuous learning and development techniques must be closely associated with the structure of the business and form part of its basic culture. Don't limit the implementation of Kaizen to unique processes or some specific occasions only. It should be integrated into the corporate culture of the company as a way of life.

Creating a Winning Mentality

When you've been employed in the past for a "no" culture company, operating in an environment where you're told it isn't possible, even though you know it is, it can leave you feeling demotivated. In the past, you might have used a new and innovative program, method, or technology just to be told you can't use it. Would you want to promote such a toxic environment inside your new business? If you want your company to prosper and succeed in the long run, destroy the "no" mentality. Train your workers to say "yes" and to always assume that it's possible. From embracing fresh ideas to helping a company grow and prosper in the long run, it can all be done with the right mentality. A "yes" culture is based on the concept of developing, modifying, and helping others move together.

Pareto Principle

To significantly improve your performance, you should start using the Pareto Principle or 80/20 rule. Taking small steps to achieve the best results is the basic feature of this tactic. Small business and start-up owners should inspire its employees to seek out big wins for the company, where the company has to make the least effort while at the same time gaining the most. That doesn't mean that you can overlook the subtle things, though. Remember that this information will do your business or break it. A range of sectors spanning from software design to manufacturing to those working within the service industry may benefit strongly from making minor adjustments or correcting small details. For example, a slight improvement in the manufacturing process will turn the reduction in wastage of 5 percent into a 5 percent reduction in the cost of input. This 5 percent will add up to become a massive sum over a period of time.

Constant Change

Improvements occur in other companies only at certain set times during the year. Let your company not follow a similar tradition, in which updates and enhancements are only welcomed at particular times of the year. You should not limit upgrades to only a few times in the year or to general meetings. Process updates and program enhancements should occur regularly without stoppage. Make it a part of the everyday culture of the organization. Develop your startup right from the start into an enterprise powered by change.

Your staff will be happy to come to work every day if they know something new can be done. They will be motivated by the development goals, principles, and ideology to keep making improvements within the company continuously. Employees will be happy to come to work every day as they discover a more productive way to do things and know they are free to adopt this successful way of doing things. They should be allowed to celebrate small victories and be given the freedom to make decisions based on what they believe is best for the overall quality control, growth, efficiency, and competitiveness of the company.

Even the most non-creative employee can often impress you with their ideas that can improve your company's total income and reduce your expenditure. It's a real win-win situation for every company when it happens, which is exactly what Kaizen is all about. Kaizen is all about simple fixes. This basic but cutting-edge Japanese theory has no magic bullet to solve the issues or trigger obstacles to vanish in one shot. Because Kaizen means "change for the better," its simplicity makes it unique because, while it might be a minor improvement, it is about continuous improvement. One change leads to another, and eventually, the whole system is transformed.

Everybody loves tales of rapid and revolutionary changes that yield immediate results. A more doable and efficient solution, however, includes making organizational and individual improvements through a series of small, systematic steps.

The way it functions on a psychological level is that drastic changes set off the mechanism of fear and resistance from our brain, thereby shutting off our ability to think logically and creatively. Tinier and streamlined actions, on the other hand, avoid making us feel tense, anxious, and scared. It does not activate the warning or reflexive defense mechanisms of our brain. Our imaginative, rational, and cognitive processes work easily when there is a gradual and steady change in a lasting and effective way. That is why people continue to believe that being slow and steady works.

Likewise, continuous repetition simplifies the transformation of behaviors into habitual activities and ultimately makes them our lifestyle. The act of doing small tasks gives the mind a deep sense of fulfillment. Keep making small and incremental regular improvements to processes and systems rather than making drastic developments that could scare you. Your emotional blindfolds are overcome when you make small and incremental changes, as opposed to making big changes that cause work-related stress to take over and keep you from accepting change with all your heart. The change will even overwhelm people who think they aren't scared of anything.

Chapter Five

Ikigai

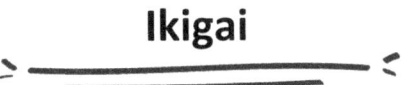

Ikigai is a combination of the words 'iki,' meaning 'life,' and 'kai,' meaning 'product' or 'value.' The premise behind ikigai is that there is something beyond your own life or something that might ultimately become part of your own life, giving meaning to everything around you: yourself, the people you live with, where you live, and your environment. That is your purpose in life, your Ikigai. Possessing a purpose-driven lifestyle is akin to knowing what to do, where to be, and how to function at all moments of your life. It's getting rid of those nagging questions that make you question everything around you.

Locating your ikigai makes life so much easier and more deliberate because you have a reason for being. In the good times, it will give you something that you want more than anything else, something that will help you get through the tough times and something to create a sense of accomplishment at the end of the day, helping you to sleep comfortably in your bed at night. You'll be free to start your day without any unnecessary questions about existence bothering you.

Many people today typically discover their Ikigai by mistake. They end up becoming a parent, land a dream career, start traveling, writing a book, finding confidence, or creating an invention, and all of a sudden, understand that this is just what they wanted to do all along. They finally get that this was what their life was supposed to lead to - they want to live and die for exactly this. This is their contribution to the universe, their commitment to the entire world and purpose in life.

Some people today learn this from a young age — a lot of teachers and doctors understand this. They were attracted to educating others or caring for others even when they were too young to understand how they could enter such professions. For them, it is a calling, a higher purpose, rather than simply a job. This is intrinsic motivation, and you know you have the ability to do something great, like becoming an artist. This may occur randomly also at times.

For some, this discovery comes after years of soul searching, though, for many people, even after years of aimless wandering, nothing happens. The overwhelming majority of people do not discover their own Ikigai until they are in their 40s or older unless they bother trying. It can also lead to mistakes, like when you end up opening a company, you didn't truly feel connected to which can leave you with a profound sense of regret. Many more never discover their own Ikigai and fail to find meaning in their lives. They end up feeling depressed, knowing that it's all for nothing. This feeling of being disconnected from your higher purpose makes you feel like life is not worth living.

Let's take the example of Okinawa to understand the importance of Ikigai. Okinawa, a small island to the south-west of Japan, has a surprisingly huge and strong population. Okinawa is situated in the infamous Blue Zone. People here live much longer than traditional Western life expectancy. Okinawans have an inner drive, intention, and a close-knit community as well. Ikigai is what makes their life truly remarkable.

If it were that simple, we would all probably live for over ninety decades. Instead, the world is teeming with numerous ailments linked to food, chemicals, emissions, and lifestyle. We're too busy to eat what we require, and we're far too caught up in our jobs to be doing everyday exercises. There is not enough time to develop friendships and close social ties. Many contemporary cultures of the West revolve around accomplishments that can be quantified in cash and popularity. Okinawa is different - a place on earth where people live better and longer lives than almost anywhere else. The island's people say that the key to their survival is harnessing purposeful energy and expelling negative ones. They continue to live a long, happy, and purposeful life.

The word "purposeful" is important to emphasize. Even retired people get up every morning with a sense of purpose, a goal in mind to achieve for that day, no matter how small it may be. Despite the island's rural and rugged environment and restricted access to modern medicine and health care, Okinawans are fitter than their Western counterparts. They don't have cancer, cardiovascular diseases, diabetes, and psychological issues like depression or dementia.

Folks in Okinawa spend all their energy building personal and meaningful relationships with each other. In a given lifespan, family and friends support each other, and no individual is left lonely and unattended. The older serve the young, and even the younger serve, the older, both living in a symbiosis that is optimistic and welcoming. Such social networks help to alleviate anxiety while also providing safety and security in everyday life, where people recognize that they have other people to rely on if they are in any kind of need. Most Okinawans have a slim, healthy, and light diet based on vegetables and tofu. They consume balanced, low-carb foods in combination with assorted soy foods. This diet lets them have a balanced existence.

Alongside sugar, fats, and highly processed foods, avoiding meat helps them to fight against cancer, diabetes, heart diseases, and obesity. Fat cutting green tea is a major part of the diet. They have plenty of ginger, mugwort, an assortment of herbs, and chilies, too. Besides eating healthy and sweet, Okinawans believe in exercising regularly. They construct their everyday routines around walking, dancing, and gardening. They spend a large amount of time in the fresh air and reap the benefits of the outdoors and the sun. They are safer, have stronger muscles, high vitamin levels, and generally possess happier moods, thanks to the daily exposure to exercise and sunshine.

Okinawan living isn't just a walk in the forest. The Okinawans have learned how to leave the past where it belongs in a strangled and dark history. Instead, they are focused on the simple joys of today. What we need to retain from this culture is that the standard of life should not be quantified by fame and wealth. Rather we should seek to promote the quality of our interactions, to find peace of mind in simple daily acts, and to lead a positive as well as active life.

The secret to the survival of these island dwellers can come down to just one term: ikigai, which roughly equates to one's purpose for living or your own internal motivation to go out of your house and carry out your job. This can also be defined as an intersection that includes four distinct components: what you're passionate about, where your talents lie, how you can make a living, and what the world needs. Most Japanese think everybody has an ikigai, or destiny; they were born to meet. Yet while some people discover their ikigai quickly, others need to figure it out as time goes by. It is very important to carry on if you fall into the latter group; after all, it is ikigai that will eventually motivate you to escape from your bed when you are too depressed.

Okinawans are also great at the work they do. They have a high degree of precision and put a lot of emphasis on detail in their daily work. For instance, a professional craftswoman in a paintbrush mill in Okinawa is famous for her brushes because she spent her whole life perfecting the craft of attaching human hair to a brush. She has managed to do her job with outstanding dexterity and skill because she believes it to be her purpose in life. Consequently, if your ikigai is the profession you are in, you will not retire ever. And if your ikigai is a hobby that gives you happiness and a sense of peace, don't give up on that ever. Okinawans obey these values and therefore stay active even late in their lives. When they are forced to retire, they will nonetheless find ways to stay involved in their communities, such as doing gardening or other alternative work.

Defining Ikigai

But how does one find one's personal ikigai? We need to start by discovering the two definitions of life and how they impact us.

Love

The first definition of life is love. Love is the ultimate purpose for why any of us exist on this planet. All of us are searching for it constantly, whether it's from our parents or a partner. Love can exist in different forms, and in many ways, it can also be harmful to us. The reason why love is a definition of life is that it can end up defining us. When you love somebody, you think that you will give your life up for them, this gives you direction, as a man you might think that protecting the lover of your life is the reason why you were born. But, the problem with this is that love can also be problematic when we don't understand what it truly is.

Love isn't about people. You can't assume that taking care of somebody is the entirety of your being. What if that person goes away or they do not want you to protect them anymore? We have all heard of break up stories gone bad where people take drastic measures when they lose love in their life. This happens because what you fell in love with was only transitory and non-permanent.

The kind of love that Ikigai talks about is love that transcends people and places. It's truly being in love with yourself and realizing that you carry a whole universe all within you. It might sound cliché, but remember that everything you witness only exists because you do. This means that the world doesn't exist beyond your own mind, and therefore, everything in a way is a part of you.

So, how do you discover what you truly love? You need to try the Kondo method. Go through the things that you own and find out the ones that have meaning. Say you own a car, what does that say about you? That you have money? Is that truly meaningful? The only way that you can find true love in your life is to look for those things that don't serve an immediate purpose, yet you keep them. An old photograph of you with your family; for example, does it help you in any way? No. So, why are you still attached to it? It clearly shows that it's the photo that you truly value. This way, you can retrace your steps to find out what is meaningful and what is not.

Talent

The second meaning of life is talent. Not talent in the sense of being able to accomplish something, but what can you create. As human beings, we find it hard to determine what our true purpose in life is because we don't have much beyond us to tell us who we are. If somebody asks you who you are, most people just reply with their accomplishments. Why is that? Because we tend to think that the things we have achieved are more real and substantial than we are. Our talent bridges this gap because it tells us what we are good at creating and how that relates to our intrinsic nature.

Some people are talented singers, what does that mean about them? That they should start a career and become rich? That would be most people's answer, but people who truly enjoy singing realize that it's a way to connect to their inner emotions. It's a form of expression that is unique to them. Similarly, people who draw art can create what they feel, and this helps them to process their emotions. Painting is considered therapeutic because it allows us to channel what we feel on the inside.

You might think you have no talents, but it's probably because you haven't looked for it. Your talent does not have to be something conventional like singing, dancing, or painting. You can do find joy in anything, even if it's something like sewing or just organizing a house. You will know something is your talent when you not only feel like doing even when you have nothing to do but feel like you're in a stride. It's like erasing who you are and becoming one with the task at hand. This way, you will know what you feel connected to.

Ikigai and Entrepreneurship
Since the beginning of time, the acquisition of a fulfilling lifestyle has been the universal objective of all human beings. We are looking for activities that offer us happiness, and that exists outside our own home. We all want to do something for the society and recreate the world in a way that suits our internal reality. Japanese philosophy

implies that 'ikigai' is not something you find outside the office to distract yourself from work, but something that should be present in every aspect of our lives. We spend a lot of our time in our office, and it can be hard to feel comfortable if we have to undertake a heroic effort every morning to escape from our bed and make our way to a place where we don't feel respected. It is the place where we embark on our personal journey with the world, and if it's not fulfilling, then it can leave us feeling disconnected. Individuals in every company should always be a priority over and above the actualization of private goals such as money or fame. While this might sound immature, the simple truth is that if you look after your employees' well-being, your profits are likely to increase ten-fold. From a financial perspective, investing in the intrinsic motivation of your workers, the ikigai of your whole team increases your profits.

One will always encounter the notion of fulfillment when looking into the question of finding a satisfactory place of work. But, there are other factors that should be considered, as well. The following are the aspects you should study to determine where you want to work:

- Trust between colleagues and leaders
- Pride in the work that you are doing.
- Comradeship at Work.

Trust is the very first place that you need to start if you wish to develop and improve; it's the adhesive that ties the workforce together. Trust is established through the worker-employer relationship. There are countless benefits that you will derive if you end up creating trust in your office: staff in the office will act more relaxed, everyone will feel like they can rely on each other for support, everyone will feel valued, and will become far more confident in sharing their views and thoughts.

Pride and camaraderie are the most important and are becoming rarer by the day. Each of these values is experienced subjectively by an individual because they depend on every person's personality and needs. They rely on the connection between the worker and his or her job (pride) and the connection between the worker and his or her colleagues (camaraderie). The expectations that each individual has from their work in order to be satisfied are personal and special, and ensuring that everyone is in a job that fulfills their goals is crucial. The quality of relationships with colleagues depends on the personalities and diverse preferences of each individual and their needs. The management's ability to match them effortlessly and put like-minded people in the same department is vital for camaraderie to occur.

Pride and camaraderie can be connected back to ikigai if you take the principle of 'living and letting live' into account. Appreciating others for their purpose in life while valuing your own makes for a harmonious working atmosphere even when people might clash with each other.

To become a business that is made up of happy employees, you first need to address the three variables mentioned above: hope, pride, and camaraderie. The best way to create a happier workplace is by listening to your employees and their inner demands. If you keep them satisfied, they will ensure that your business is successful. What you need to remember is that what other people are saying is more important than what you have to say. Many people believe leading others is all about being dominating and capturing as much space in meetings and conversations as possible, but that's a lie. As a leader, you should never forget the fact that you don't do any work, you aren't the one who is producing value for the company, and all you are doing is directing and supervising the labor of others. Your job is to listen to what they're saying – let other people speak as much as possible because it will give you more information on their inner state, and this way, you can use that information to help them work better. You want your employees to share what they are thinking, not hide it from you.

If you want other people to speak their mind, your first task is to make them feel welcome. Don't use your phone or your laptop, or keep constantly being distracted by others – the other person has to feel like their emotions are welcome within that space. Being a good listener also means getting to know your employees better; you can't expect to understand what someone means unless you know their personality, background, and what kind of person they are. As a leader, remember to interact with your employees on an equitable plane, share something about yourself as well, and this way, the personal connection you form will enhance the empathy quotient. It's also the best way to humanize people; if the purpose of leading people is to see them as a herd, you can counter that only by individualizing people. You have to see them as people who have families, aspirations, and a life beyond work.

The one thing that most leaders tend to forget is that you can only motivate people to work harder by making them feel part of the team. When you appreciate their work and promote them to better positions, your employees will start to feel a sense of pride in what they do. More importantly, the best way to generate pride is by allowing your workers to do something meaningful. If an employee cares about the planet, you should let them work in a field that focuses on saving the environment. This will create a motivation that will push them to work even if you don't pay them (although you must). Solidarity within the workplace means ensuring that everyone feels like they can say anything without hesitation. Even if you are the manager, you have to make your workers feel like you consider them to be part of your family. They shouldn't be scared of you because that won't make them feel like they have a purpose, but will instead demotivate them.

Locating your Ikigai

There are people who say they can't find the satisfaction of life within their individual abilities or thoughts. Most people find themselves enduring the reality of forcing themselves out from their bed and laboriously dragging themselves out to get the job done. To work with the feeling of energy and passion is now just a distant memory for many of us. Individuals find it very difficult to get that spark of life in their work, and the idea of finding their ikigai hasn't even had the chance to surface.

According to a study on ikigai, among the research's main findings was that extrinsic motivation is unachievable, in different terms, encouraging people with material things is non-realistic. Scientists find that people respond only to inspiration intrinsic to them. Japanese Philosophy asks individuals to ultimately work out their ikigai. When you look back, you'll remember that as a kid, you might have had an extraordinary inclination towards something. Once maturity arrives, who we become depends on socio-economic variables like, what we do, what our parents think we should do, and what kind of income we think we want to achieve our ideal living standards.

There are four questions you must ask yourself for enhancing your daily orientation. Immersed in the everyday haze, it isn't always easy to discover our abilities. There are four questions that could help us find our way. Write them down in a place where you will often come across them; you can use them as a compass that takes you closer to your target. These questions are:

- What is my part in the play that is life? Can you say you are an extrovert or an introvert? Will you end up enjoying doing the task by yourself or in a group? If it's a mix of both, would you still enjoy the situation? Make sure you write your answers to these questions every time you come across a potential place where you can work and find a community.

- What acts do I experience fulfillment with? When is it that the time flies? What is something you might deliberately spend hours doing without feeling bored? This can be an activity in which you will feel completely involved, and will not feel like giving up.

- What kind of work comes easy to you? Could there be something you personally consider easy, with which others seem to be struggling? Most people today find it very easy to arrange documents in a straightforward manner; others are exceptional at considering multiple viewpoints. You need to find what you are naturally good at.

- What did you really enjoy doing when you were a kid? This query helps build your ikigai's base. Was the activity you enjoyed intrapersonal, psychological, moral, physical, linguistic, aural, or maybe visual? This will help you to understand what kind of sense of experience you are inclined towards.

Ikigai is the union point of four fundamental elements of life: passion, vocation, career, and the daily. In other words, what we are all looking for is eventually the perfect place that represents the perfect union of all these four elements. A place where all that you love meets what you are good at, suits what you value within yourself, and has a larger meaning that connects you to the universe. Ikigai is complete only if the purpose you find implies some sort of community service. This happens because we always feel more comfortable giving gifts than receiving. When you have defined these elements, the next move is to start with your compass. Start working on your questions, and see if there is something that suits your responses.

Chapter Six

Other Applications of Kaizen

Kaizen is not just a business principle, but one that can be applied to almost all aspects of life. In this chapter, we're going to discuss how Kaizen as a theory can help you in different aspects of your personal life.

Personal Development

In addition to Kaizen's organizational philosophy, there are broader aspects of Kaizen than what is applied in the corporate world. Every person is said to have an instinctive drive to want to better themselves in one way or the other. Kaizen provides the grooming that workers need for their personal growth through different ideas and methods. It helps them to measure their lives against set standards of physical, social, emotional, and psychological existence and, where possible, to make recommendations for improvement. Many people that take part in this journey prefer to focus on strategies that require small steps that will make their lives easier.

When a person starts to go through Kaizen practices, most of the behaviors they want to improve are physical, including sleep, exercise, and diet. If these new behaviors are implemented, they are then motivated to move to the self-improvement stage where their emotional dimensions are focused on. Any worker who joins in for the Kaizen initiatives will note an improvement in their behavior, and every day they get will feel happier. It will improve their workout habits, eating habits, and even sleep. They will also start exhibiting more complex habits related to their interpersonal skills and even spiritual commitments. They will also be able to establish a Kaizen mentality in their personal lives, and greatly benefit from this in every other aspect of their life.

Transition is said to be a never-ending process. If one has achieved success in a certain specific aspect of life, he or she will be encouraged to apply the same strategies to the other aspects of life. The theory of Kaizen makes it easy for individuals to change by setting short-term, long-term, and mid-term targets and to think about making small improvements as they work towards reaching those targets. The need to be successful in more fields than one does not end once Kaizen is adopted. This is why the acceptance of the theory of constant improvement is encouraged. You have to remember when attempting to change behaviors, that not all behaviors are harmful or have adverse impacts on your health. Habits are not necessarily negative; it's our relationship with them that makes them so. They are necessary for us to be able to work every day on some level. Our negative feelings can be turned into healthy ones, ones that can be used when we feel drained and stressed to keep us secure and support us. Escape from our habits' safety zone can be daunting, and as a result, we prefer to go about our everyday lives like we are some sort of robots.

You might wonder why changing habits are difficult. Did you know that repetitive behavior saves us a lot of energy and time? It can seem frightening and intimidating when it comes to altering them because they act as sedatives that calm us down by recreating familiarity. For there to be a shift in repetitive habits, the first step is to learn how we first got socialized into such behavior. The next thing you have to do is address the patterns by finding the triggers for undesirable behaviors. Besides knowing the trigger for these habits, you must become aware of the incentives that we often temporarily receive from such behavior. Consider how such incentives determine our future actions because we wish to replicate the same reward in the future, and how these habits can offer permanent rewards if modified.

The next thing you'll probably ask is, how long does this shift take? The amount of time needed for one person to achieve automatic processing varies from one person to another. It depends on the individual, the environment they have been brought up in, and the attitude of the individual towards change. To change habits, one must learn the new behavior by constantly increasing the intensity of the connection between the circumstances of the individual and the specific habit being performed. The more a pattern is replicated, the more probable it is to become ingrained.

Dietary Habits

Applying Kaizen strategies to your eating routine can be helpful to those who want to improve their attitude towards food. Rather than limiting or eliminating the enjoyment of eating, you should seek to make small adjustments to the way you eat food to build a healthy mindset to improve your mind and body. Let's look at how Kaizen can turn your dietary patterns into three separate term goals: goals for the short, medium, and long term.

Drink More Water

The amount of water you drink each day will rely on your gender, what you generally eat, the number of workouts you do, and the environment as well. Including milk, coffee, tea, and sugar-free beverages into your diet while at the same time, drinking water is fine. Many people forget to drink water, but with the advent of Kaizen, it will become a habit, and therefore help the body even when you forget to. Don't forget to listen to your body's water needs just remember to rehydrate every few hours. You should not overhydrate because it may be harmful to the body.

There are plenty of meat-eaters in our planet as of now. Reducing the level of meat consumed by the body has many definite benefits for your health. Kaizen is an ideal method for such a transition because it is a slow process of improvement. All you have to do is slowly transition and start eating more vegetables and fruits. Within the Japanese diet, vegetables play an essential role. It's also a cheaper diet that includes all the nutrients that your body might possibly need.

Kaizen is a perfect way of bringing fruits and vegetables into your diet. You must cut down on sugar as a vegan. It's said the sugar and soft drink intake is really dangerous, and it's true to a certain extent. So, remember to stop drinking fizzy drinks. This doesn't mean you can cut back completely on sugar because the fruits you eat as you continue Kaizen implementation contain only natural sugars. Since it's a gradual process, you should start cutting back on the amount of sugar you usually take, just reduce your consumption by half and then slowly phase it out. Your body needs time to adjust to a new source of energy like natural sugars, and that takes time. Do not eat cereals because added preserved sugar is present in them, which are harmful to your body. Also, stop adding sugar to your hot drinks like coffee or tea.

Limit the Portion of your Diet
This relates to reducing the amount of food you consume. We tend to eat too much because we don't measure our food based on the correct portions. You can start by calculating the calories in your food, using small bowls; after cooking and eating, make sure there are no leftovers and observing your hunger levels.

Eat Attentively
Focus on and truly enjoy every mouthful you consume. Try to eat with little to no distractions at a meal, switch off your TV, and don't eat in front of a laptop. Concentrate on preparing the meals rather than ordering things from outside. When we don't pay attention to the food we eat we are left feeling hungry because we didn't really enjoy the food and instead just ended up swallowing it down. So, even when your stomach is full, you still feel like eating, and this is what leads to overeating.

Mindset
Your mental disposition and temperament are either the greatest asset or the greatest barrier between you and your objectives. Our inner problems continue to overshadow our abilities and talents, no matter how much we try to overcome them. This is why we often struggle to accomplish goals even when we are capable of achieving them.

Changing your attitude is not a job for a single day. You've imbibed your convictions, ideals, and behaviors over years of practice. Those bad habits and assumptions have taken years to merge well with your temperament. But once you embraced them, they started controlling how you behaved. So, to substitute those unhealthy habits and wrong values with good habits and true beliefs would take a constant positive improvement in your daily persona. Luckily Kaizen's going to help you with this mission.

Getting to Learn About Yourself

It all starts with the first step of getting to know yourself. You need to work with Kaizen to try to improve your habits, and you can understand more about your actions by tracking your attitude every day. You should be able to learn how and why you are reacting to certain situations in the way that you are, like responding to your Internet going down with anger and stress. And, hopefully, you'll be able to acquire the ability to regulate and monitor your emotions in time.

Changing your Convictions

Your values will stop you from carrying out a positive change in your life. Nevertheless, even though a positive shift challenges your current negative views, you are less likely to accept the change in your life unless you change the way you think. If you believe that yoga doesn't work at all, the chances of you practicing it as an exercise to heal your body are close to zero. A negative belief that contradicts a positive action prevents you from bringing about meaningful change. This is a challenge that holds back the potential of Kaizen to change your life.

You use Kaizen to develop little habits incrementally, but you can also create little beliefs incrementally. An individual who has no confidence in something by using the power of a positive belief can end up creating a habit. If you don't think you're going to have the stamina to run just seven miles, then start by thinking you can run for 3 miles. If you believe that and achieve this amount of physical exertion, do you think you can run for seven miles then? Whatever the number is, don't think that Kaizen can make the impossible real. Kaizen teaches you that by taking small steps, everything is achievable, but only if you take one step at a time.

When we see evidence, our beliefs alter. If you start doing yoga and it benefits you, there's no way you can deny its healing power. Since Kaizen's whole point is to provide the subconscious mind with tiny regular proofs that it is working, it ends up bringing transition at a slow pace. Yet, it does have the power to alter your personality and values forever.

Changing your Patterns

We all have certain patterns of behavior that determine how we respond to things that happen around us. Those fixed patterns are triggered into action by changes in our environment. Many trends are positive, such as seeing the good in a negative situation, getting empowered when things go south, and dignified treatment of people no matter what. Yet other patterns of actions are negative, such as getting upset in stressful circumstances, losing all faith, ignoring essential tasks, and disregarding connections. In a life-threatening situation, one person may feel energized while another may feel overwhelmed with fear. That's why some people are looking for adventure in life while others are looking for stability. A person seeking a healthy environment will find it hard to leave their town or nations in hopes of a better job and a better life. It's a huge deal to change your entire position in life, and it can scare people. With Kaizen, these scary situations can be diffused by dividing them into smaller parts.

Imagine being part of a situation that makes you feel horrible and out of control or an activity that is outside of your comfort zone. Perhaps it's elocution or maybe even skydiving. It doesn't matter what kind of situation it is. We build upon our personality and strength by opening our minds to such discomfort. If you're going to move to a new city, for example, you can brace yourself by contemplating your life in that new location. To familiarize yourself with the transition, you can also visit the city many times. The purpose of this is to not allow the brain to overthink every situation. By controlling your fear, you control what your reaction will be. No situation can be so daunting that it cannot be faced – it's your reaction to such situations that determines your character.

The Kaizen approach through gradual change prevents you from becoming frustrated with things because instead of taking the whole task on your head, you just tackled a part of it. You should pick only a part of a stressful event and tackle that first until the fear subsides. Only then move on to another part of that situation.

Managing Private Time
Managing their private time is a big life issue for most people. Twenty-four hours a day doesn't seem quite a lot to do all the tasks

you need to do. Yet, this is not about how many hours you have; what is important is how you use those hours. Time management is an ability that every individual needs to learn to improve their performance at work or home and attaining a higher standard of living.

You can use the Kaizen approach if you wish to find more time. List out all the important things you'll need to do this week. Such tasks can vary from day-to-day duties to tasks you need to complete in order to fulfill your long-term goals. List out the things you usually overindulge in after that and end up wasting your time doing so. Such habits may be things like watching television, playing video games, or napping. Of course, with Kaizen, you don't have to get rid of all of your frustrating behaviors at once. Instead, you need to slowly delete one item from your list of harmful activities and add one item to your list of positive activities. You can cut down by twenty minutes on your TV viewing time, and this time you have gained can be utilized for a twenty-minute walk or brainstorming session. The aim is to make time for healthier things by reducing the time spent on unhealthy habits.

Realizing the Perfect Self

What is your ideal version of yourself? Responding to this problem with introspection will lead to a form of enlightenment where you will realize what you value within yourself. We all hold in our minds a dream of the person we want to be able to become. Your ideal self can be a lofty person or a humble one. You may find yourself adopting the characteristics of a popular character in a movie. Whatever the case, the ideal self is a dream we're all pursuing in our lives though most of us never really each there. And, while the ultimate stage of self-actualization will remain elusive no matter what, the Kaizen approach can provide us with a way of life that facilitates continuous change, bringing us closer to this perceived self.

You're concentrating on one specific part of your personality with Kaizen, and trying to replace it with something stronger. For instance, suppose you want to be more confident, how do you go about that? For most people, confidence is only a reflection of their current financial status. But, such a metric of confidence restricts you because if your bank account doesn't expand, then neither does your confidence. Do something else, then. It's possible that money will always be a highly volatile part of your life. So why not align your faith with something that will always stay with you. You may have a talent for music, or you are highly knowledgeable about a specific subject, or you are a social person who is the life of the party. Whatever your talent is, learn to interpret that ability as the ultimate source of your confidence. Then remove the assumption from your head that your bank account's size determines who you are.

Try leaving the house in everyday clothes, with only a small sum of money to practice this. Try to get close to people and participate in discussions that are totally disassociated from your monetary interests. But, just tell people right away that you are struggling monetarily and record how they're responding. What you will find is that, usually, people's perception of you is not wrapped up in such shallow stuff. If people only care about you because of your money, you should not surround yourself with them, to begin with.

Saving Money

We all want to make as much money as possible. Everyone understands that wealth is the global metric of success – it allows you to feel secure, makes your feel confident, and gives us a sense of peace. It's the most appealing idea there is; people are crazy about it and will do anything to get their hands on some money. Amassing wealth doesn't have a short cut. When people think about earning money, they directly jump to dreaming about having a big house, a car, and a huge bank account balance. What Kaizen teaches us about money is that it is in the small things where money can be saved. And while it might not seem like an attractive idea to save little by little until you have a lot, it actually is the best way to amass wealth.

We don't realize it, but we waste a lot of money. It's because we don't pay attention to the money we are spending and where we are spending it. Once you start paying attention to the small things and focus on gradual improvement, you'll be able to make saving money a habit. Since Kaizen is all about the small steps, start thinking about what you can do to save money this week and then move on to thinking about where you can save money this month. Just go through expenses and identify the places that are hitting your bank balance the hardest. Here are a few areas you can work on:

Credit Cards

Credit cards are a scam; they are made to make you feel rich so that you keep on buying things until you realize that all the money you thought you had was only fictitious. The first thing that any financial advisor will tell you is to get rid of your credit card because it makes our brain see money as a plastic commodity and not a painstaking resource that is hard to get. Most people in the world don't actually have money; everyone is just living in debt and assuming they are rich. The fastest way to get rid of your credit card is by consolidating your debt. Throw away your card and turn the leftover debt into a loan that you can gradually pay off. Alternatively, just pull up your socks and get to work so that you can pay off those debts as soon as possible.

Phone

Phones have an aspirational quality to it, and all of us want to get our hands on the new technology that everyone is talking about. But do you really need the new version of the same phone just because it has a few better features? The answer is no. Opting for a cheaper phone might make you feel like your friends will judge you, but it's better than constantly living in debt and skipping meals all for a better camera. Phones are also expensive because they rack up additional payments. Try to cut out your data plan and other similar things that you don't really need.

Food

We all love spending on food. Even when we don't have a lot of money, it's hard to stop spending on that one meal from your favorite restaurant. The first thing you need to do is stop eating out. Even if you are forced to eat out a lot because of your job and social obligations, try to minimize this as much as you can. Designate only a few days a week when you're allowed to spend money on food. More importantly, start getting up early in the morning and making yourself the meals you might need during your working hours. This way you don't have to go to the canteen or some restaurant for your lunch.

You should also opt for smarter grocery shopping. Buy everything you might need for the month in bulk. Try to find the cheapest grocery store around you and the ones that have the best offers or discounts. These are simple things that most people forget because they're just too lazy to change their ways. It might take an additional half an hour to travel to a grocery store that it's cheaper but further away. But at the end of the day, it's going to save you money, so it's worth the effort.

Subscriptions

Everyone now pays for their Netflix, Hulu, and Amazon without thinking about how much these subscriptions end up hurting your pocket. If there are monthly bills that you don't think are essential, you should eliminate them. Ask yourself if you really need them? Are there ways to find an alternative to such a subscription? Perhaps you can split the subscription money for a Netflix account with a friend or a coworker, saving quite a lot of money by the end of the year.

Electricity

Most of us don't pay attention to the amount of energy we are consuming because it seems like an endless resource, but it's not. Heating and cooling waste so much energy that you can reduce your monthly electricity bills by half if you just started closing your air conditioner or heater when you don't need it. Even closing power sockets and light bulbs when they're not needed can be extremely helpful. The fact that most people switch on light bulbs even when there is direct sunshine they can sit in is baffling. You have to be smarter about the small choice you make because they can add up to a lot.

You don't have to suddenly make all these changes happen and some changes you might not be able to handle. The important part is to keep trying – every day, you can find one area where you can potentially save money, and all you have to do is exercise that choice regularly until it becomes a habit. If you do end up saving money, don't waste it by using it to buy something wasteful or spend it on some home upgrade. You should start saving and investing your money so that it can replicate itself as quickly as possible.

Investing
Living paycheck to paycheck can be really hard because you're always stressed about not having money. The fear of missing one day of work can be harrowing, and it can eventually lead to long-term harm to your physical and mental health. The best way to get rid of such fears is to start working on saving some money so that you always have some backup. This will give you a sense of security as well, which can go a long way in helping you deal with your money woes. Investment is a gradual practice; unlike movies, you don't have to find some brilliant stock and become rich overnight. All you have to do is find a reliable and stable financial instrument that you put some money into little by little. Once this becomes a habit, you might even forget you had all this money saved; eventually, it's going to become a larger sum that you can use in case of emergencies.

It's your choice to decide what kind of instrument you want to pick – it can be stocks, mutual funds, or even a savings account. You should never invest without complete knowledge of what you're doing. Try to consult a financial advisor, and if that is too costly for you, then there's always the Internet. Make sure that you do your research thoroughly before you spend any money. Just don't end up wasting your money in trying to replicate it. Start by investing only a small amount, once you feel confident that your money is safe, start increasing your investments gradually and keep on doing those little by little.

Using money to invest can put a lot of pressure on your pocket. The best thing you can do is to assess how much money you have and what are future prospects are of this money being stable. This will tell you if you can afford to invest money or not. If you work in a job where money fluctuates a lot, then it's not a good idea to invest a lot of money. If your income suddenly increases, then you can also increase your investment. Just figure out your financial situation and, based on that, decide how you want to go ahead with investing. Just study your income every month, and for every rise in income, invest 5 percent more, and whenever your income falls, just don't invest that month. What Kaizen really wants you to do is to have patience. Take your time with your investments and take small steps only even if they are months apart. This will reduce the risk you're taking while at the same time, increasing your potential gains. Investment is also a game, so always be on the lookout for potential places to invest in.

Health

Mastering the Kaizen approach will allow you to lead a healthy lifestyle. You must have definitely promised yourself thousands of times to eat healthier and better. You must have wanted to exercise more and live a healthier lifestyle without smoking or drinking. But somehow nothing seems to have worked. Mostly, this is because your target seems too big, and the two-hour exercise routine video you tried to watch was just too hard to do every day. Luckily, you can learn to develop your wellbeing gradually with Kaizen, without placing too much pressure on your mind and body.

Even a tiny bit of weight loss and lifestyle improvements carry a lot of health benefits. If you engage in moderate exercise sessions every day for just twenty minutes, it decreases the risk of health problems such as diabetes, heart disease, and high cholesterol. Since Kaizen is a holistic approach, weight loss and exercise are inextricably linked with the overall lifestyle benefits of Kaizen. Suppose you want to lose twenty pounds just like everyone else in the world. If you don't work out at all, it can be a huge target. So, you can break the target into smaller, more manageable two-pound targets per week. This way, you are giving yourself ten weeks to achieve your goal, rather than expecting instant results. After you have come up with your weekly target, you will need some small steps of Kaizen to achieve your aim. Here are four of them:

Measure your Weight Daily

This tiny habit will remind you every morning of your current weight. Research shows that people who look at their daily weight often practice healthy eating and exercise significantly more; as a result, weight loss is easier to achieve. You should develop this habit to get yourself ready for a workout and diet. This practice will also inspire you when you begin your work out and diet. This will also give your brain a feeling of reward every time you see that your weigh is less than yesterday. So, you will end up feeling inspired to continue to follow your diet and exercise schedule.

Stand up More

How many hours a day are you spending just sitting down? Most people do jobs that require them to sit for nine to thirteen hours, depending on their work and lifestyle. A few people are able to muster enough motivation to go out and buy a standing desk.

Instead, try to stand up every thirty minutes or so only for a couple of minutes. Take a quick stroll around the building, or simply do some stretches. Then just go back to work. Slowly try to increase it from two minutes to four minutes after some time. Ideally, it's best to find little ways to increase the amount of time you stand, especially for people who sit a lot at work. /This also applies to you if you spend a lot of time playing video games or watching television. You can just walk around the room during the advertisement breaks of a TV show if you spend too much of your time sitting all day. These little habits will bring big changes to your lifestyle and allow you to live a healthier life.

Take the Stairs

Your apartment or office building also has stairs. So, just continue to use them. If your office is too high to climb every single flight of stairs, just use only half of them at first. And incrementally in the coming weeks keep on adding more flights of stairs. The goal is to raise your step-count every week, slowly. You may be shocked to see your improvement in a few months; what you'll remember is how winded you felt in the first few flights when you began.

Park your Car Away from your Destination

You can do this with your car everywhere you go. Pick a parking space that is a bit farther from your destination each time you park. That way, you will have to walk, and this will give you some required exercise on the way to each destination. Just a 3-minute walk through a parking lot can weekly add up to 20 minutes of steps.

Healthy eating is an important part of life, regardless of whether you want to lose weight or protect yourself from potential illnesses. Today most people know that there are many safe food options they can make at home. But it can be daunting to change your habits and get the right kind of food into your lifestyle. Approaching this fear, Kaizen can be helpful.

Tips

Here are some tips for balanced eating with Kaizen:

Write Down the Food you Eat Every Day

Keep a diary of any meal, drink, or snack you consume during the day. This will help you to count your calories and will remind you of how much you have eaten so that you don't indulge in overeating. Now, use a green pen to highlight all the good food items like vegetable salad, grains, greens, eggs, and others. And use a red pen to illustrate unhealthy food items such as pizza, cake, fat-rich foods, sugary drinks, alcohol, and so on. Count the number of green foods on your list, and compare them to the red foods. Is your list full of red?

From a Kaizen perspective, we aim to improve our eating patterns incrementally so that our journal includes more green marks and less red marks. The aim is to change our dietary habits each week by eliminating one unhealthy food item and replacing it with one safe food item. You may substitute a cup of soda with a glass of green tea, for example. If you eat a pizza slice, then you should replace that with a healthy vegetable the next time you eat.

Eat a Little Less

Eat a little less every time you do and rate your level of hunger satisfaction on a scale of 1 to 10. The goal is to achieve a 7 or 8. So, you get relaxed, leaving you a little hungry — every time you eat. It is because it takes your brain time to know that your body has eaten only now. So the sense of satiation won't be excreted until many minutes have gone by. So, if you're inclined to stuff yourself at breakfast or dinner, then seek to reduce the amount of food you consume every meal incrementally until your satiation level is lower — but not too small.

Physical Workout

Regular exercise is a vital aspect of a healthy lifestyle and keeping fit. Depending on your weight goals, your fitness goals can vary, but with Kaizen, any form of physical training becomes easier. The biggest obstacle that we face is beginning the physical routine. Starting anything is tough because the effort that we know it'll require from us is daunting. It's hard for most people to hit the gym every day, particularly during the first few sessions. Most people stop going to the gym in the first week itself. The fear of failure and the nostalgia of the old sedentary lifestyle keeps people from ever committing themselves entirely to fitness. If you are dealing with the same issues, the Kaizen work out method will certainly help you. Here are a few tips for getting started:

Monitor your Daily Exercise Activity

The goal is not to just join the gym nearest to you; its physical training. You can fill several parts of your life with small bursts of physical activity such as walking for five minutes, stretching your body (after every few hours spent in front of your computer), and swapping the stairs in your office building for the elevator. Whatever set of tasks you select for physical exertion, it's crucial that you do those same tasks every day. And, most importantly, we want to monitor certain activities with Kaizen so that we can increase our everyday physical exertion levels incrementally. Note, with Kaizen, the amount of time you are active in any given day is not as important as the fact that how active you were today is just slightly more than yesterday's activity.

Start and Finish the Day with Physical Activity

Most of us get only two primarily free moments every day. It's the moment we wake up in the morning and the time just before we go to bed in the evening. Both of these moments in the day are good for indulging in small and efficient physical workouts. During these times, just do some really gentle exercises like stretching your back, your legs, and your shoulders. And, just walk a little; perform torso bends, hand rotations, and other strategies for lengthening the limbs. Having a regular morning or evening routine can benefit your health a lot because you will slowly build up a habit. Plus, you will start and finish your day free from physical stress. Exercise allows our body to expel stress and tension, which will keep you fresh and rejuvenated as you start your day, and when you go to bed.

Pick a Hobby that Involves Physical Exercise

If physical exertion that is intense in nature like lifting weights is not your thing, it's perfectly fine. There are other ways to make your daily workout a well-rounded one. Consider joining a party of hikers, a dance class, or some other enjoyable outdoor activity. Play tennis, or soccer, or any other sport that requires extraneous activity. The main thing is that you're working hard daily to get your body into action so that your calories are burnt off quickly. Just as in every other Kaizen related task, focus on incremental efforts to integrate these new hobbies into your life slowly. You can pick multiple hobbies, for example, and attend them on a regular and weekly basis. Start your Saturday with a jog in a local park, hike every weekend, and schedule one adventure trip every three months with your friends.

Relationships

All of us are looking for a perfect and honest relationship with our partner, relatives, employers, acquaintances, and others. For many of us, the notion of "a good relation" is nothing more than a lie. So, we try our best to make it work and not let those everyday anxieties destroy what we have. We try to keep the relationship running smoothly, as long as it is possible. But gradually minor disruptions keep on getting worse, and many of our relationships break down. Is there any way this could be prevented? Is there some way we can save all our ties from going downhill? Luckily Kaizen can also offer support in this area. There are two reasons why relationships suffer and fester, turn into grudges, and eventually destroy any hope of retaining some good memories from these past associations. First, you never properly discussed anything with the other person and choose not to register your complaints. And secondly, that your own interpersonal skills aren't strong enough to try to settle the problem by trying to talk it out. Discussions can work, but only when we are able to have mental clarity ourselves. If you don't even speak out when you feel bad, then there's no hope for any communication to occur.

Our definition of a "good relationship" is based on some generic ideals and is usually extremely incorrect. You might think there's a great person who is waiting for you, and once you meet that person, your life will turn into a fairy tale. Or, maybe you think there's a great boss who resides within the other person who will appreciate your creativity and show you the respect you deserve. These common assumptions exist in all forms of relationships. But there is no relationship that can be ideal and meet all the expectations we have daydreamed. A relationship may initially seem ideal, but it sometimes transforms into a difficult and complex partnership. And that's natural because, with time, we all adapt. We can grow to become better or worse, depending on the events in our lives. Every partnership calls for constant effort. You cannot achieve perfection, but slowly you can reach for it and work towards it – that's Kaizen's core. You've got to recognize and accept this fact of life. You have to come to terms with the fact that constant evolution and change are universal truths, and therefore, in any relationship, you will have to leave some room for people to change. Every partnership, from your spouse to your colleagues, is about resilience and cooperation in the face of adverse events that keep occurring in life.

Here's what you can do to tackle a relationship that has become difficult to handle:

1. Think of the most frustrating relationship that you have right now in your life and write down a list of reasons why you

find this relationship difficult. Then write down the things that you think you do right in this relationship. And then, write down all the mistakes you have made in the relationship as well - Were you too busy to spend some time with your spouse? Does your partner want you to spend more time with the kids?

2. Now, make a list of mistakes you think the other person has made in the relationship.

3. Act on one of your mistakes every week. You may set a mobile alert, for example, to call your spouse at lunchtime or devote time to playing with your kids after dinner. Your significant other will finally note these little changes in your daily behavior, and that will inspire them to focus on their own issues. Relationships are a two-way street; it's only when you show the other person that you are willing to change for them that they will try to change as well.

4. But, if you still feel that your significant other is treating you in an abhorrent way, then it's time to seek an alternative form of patching things happen, which we will discuss in the next section.

Keep the Balance Between "I" and "We"

Depending on the type of relationship you have, the balance of 'I' and 'We' is always in flux. The "We" defines the strength of your relationship with another person. The "I" defines your capacity within the relationship to preserve your individual identity. Too much "I," which is normal in a casual friendship or a professional relationship, can undermine your relationship. Too much "We" makes a relationship hard to deal with, and you lose your personal space. How much is too much? That depends on your own personality and your significant other's personality. You need to focus on finding a balance between "I" and "We" in every relationship. Individuality should exist in the midst of the feelings you share for each other. Nobody should think that they should erase themselves in a relationship.

How to Fight

Disagreements, disputes, and debates are a part of all human ties. Your fights might shift in their size and gravity, but you cannot avoid disagreements. The best way to come to grips with a dispute is to learn the art of fighting in a fair manner. Justice is what we all want at the end of any conflict, and it is only possible if both parties are trying to fix the problem and not win the argument. A healthy and reasonable discussion involves love, loyalty, and integrity so that a shared agreement can be reached. Fighting is another aspect of love in a way; think about it, would you be fighting if you didn't care about each other? If you really didn't care about the other person, you wouldn't waste your energy to even fight with them.

How can you have a respectful fight? Unfortunately, in our closest relationships, we tend to feel more at ease and get angry far more quickly. This happens because we feel close enough and comfortable around the other person to express all our emotions, even if they are ugly. That's why our problems with partners, parents, and friends can take a serious turn quickly. The Kaizen approach to relationships is about developing a habit of expressing your love and appreciation, especially when you fight. Seek to fill your fights with sentences that emphasize your appreciation and love while at the same time making your point. Tell the other person that you love them, and your respect for them will not dwindle if they accept their mistake if you want to blame them for something they did that hurt you.

First of all, expressing your love and admiration is a common way to make others understand your point of view. This approach immediately brings down the intensity of a fight because both sides begin to consider each other's point of view. For people with self-centered personality styles, this degree of understanding doesn't come easily, and you have to work with them slowly. It is here that the Kaizen approach comes into play. Try to work to minimize the amount of time you spend blaming the other person during any fight you have and increase the amount of time you spend expressing your respect for the individual. Using words like love and respect properly and sincerely will calm down everyone's anger. Ultimately, saying these words does make you listen to what the other person is thinking during an argument because you are reminded of your empathy for the other person. At the same time, your significant other will be encouraged to listen to your points too.

Communication

Every relationship is different, and the way you communicate with one person is not the same as how you communicate with another person. You may feel close enough to converse openly with certain friends or near family members while with other friends, you might have a superficial relationship. It depends on how close we become with people and who we allow seeing through our walls. It also depends on how close people let us get into their lives, at the same time. It is a joint agreement that both parties make each time a relationship starts. Below we'll talk about some strategies to promote a healthy and open communication atmosphere with the people in your life.

What's Hurting You?
As with any other approach to Kaizen, this one begins with self-reflection too. When you become a hard person to connect with, it has repercussions that become visible in your relationships. Your goal is to be aware of the change in your emotions caused by certain triggers that make you shut down and put up walls that shut other people out.

Try to recall the time when you disagreed with an individual, and it turned into a heated debate. What were the phrases that were said that made you angry? Write all those phrases down on a sheet of paper and keep the file with you. Take note of the interactions or environmental factors that make you feel anxious as you go about your day and bring up all those negative feelings. This study will help you understand how you are not as logical as you would like to believe you are. You'll learn to recognize individuals, locations, thoughts, and situations that make you shut down and become a tougher person. Hopefully, over time you can develop a new sense of consciousness that allows you to become more aware of your emotional reactions. Your list will help you to study the different changes in your moods and how your thought patterns function to make you react a certain way.

Tackling Violent People

Some people just do not understand relationships in any way other as a way for them to get what they want. They are only there to fulfill their needs no matter how oppressed and horrible the other person might end up feeling. They're pushy, arrogant, and just craft relationships to get what they're looking for. Such people have no comprehension of the meaning of love, reverence, and dignity, and therefore, it can be difficult to tackle such men. To deal with these people, you have to look into yourself and why you're still around them. You have to remind yourself that you deserve self-respect no matter what and that if any relationship your individual autonomy is being violated, then you deserve better.

If possible, avoiding these people clearly is the best way to exclude them from your life. But, usually, because of work or family, we are sometimes required to sustain these relationships. It's best to have a set of methods in your mind that you can switch to when reacting to such aggressive people.

- Try to sit with your eyes closed, and speak to an angry person in your head. Imagine something they've told you that makes you feel furious. Do you feel like they have power over you? Do you feel afraid and incapable of speaking with them?

- Now, imagine yourself going through different types of retort. It's kind of like training your mind to just say whatever it can so that when the situation occurs, you are able to push through the impact of their aggressive demeanor on you and say what you need to.

- Try standing up for yourself, confidently and vigorously, in the face of this assault. You have to be strict with such people and not let them get the better of you. If they ask for your compassion, study them, and see if they are honest.

If you don't have the patience to listen and understand other people, you can't connect and develop good relationships. Listening lets you know how and what others think, feel, and what their viewpoints are. If you work on listening and understanding, then handling difficult scenarios will become easier. Listening is also about seeing beyond the façade the other person is putting up. It is essentially a skill that you have to acquire by continuously trying to hear what people are conveying to you. Listening doesn't just involve what someone is saying; it goes beyond that. It includes body language, tone, and even the emphasis that people put into certain words. We tend to only hear what we want to hear, and our brain takes all the information that it doesn't see as relevant and filter it out. This will harm your relationship because essentially you're just convincing yourself that the other person is bad, simply because you refuse to hear them.

Conclusion

It can seem daunting to begin your Kaizen journey, but just remember what this book has taught you – all you need to focus on is the small steps. All of us have an intrinsic need to do things quickly and skip all the hard work, but that's not how you achieve success. You need to focus on the small things in life and start finding meaning in them if you want to achieve anything.

Once you have started with Kaizen, there's no stopping. You might have to wait some time to see positive results, but make sure that you collect the right data and study it to see what kind of impact Kaizen has had on your organization. This will also help you to analyze what kind of changes worked and which ones didn't. So, if you see that some departments started to perform better, while others were still struggling, then you know what area to focus on next. This might also be because the workers of that department still haven't opened themselves up to the emancipatory potential of Kaizen. Your task is to keep on pushing for change, no matter what.

You might find a lot of challenges with Kaizen, but you should never falter. Remember that whatever the problem is, all you have to do is break it into smaller things and then tackle them; eventually the whole problem will get solved.

References

7 Kaizen tools to reduce waste and improve Lean Process. (2019, August 9). upKaizen website: https://upKaizen.com/en/2019/08/09/7-Kaizen-tools-to-reduce-waste-and-improve-lean-process/

A Brief History of Kaizen: The Key Players. (n.d.). Creative Safety Supply website: https://www.creativesafetysupply.com/articles/a-brief-history-of-Kaizen-the-key-players/

DeShaw, J. (2017, June 2). Kaizen for Healthy Lifestyle Changes. ZUM Fitness website: https://zumfitness.com/Kaizen-healthy-lifestyle-changes/

Dolcemascolo, D., & Trout, J. (n.d.). Kaizen Events: When and How to Use Them. www.reliableplant.com website: https://www.reliableplant.com/Read/8904/Kaizen-events

Howard, A. (2019, September 24). Kaizen Events 101 - Before, During and After. Kaufman Global website: https://www.kaufmanglobal.com/Kaizen-events-101/

Kaizen Gaining the Benefits of Continuous Improvement. (2009). Mindtools.com website: https://www.mindtools.com/pages/article/newSTR_97.htm

Kaizen – Lean Manufacturing and Six Sigma Definitions. (2019). Leansixsigmadefinition.com website: http://www.leansixsigmadefinition.com/glossary/Kaizen/

Kaizen Creates a Culture of Continuous Improvement | Lean Production. (2011). Leanproduction.com website: https://www.leanproduction.com/Kaizen.html

Planning and running Kaizen Events. (2012). Lean Manufacturing Tools website: https://leanmanufacturingtools.org/625/planning-and-running-Kaizen-events/

Roussel, J. (n.d.). Kaizen Event Planning in 7 Simple Steps. blog.kainexus.com website: https://blog.kainexus.com/improvement-disciplines/Kaizen/Kaizen-event/Kaizen-event-planning-in-7-simple-steps

Sherman, P. (2018). Understanding Kaizen Events | APICS Magazine. www.apics.org website: http://www.apics.org/apics-for-individuals/apics-magazine-home/magazine-detail-page/2018/10/10/understanding-Kaizen-events

Thakur, S. (2010, December 23). Seven Best Kaizen Tools. Bright Hub PM website: https://www.brighthubpm.com/project-planning/100412-a-survey-of-Kaizen-tools/

The Seven Wastes | 7 Mudas. (2011). Lean Manufacturing Tools website: https://leanmanufacturingtools.org/77/the-seven-wastes-7-mudas/

Wilding, M. (2018, January 22). The Japanese philosophy of Kaizen can reinvent your daily routine. Quartz at Work website: https://qz.com/work/1183536/the-japanese-philosophy-of-Kaizen-can-reinvent-your-daily-routine/

What is Kaizen? - Five S of Kaizen. (2015). Managementstudyguide.com website: https://www.managementstudyguide.com/what-is-Kaizen.htm

KAIZEN

Advanced Guide of Effective Kaizen Methods and Strategies in the Information Era

ROBERT MILLER

Introduction

In the past fifty years, both the market and how we approach entrepreneurship have changed drastically. In the past, the only people who could start a business were those that had a large amount of capital, something that few people could have done. It was also a sign of power. Even the smallest of businesses appeared as if they were something incredible.

It was also much more difficult to start a business. The information that you worked with was far more limited than today. Before starting your own business, you need to make sure that your product has a market to be sold and that it can grow. The number of information people worked with back then was extremely small. On top of that, the market was also much more volatile and harder to work with. Luckily, with the internet and wide-spread media, a new age in business and entrepreneurship has started.

Right now, the market is much bigger than it ever has been, no matter where you are working from. Globalization made sure to unify every individual financial cell of the world into a huge network. Though it might seem overwhelming, the market is now more diverse, wider, and easier to deal with. Though, it is worth noting that this only applies if you know how to use this diversity and width and that you know how to deal with it.

If that isn't you, you might instead feel as if you were lost on the high seas with waves crashing all around you.

Before you set sail, you can easily determine if the market will be good for your business. It is also much easier to get over the limitations of your location. Fifty years ago, you were tied down to the place you were working from, thus limiting your options. While you might have been interested in making a washing machine company, you would be limited by the number of companies that are doing the same near you, making the competition extremely hard to beat. Having an incredibly saturated market will make your business much less viable to succeed, turning your dream into a nightmare. Today, shipping is much easier to work with. Communication technologies have progressed so far that errors in communication almost never happen. You are always in tune with everything that is going on, making sure that you can avoid any issues that might arise on the way. This makes it much easier to connect your business with another market in another place.

This is not to say that it is easy to do a business of your own. The global market is much harder to track. Everything is so neatly intertwined in such a way that pulling on one part of it will affect a lot of other fields. The field of financial analytics has become much more important, and harder to master due to the width of elements that go into it.

What this means is that it is important to stay informed in this age where information is so abundant. It is one of the keys to any successful business. Disinformation can lead to catastrophic consequences. For example, making a company that deals with making low-quality type-writers would not be the best idea ever. The reason why is obvious as we have computers that can do the same job, and for people that actually want a typewriter, a regular typewriter will not do. This is due to the fact that the market has changed drastically since personal computers started being mass-produced. The only typewriters that are worth their buck are those that have a story, like antique ones, or those that are extremely luxurious. A similar example can be given in most industries.

The importance of being well informed cannot be stressed enough. You need to know what you are doing and how you need to do it. That being said, it is not the only factor in success. You can work with whatever amount of knowledge, but if you do not have the proper finances, it will do little to make your dream come true.

When starting a business, it is important to start small. Starting small, however, is not cheap, either. There are many costs that you need to take into consideration. Marketing is something that you want to put money into. This is especially true because quick, in-your-face social media marketing became a factor in success. You need to be ready to lose some money at the start. Most businesses start like that as it takes a bit of time to get your money flowing.

Another important thing to think about, and, perhaps, the most important factor is manpower. While it is true that with the rise of technology, less and less manpower is required for most work, the quality of your workers is something that you need to keep in mind at all times. In large companies, CEOs are cautious when it comes to what job is given to who. This is for a good reason. In small businesses, the boss can control everything with relative ease. When there are fewer parts in your machine, you can fix it more easily when it starts working. However, when it starts getting larger and more complex, it gets harder and harder to control everything. Having good people at the top of your ranks, people that you trust with oiling up the parts will make your job so much easier and more efficient.

Similar is true for every person working for you, even those at the lowest position. While having a good spokesperson working in your car dealership will not make the car faster or newer, but it can make it look like that. You have heard of: "The chain is as strong as its weakest link." The same can be said here. To truly succeed as a businessperson, you need to make sure everyone is doing their job as best as possible. You can see examples of the importance of this everywhere.

In this book, we'll be going over every facet of Kaizen, ranging from beginner's issues such as "what is Kaizen" to professional-level tips on how to improve production speed by applying Kaizen in places critical to the process.

If a cog stops turning in a watch, the watch will stop working. In chemistry, you cannot have a proper molecule without every atom being in place.

Chapter 1

What Is Kaizen?

This is where the Kaizen method comes into play. The Kaizen method is one of constant improvement. The name itself means "change for the better." It is an incredibly simple method. It would seem very obvious from a third-person perspective that such a method is beneficial for any working environment. Still, the method is relatively new, developed in the 40s as a part of the Training Within Industry program. Japanese businesses first applied it after World War II, and ever since then, it has been growing in popularity. Even now, more than sixty years later, the method is relatively foreign to most people.

So, what is Kaizen? To put it simply, it advocates the progress of small changes. Most people think that in order to improve a business or save it from failing, you need some huge dramatic changes. And, while this is often true, that is not always the case. It is very obvious that a huge change when it comes to how you approach work will make a significant difference in how your work is going to be affected and, in turn, affect you. Firing a huge amount of excess workforce will save you a lot of money. Finding a new, cheaper source of materials will also save you money. However, these drastic changes can have some unforeseen consequences.

As I mentioned before, pulling on one line of the net you create will pull some more. While it is often possible to predict what will happen when you make your huge decision, this can often lead you astray and, more often than not, cause consequences that you could never have foreseen. Making huge movements from out of nowhere is a very brave thing to do. It is a hit-or-miss kind of situation really. The profits you might obtain this way will be huge, but the failures will hurt more as well.

Such endeavors may be easy to decide upon with smaller businesses. After all, if you fail, you are not losing as much money as you could. On top of that, if not now, when? If you do not get used to high-risk-high-reward situations in the early phases of your business, you will be less likely to succeed. That being said, it is easy to say that huge decision is important for success. That is obvious enough to see. However, one should never underestimate the importance of the smaller pieces of the puzzle.

The Kaizen method accounts for the pieces of all sizes. In a factory, you will rarely be able to make huge changes in order to fix small problems. If an assembly line malfunctions somewhere, you will not be able to replace everything and everyone working on the line. You do not have the luxury of ignoring the problem either, as it can lead to a deterioration in the quality of the product. In turn, the good name of your company comes into peril.

The Kaizen method suggests that, no matter how small a problem is, you should attend to it as efficiently as possible. No problem is too small or too insignificant to ignore. It pushes you to improve continuously. It follows the Japanese belief that there is no perfection and that "enough" does not exist.

It relies on you being ready to improve infinitely. Not to a certain point. There can never be a goal within your head. You are not aiming for anything specific. The only way to move is forward without stopping. This model is what the Japanese have been applying for as long as we can trace. While it did not always have a name, the effects of that mentality can be seen in every aspect of the culture.

It is easy to underestimate how important it is to point this out. After all, it might seem like an insignificant forethought. However, this strategy is not something that you need to keep in the back of your mind. It is there to be the main focus of your planning.

That being said, the changes that happen due to the Kaizen method do not necessarily have to be slow. Even though it mostly deals with small optimization that works towards future benefits, as well as making a working environment with less waste. The changes will mostly be very fast and small, barely noticeable, but they aim to build over one another in order to make something amazing.

If you need evidence of the power of Kaizen, look no further than Toyota. To emphasize this even further, Toyota uses this model as one of its main principles. Toyota does not see improvement as something that "can be done," rather something that "must be done." They leave nothing to coincidence and do whatever they can to do right by their buyers. Kaizen is not a thing that only the administrative staff needs to continue, rather every single employee. Toyota gives a very interesting Kaizen system that you can learn a lot from.

Types of Kaizen

Being not only a management tactic but also a philosophy, Kaizen has many different forms that are being applied in different areas. As with any philosophy this broad, there are small differences that can be recognized between the basic types of Kaizen.

Point Kaizen is perhaps the most common type. It aims towards making small changes very quickly with as little time as possible elapsed on planning. It is a very simple principle to work with. If you happen to discover something that is not working as it should, you take quick action in order to make sure that the error you detect is corrected. Though this might seem slightly irrelevant, due to the scale of the corrections that you make, they can make a huge impact in the long run. An example of this principle would be finding broken materials inside of your shop and immediately taking action to either repair them or replace them completely.

There is a downside to point Kaizen, however. It has been seen that any positives achieved through this method can stagger or completely remove the benefits of the same method being applied in other areas. For example, if you find a product that is poorly made, you can fire the worker that is reducing the quality of your product. However, this might have an adverse effect on you being understaffed.

Another kind of Kaizen is called system Kaizen. As the name suggests, it is an upper-level method. This means that the strategy is much more complex than with point Kaizen and requires more careful planning. The method is devised in order to repair system level errors inside the workplace in an organized manner that will not disrupt the work of your employees.

While point Kaizen works towards discovering small flaws and issues inside of the system and quickly dispose of them, system Kaizen elevates this to a higher level. It aims to bring huge changes to the company through a series of well-planned Kaizen events. It will usually take a while to see the benefits of system Kaizen, as it is a process that occurs very slowly.

Line Kaizen is usually a term that refers to two instances of point Kaizen collaborating. Usually, this is done by spreading Lean from a point to a line.

Lean production or lean manufacturing is a method of production that was first used by Toyota. The "Toyota Way" gave rise to the model that relies on five key principles. James Wommack and Daniel Jones devised it. It is defined as a way to come closer and closer to exactly what the customer wants while expending fewer and fewer resources.

The first principle is "Value." It encourages you to speak to the customer in order to determine the market value of what you are putting out. After this, you should form a team that will stick to the production of the product during the whole cycle.

The second principle of Lean production is "Value Stream." You are to identify how the value stream mapping of each product looks. By assembling a diagram or flowchart of how the product works, accounting for spent time and materials, as well as manpower, you can more easily see which steps are flawed and improve upon them. This is where we can see how it intertwines with the Kaizen method the best, as it encourages meticulous striving for perfection.

The third principle of Lean production is "Flow." This one is self-explanatory; The production of the product must continuously flow through the chosen steps with the greatest efficiency possible. Or, in layman's terms, the production must be done at a steady pace, exactly following each step.

"Pull" is the fourth principle. It instructs you to connect as many steps of the production together, letting them pull one another for increased efficiency,

The fifth and last principle is "Perfection." This one might be misleading as, in this philosophy, there is no measurable perfection. The "perfection" here is decreasing the time and resources that are required to give the customer what they want.

Line Kaizen will help you introduce Lean not only to the production line but apply it to your procurement and planning processes.

When several instances of line Kaizen are connected in a net, we get what is called a Plane Kaizen. This one is quite easy to visualize. Imagine a net in which whenever you make an improvement to one or two lines, the benefits of the improvement go down the other lines as well. Instead of traditional departments in a value stream, here, the structure is divided into families or product lines.

Cube Kaizen is the most complex and the most effective of them all. It is a systematic step-up from plane Kaizen. The term is used to describe a system where all planes are connected to each other, and no part of the system is isolated from the rest. An example of this would be a company where Lean is spread over the whole organization. Such a structure might often require many changes in how the business works, down to even the most basic processes. In such a system, there is no constant pattern of how improvements are made. The changes spread as far as the whole organization, customers, and suppliers. They are made upstream or downstream from plane to plane or down and up through the planes themselves.

This kind of organization shows the true spirit of Kaizen as it not only goes towards improving productivity but also turning the workplace into a safe environment. Workers are not treated as workers, but people as well. The input of workers means as much as that of the administrators would. It also goes towards eliminating "muri," also known as overly hard work. It encourages workers to use the scientific method in order to perform experiments in the workplace, aiming to eliminate waste and improve their skill, as well as the workplace itself.

The Kaizen method is not only about encouraging the method to be used, but it is also a way to increase productivity while not dehumanizing the working class. In order for the Kaizen method to be properly implemented, it does not require only the administrative sector to work towards it, but the workers as well.

Every part of your company needs to be involved with your changes. The CEO works as much towards it as the menial workers, sometimes going even as far as stakeholders at times.

While the Kaizen method is usually connected to Toyota, especially the manufacturing method, it is not the only place where it is applicable. It can be applied to an individual as much as a large group.

At the Toyota workplaces, it is usually about small groups improving the local workstations. This group will, more often than not, have a line supervisor. This person is usually in charge of recognizing and analyzing problems, often fixing them as well.

When we are talking about Kaizen applied on a larger scale, it is usually about creating total quality management. It reduces human effort by using machine and computing power in order to improve productivity.

In Toyota, Kaizen is usually about small improvements that stack up over time in order to, through standardization, generate large amounts of value in overall productivity.

While similar to the "command and control" method, it is quite different in the way it is executed. The Kaizen method is all about making changes and adjusting after some time. There is usually little large-scale pre-planning. This, instead, is replaced by smaller experiments. This makes it easier to adapt to processes if there are unpredictable events.

In the 21st century, the method is mostly applied as a way to fix an issue over the course of a week. This kind of action is called a "Kaizen event" or "Kaizen Blitz". They usually have a smaller scale, and any issues that may turn up after them are fixed in other blitzes that may come later on.

Kaizen events can vary in size and scope due to how broad the Kaizen method is. However, they can usually be recognized due to the specific line of events that occur. Any Kaizen effect will usually go as follows:

1. Determine your goals and provide any necessities for achieving them
2. Compare the current state with your goals and recognize how you can get there

3. Start improving

4. See the effects of the improvement and adjust your plans

5. Gather reports of the results and determine what actions are to be taken next

This is also known as a PDCA cycle. This is a scientific approach that can be used for making improvements by following the pattern:

- Plan (determine the issue and find the potential solution)
- Do (start the experiment)
- Check (accumulate the findings)
- Act (reassess your plan and start the cycle over)

The term "Zenkai" is used to refer to a person who made a huge contribution when it comes to implementing Kaizen. Recently, there have been more and more business consultants all over the world that work on spreading and building on the Kaizen network.

The History of Kaizen

When we talk about Kaizen, it is important to note how interesting the path it took from the day it was created until today is. The story starts in America, then goes to Japan and from there it spread through the whole world.

Walter Shewart was a statistician and engineer, working at Bell Labs during the 1930s. This is where he worked on PDCA, which is also known as the Shewhart Cycle. This system was designed as a test for any organizational change to see if they deliver actual improvements. The roots of Kaizen started here.

In this system, the "Plan" phase is perhaps the most important for its success. This is where you look at the core problem that troubles you from as many angles as you can. This is also where you identify the solution that you deem the most effective at solving your problem. You also need to identify the necessary resources that you are going to have to expend to reach your end-goal.

After this, you "Do." You take action to follow your plans as much as possible and as precisely as possible.

After this, you need to "Study" the effects of your plan in order to determine if it worked. This also helps you identify where your plan was lacking, allowing you to fix the parts that can be improved or fixed and ditching those that can't.

The last step is the "Act." It involves placing your plan into a full application. Of course, you only do this if you deem that it gave you the expected results in the "Do" phase. If not, you need to go back to the "Plan" phase. This gives you more insight into the nature of the problem and provides you with a new point from which to start.

The PDSA cycle was groundbreaking as it turned the employee into more than just manpower. The regular employee now becomes a source of critical thinking and potential improvement. It makes sure to make the most efficient usage of the collective brainpower of your company.

This has been the main method of quality control in clinical laboratories for more than fifty years. These ideas were taken even further during the 40s by Shewart's student, W. Edwards Deming.

Deming added several more concepts to the system. The first being "Total Quality Management." This concept dictated that if you focus on improving your management and product quality, this, in turn, would result in your costs getting lower and lower over time, thus increasing the efficiency of production.

In Deming's view, increasing your profits by being cheap is the opposite of the way you should go. Rather than decreasing the production cost by cutting down on the quality of the materials used, you should focus on making your system as good as possible. In the short-term, the difference will not be very noticeable; however, you will make much more money and have a better market value in the long-term.

Understanding information variation is one of the keys to improving your quality management. That is why we have a differentiation between "common" and "special" causes.

"Common" causes of variation are those that happen inside of the system. These are events that happen every day. They are usually small and very hard to see unless you get up close and personal with the processes in the system.

"Special" causes are events that happen outside of the system. They are usually the results of big changes. This category includes things like natural disasters and changes in international trade policy. These are things that are very difficult to take into account as they are very unpredictable and out of your control.

There is also a third category of causes of variation. They are usually extremely small and hard to see. They are usually visible only to those who work in the most micro-level sectors of a business every day, usually the workers in the lowest level of the hierarchy.

Deming claimed that eighty-five percent of all processes are caused by management. As he claims, this is usually because management did not pay attention to the common variation issues that are identified by the workers.

Strangely enough, Deming's ideas did not see warm reception in the United States at first. This is due to the production mentality of America in World War II. The American market was all about producing as much as possible as fast as possible. The mentality did not mesh with the ideas of extreme quality control well.

Luckily enough, Deming had a much easier time spreading his ideas in Japan. Starting from 1945, he was involved with the American occupation government.

After the war, the States had a huge interest in the economic recovery of Japan. In order to get to that point as soon as possible, America dispatched a group of visionaries to help the country's economy get going again.

Among the group, Deming was probably the most important for the goal. His importance was so great that in 1960, Nobusuke Kishi,

Japan's Prime minister at the time, awarded him with a position in The Order of the Sacred Treasure. He was made into a second class member and had an award named after him.

This is only a part of the story of the "Japanese Economic Miracle." Deming was given complete freedom to try whatever ideas he might have, and thus he gave them a smart miracle to solving the crisis. His ideas were applied by many managers in japan and spun them into the Kaizen ethos.

The economy started to boom from that point on. From one year to another, the quality of Japan's export increased, as well as the GDP. The changes were so explosive and drastic that, by the 1980s, Japan's economic power became globally recognized.

Japan was known for its dedication to craftsmanship up to that point. Their production techniques are world-renowned for being meticulous and detailed for as long as we can trace it. After Deming came into the mixture, bringing a new method to their mass production, Japanese companies superseded their Western counterparts, in both quality and efficiency.

The first to catch on with Deming's ideas was Taiichi Ohno. Being the savvy businessman and industrial engineer he was, he immediately saw the potential in Deming's method. Ohno's greatest achievement is the TPS (Toyota Production System). He started the development of the system in 1945 and, with the new method presented to him, perfected it around 1965.

The TPS has many names under which it can be recognized. One of the names is "just-in-time" manufacturing. This system, like many other Kaizen systems, aimed to perfect efficiency by continuously improving. Another thing it can be recognized for is its importance to Lean manufacturing studies.

It was a last-ditch survival strategy at the time when it was devised. Toyota was in an incredibly dire situation after the war. Both its survival and future were questionable, to say the least. Resources were scarce all over Japan, and the same was true for Toyota.

The fact that Toyota even worked was a miracle. Their plants used incredibly outdated and low-quality equipment, literally taking them from junkyards. It was ingenious, really. The heap of steel that they called a factory pumped as hard as it could.

Due to how weak the company was materially and financially, Ohno's only solution was to make the best use possible of what he had. He aimed to use the workers to their full potential, working with them to think of solutions.

Ohno summarized his system into "Ten Precepts" of winning:

- Reduce waste, even you yourself are a cost.

- Try as hard as you can whenever you can. You can do it.

- Before turning anywhere else for answers, turn to the workplace. It is the best teacher.

- Postpone nothing. Winning is only possible when you start working immediately.

- Persevere through hardships. Giving up is not an option.

- If something is hard to understand, make it easy. If it is easy to understand, repeat it.

- Do not hide problems. Make them visible.

- All of your motions must have value. Waste nothing.

- If you have improved something, continue improving it.

- Wisdom is not the treasure of only one man. Share and use it.

While Ohno was a white-collar manager, he was always reluctant to be such. He always liked to be where the problems are. He liked a hands-on approach, never being scared of getting his hands dirty.

The TPS wanted you to understand and monitor even the smallest details of the manufacturing process, not just in papers and in the offices, but on the line itself. It wants you to ask your workers as many questions as possible, as they know the most about what is working and what is not. This is extremely important due to the fact that the hidden processes might conceal the most waste.

The system did miracles for Toyota. The company grew quickly and promised to grow faster and faster. Their sales grew dramatically, and it even surpassed General Motors in 2008, taking the position which was unchallenged for 77 years.

Ohno's mentorship worked towards spreading TPS even more. He taught his students, and they mentored a new generation of managers. As with most groundbreaking discoveries, it spread overseas, further and further away from Japan.

The cliché of Japanese cars being cheap and immortal had their roots in Ohno's innovations. It is nothing new to say that Japanese cars work perfectly for a long time, even being passed down from generation to generation. This is the product of the TPS philosophy,

Nisan, Suzuki, and Honda all work with a derivative of TPS as a base. As you are probably aware, they work incredibly well, as all of these companies saw a spike in quality and efficiency of production ever since they started implementing TPS.

An important name for the spreading of Kaizen to the west was Masaaki Imai. He was a management consultant in the 1960s. He worked with many companies both outside and inside of Japan.

In his best-seller "Kaizen: The Key to Japan's Competitive success," he detailed his take on the Kaizen ethos. He proposed a few more solutions and took in the 90s with the book "Gemba Kaizen: A Commonsense, Low-Cost Approach to Management."

He was also the founder of the Kaizen Institute. The institute was founded in 1986, and it works towards helping organizations apply Kaizen practices in the most efficient ways in relation to the local practices in the fields of business and culture.

The concept of Kaizen that Imai focuses one is one of both improving and maintaining operations. It opts for a slower, more steady process of moving up, rather than going for an all or nothing gamble.

Specifically, he gives importance to the "value-added" component. Delivering value is everything in the world of economics, and Imai makes sure that you are aware of that.

Another important term in Imai's methodology is "gemba." Gemba refers to the place where you are working. It does not matter what this place is. Even if it is a doctor's office or a shop room floor, Gemba is something you need to put a lot of time into, according to Imai.

What this means is that managers need to stop being afraid of learning. Being exposed as ignorant due to asking questions that might come off as elementary to other people is far from the worst thing that can happen to them, and they need to face that reality.

Imai always found it interesting how the companies in Japan focused on the process, while those in America focused on the results more. In his studies, he broke down the Japanese obsession with quality control. He noted that this kind of production promotes transparency.

In the 1950s and 60s, Japan was popular for producing low quality, but cheap products in every field of production. Despite this, the Kaizen method was applied in many large companies, and, by the time the 80s rolled around, the global consensus over Japan's product greatly shifted. During the decade, "Made in Japan" became a synonym for affordable high quality.

Japan had a reputation for cheap but "not so great" products in the 1950s and 1960s. But Kaizen principles kept being applied year-on-year at major firms.

To summarize, the Kaizen project yielded great results. Huge firms used it, and by the 80s, they managed to outperform their Western competition.

The Americans regretted ignoring Deming. They saw the value of his ideas far too late, and only after it worked for Japan. In 1980, NBC introduced Deming to many Americans for the first time. The segment was an hour long and was called "If Japan Can, Why Can't We?". It was a form of awakening for Western businesses.

In 1981, Ford was struggling like never before. They had lost three billion in three years. Single-Handedly, Deming saved the company by 1987. Regan awarded him the National Medal of Technology. After that, Deming's teachings spread in America and helped the economy make a comeback. In 1997, the Lean Enterprise was created and started spreading Denim's ideas in many other fields.

Chapter 2

How Does Kaizen Work?

How do things "change" in your workplace? Does change occur as a result of major initiatives, or does it happen as a part of your working process? Of course, some kinds of changes cannot happen unless they are a part of a major project. Changes like this require large amounts of time, money, and upheaval. The slow and steady continuous improvement of Kaizen can be both an alternative and a complementary approach to general improvement within each area of your company. This approach is often undervalued due to the fact that changes gained through continuous improvement are often less impactful and harder to see.

Once you make a major change, it might seem as if it is as good as it can be, but is it really? Will your changes last long enough to be impactful until the next project, which might happen only in a few years? Usually, the answer to these questions is no. In fact, if you base your changes on such a principle, you will most definitely see a decline over time. While it is true that it will start off as a burst of positive effects, you will soon see it plummeting, letting inefficiencies and bad practices inside.

You must always keep in mind the fact that there is always room to improve. The status quo is there to be challenged every day. There is always something that can be further tuned and improved. The thing is that this process is something that everyone in the workplace does subconsciously. You are already benefiting from it as well. Everyone intuitively works towards constant improvement without being told to do so.

Kaizen is a word that is derived from two others. The first word is "kai," meaning change. The second word is "Zen," loosely meaning for the good. The single sentence that can describe the Kaizen method the best is that it is a philosophical belief that everything can be improved. Mostly, corporations look at a process that is working fine and assumes that this is good enough. However, for the Kaizen philosophy, this is unacceptable. In Kaizen, the status quo does not exist. You are expected to make constant improvements, no matter how small and imperceptible. These changes will add up over a period of time and turn into substantial changes in the long term, without any radical innovations, all while being as gentle and employee-friendly as possible.

Kaizen is not a specific tool that is used to fix a problem. It is an approach that can be applied to any process in your corporation, from the lowest operational units to the highest. Kaizen suggests that it is the responsibility of every employee to identify any inefficiency in the workplace. This is supposed to result in anyone, no matter at which level of organization they are, should have the right to make a suggestion for how it can be improved.

The Basic Effects of Kaizen

- Less waste - In Kaizen, waste is an extremely wide category. It almost always refers to any factor that makes production more costly or inefficient in any way. By applying Kaizen in your business, you will use the skills of your employees more efficiently, as well as the inventory you are working with.

- People are more satisfied - Your workers, as well as you, will end up happier with the new workplace. This will make your production more efficient as the quality of life improves.

- Improved retention - No business can truly succeed by servicing a customer only once. Every business wants to retain the customers that they have. By improving the quality of your products, you will make your customers happier, and in return, they will be more likely to stay.

- Improved competitiveness - You will become a more viable competitor in the market as lower costs, and higher quality products tend to increase the value of your company.

- Improved problem-solving - By employing every sector in the problem-solving process gives you more angles, as well as a more hands-down approach.

As mentioned before, waste is a very important thing in the Kaizen method. Waste, also known as "muda," is something that Kaizen aims to eliminate completely. The original usage of the philosophy was improving manufacturing processes. However, it can be applied to almost anything.

The "Waste" Takes Several Different Forms

Movement - Moving materials around without a higher function in mind. This could be moving wood from one storage area to another even though they would be moved to the same space if they were needed. An example of getting rid of such waste would be adding a telephone line instead of letting your workers move from building to building in order to do their jobs. In the method, there is such a thing as "Mental" movement that can also be waste. For example, a person being distracted by a job before finishing another one will decrease the efficiency of that worker. Concentrating on each task is the best way to avoid this, switching between different jobs as rarely as possible.

Time - This can be another type of waste. Time spent waiting will give you no value when compared to the time elapsed. For example, you should never wait for latecomers to meetings. A meeting needs to start at the allocated time and end when such is deemed possible. Good timekeeping is very important. Remember, time is money. An example of getting rid of waste like this would be organizing your files into neat folders in order to spend as little time as possible looking for them. In workshops, this can be done by adding boards where you can add hooks for better tool storage.

Defects - Redoing any work that should be done at the point is a huge waste of resources. An example of such waste would have to rewrite a report due to faulty information or errors. This can often be avoided by being meticulous before you make key decisions that will affect your work.

Over-Processing - Doing more than necessary in order to give as much value as possible to the customer for the allocated price. Printing your graphics in color is not necessary. Neither is calling as many people as possible to meetings. Always find solutions that will save you resources without dropping the quality of your services.

Variations - Giving make-shift solutions that will do the job as well as a standard one. Producing different kinds of reports for different

There are many ways to implement Kaizen in your company. Most of them, however, follow a pattern more or less. It is always recommended to keep a log of your ideas. It is very important to have a hands-on approach to your company. It is often easier to spot flaws in the spur of the moment that it is while analyzing your production. You should do so as often as possible. Identifying areas where there is waste is produced of key importance as this is where applying the Kaizen method starts. You can often do so relatively easily. However, the tricky part starts when you start asking questions. "How do I fix this?" or "How should I make this better?" are often not simple to answer.

You will have to consider "change overload." If you implement too many changes in a short period of time, it can quickly get out of control, and the consequences of the changes can be extremely unpredictable and chaotic. It is very important to balance out the time elapsed in making changes with the time elapsed planning them. It is also important to work together with all of the people that are affected by the changes. They can give you useful insights, as well as offer solutions that you might not see yourself. This will also create a healthier work environment and a closer bond between the worker and the workplace.

It is easy to apple Kaizen as an individual; however, if you are working with a group on a wider-scale, a fair bit of effort will have to be expended.

You have to grow with your team. For Kaizen to be implemented properly, everyone has to have a solid grasp of the ideal. It is not just about one individual knowing what needs to be done, but the team synergizing in order to develop ideas.

The next step would usually be figuring out how ideas should be gathered and evaluated. Set up a system that dictates how changes should be implemented to avoid the chaos of everyone implementing them freely. Make sure that everyone knows that their ideas are welcome and heard, as this will encourage them to give you more ideas to work with.

Toyota's Kaizen

Toyota applies Kaizen in the form of a set of three principles. The first principle is the five "S." The five "S" references the abbreviations of the five Japanese keywords that define it. The words are Seiri(Sort), Seiton(Set in order), Seiso(Shine), Seiketsu(Standardize), and Shitsuke(Sustain). Though the principle is very simple, this is what makes it so special. It is very easy to follow, and Toyota makes sure to encourage employees to live by it even outside of the workplace.

The first "S," Sort, refers to removing any items in the workplace that are not necessary. This is done through a few important steps. For this step to be implemented properly, it is important first to set up a set of criteria that will determine which objects need to be removed and which need to be kept. In Toyota's case, this also includes planning what they will need ahead of time.

The second "S" is Set in order or Seiton. It invites you to classify your inventory into specific group action. In Toyota, this step is used to make sure that every item in your inventory has a determined function. This can simply be done by making sure that all of the necessary tools are near the workplace and are easily identifiable in their surroundings. Thus they arrange their workshops in such a way that every item has its own specific place. This keeps the flow of work uninterrupted and easier to get into.

The third "S" is Shine or Seiso. It refers to the cleanliness of the workplace. This encompasses not only the regular cleaning of the workplace but also avoiding uncleanliness as much as possible. This is a way to save resources, but it serves a higher, more conscious role of reducing pollution and waste.

The fourth "S" is Standardize or Seiketsu. It motivates you to turn Seiri, Seiso, and Seiton into standards that you hold up on a day-to-day basis. Toyota does this by constantly stressing the importance of the 5 "s" by making a clear set of rules for its employees to carry out.

The last "S" and perhaps the most important is Sustain or Shitsuke. This is a principle of self-discipline. The five "S" methods requires you to apply them consciously in order to succeed. There cannot be a need for a supervisor. Everyone is expected to follow the principles as best as they can, so, in a way, this turns the company into something that supersedes a workplace. It becomes something that the community consciously built up through a certain period of time because every member of the company works towards continuous improvement.

The second pillar of Toyota's Kaizen is the five "why." Every member of the company is always encouraged to give their own ideas to help the company progress and become better. This is because Toyota values each member of the community equally and because they realize that the lower echelons of the hierarchy might spot problems that the higher-ups cannot. This means that with different points of view we can come to more efficient solutions more quickly. The Kaizen methodology encourages you to ask the question "why?" on five levels.

In the simplest terms, Toyota aims to find the problem in the easiest way possible and then fix it in the same manner. The five "why?" are the idea that in order to fix a problem, you need to ask "why?" as many times as possible until you get to the core of the problem. The five "why" system is not only used by Toyota; rather, after the 70s, it started spreading through Japan as it was slowly knitted into the Kaizen ethos.

There are many ways to develop the five whys as you might imagine; these are not some mundane questions that you just throw around. No, there is a system behind that as well. The most popular methods are the tabular format and the Ishikawa diagram. The Ishikawa Diagram gives you a rough graphical descriptor that shows you how a few small factors that lead to many lines of functioning get to the same resolution.

Of course, the five whys technique has its critiques. It is very meticulous when it comes to finding the core of the problem, but it opts to leave out and ignore other side factors that might have played into the problem actually coming into existence. Currently, Toyota does not use this method only to solve problems, but to avoid wasting resources on new plans that are not properly justified as well.

Though very important, the technique is relatively simple. For example, let's say that the office has no coffee. You ask the first why and get to the conclusion that your machine is not working when you ask the second why you come to the conclusion that it has not been properly maintained. After asking the third why you will see that the person who was tasked with the maintenance is absent from the company for whatever reason. The fourth why will lead you to believe that this is due to the person not having a replacement; thus, there is no one to attend to it. Finally, the fifth why will show that the person on top did nothing to replace the worker, leaving the position empty.

With the five why technique, we came to the root of the problem. The root being lackluster management. In order to ensure that no such thing will happen again, the manager got the memo that a person should always hold said position.

The TPS, an abbreviation for Thinking People System, is yet another key principle of Toyota's success. Kaizen is not an improvement philosophy that only involves leaders and experts. Rather, it involves all of the units within a company. From the janitorial staff to the CEO, all take equal part in continuous improvement.

Toyota does not banalize anyone's skills or ideas. They are all valuable in one way or another and can immensely improve the workplace if applied correctly. By the standards of TPS, everyone is expected to be able to take part in the devising of solutions. This is why Toyota does a practice out of morning meetings where everyone can give their opinion on how the company is running at the moment.

The system provides you with another initiative. It makes sure that people know how important their work is to the company, giving a better quality of life to the workspace. It also lets the workers take a bit more control over the production, using their experience to improve upon it. For Toyota, one of the most important things is for the staff to feel valued. This is why the company has been successful and why it has been able to keep going for so long.

While it is true that Toyota is the most prominent example of Kaizen working as intended, it is not the only one. Toyota did rely on Kaizen the most and yielded the most results out of it; however, a lot of other companies have also seen great success with the methodology. We have mentioned how Kaizen saved Ford from going bust; however, this is not the end of Ford's implementation. In 2006 Alan Mulally became the CEO of the company. Following the lead of Mark Fields, he brought a new age of prosperity to the company.

These processes gave them a quick edge over the competition, and, in a truly Kaizen fashion, Ford decided that more can be done in that regard. Even now, they put great efforts every day in order to find ways that will save them resources in the future. Every day they find even the tiniest of flaws and correct them. Every time they repeat the process, it becomes faster and faster and more efficient. The effects are nothing to scoff at. Today, Ford is a name that everyone in the world will recognize.

While their legacy and historical impact on the world of automobiles is something to marvel at, the quality of their services is admirable, to say the least. The Ford Motor Company is one of the biggest brands today, and it just keeps on growing and growing despite the amount of competition it has to struggle against every day.

Nestlé is yet another amazing example of Kaizen being used efficiently. It stands to show that the methodology can be applied in other industries. In this case, specifically, the food industry is represented by one of the most impactful brands in the field worldwide. Nestlé is extremely serious about their Lean Production.

As we have discussed before, Lean production is a big part of the Kaizen way. Since the company started running, it has, on multiple occasions, found ways to drastically decrease their waste, specifically in the time and materials required to create a product. Of course, there is more than that one aspect to lean production. It is not all about reducing waste. It is also about maximizing efficiency with the resources and space you have, as well as combining human efforts with available technologies in order to bolster the company's success further. Nestlé's upper echelon admitted that implementing Kaizen is often a very difficult thing to do. As they put it, it is very hard to develop a mindset while having such a high focus on the tools of production. This is why they set up several overseers that function as role models. They work by applying the Kaizen methodology to everything in the hopes of leading their coworkers to do the same. More often than not, it is very successful. This, however, goes a bit against the Kaizen ethos. Having an authority that dictates the pace of the changes is seen as bad. Nestlé takes an approach that is somewhere between the two. It respects the teachings of Kaizen and adds something of its own to the mix. They do not place an authority, rather an organ of encouragement. They do not tell their workers what must be done; rather, they show them by example. This goes to show that Kaizen has some downsides. All change is hard to achieve, especially in a larger or more complex system. This is not to say that Kaizen is bad, far from it. You just need to keep in mind that it is not going to be easy to succeed.

You have probably heard about Mayo Clinic.

It is extremely famous for being a nonprofit group that works with medical practice and research. Their goals are obvious from the start when it comes to how they want to function. Being nonprofit shows that money is not a factor. They do not aim to make money; however, they do aim to cut down their costs while keeping the quality of their services as high as possible. Influenced by Toyota, they closely studied Kaizen in order to find ways to improve their practices. Though the company isn't as big as Toyota, the system it works on is quite complex. Their manufacturing operations are nothing to scoff at. They saw Toyota and thought, "If Toyota can do it, then so can we," and indeed they could. They applied the philosophy to health care quite efficiently. With how complex the health industry is, many moving parts can be seen that can greatly benefit from Kaizen. Parts like waiting times, sorting patient records, etc. are all areas where Kaizen can be applied for additional efficiency. After Mayo Clinic, many other healthcare companies followed the example and implemented Kaizen in their workplaces.

Lockheed Martin is a huge company, to say the least. As you might know, it deals with global aerospace, security, defense, and advanced technologies. It employs more than a hundred thousand people. It works in such a tightly knit network that just one misstep in the protocols could prove to be very damaging. Within a period of six years, specifically from 1992 to 1997, there was a notable reduction in their production costs.

On the other hand, their defect rate decreased substantially, and the time elapsed between ordering and delivery was cut down by 20 months. Even more notable is the decrease he made to the time it took for parts and materials to be transported from receiving to stock. The change was severely drastic, cutting it down from a month to four hours. Lockheed Martin was successful in applying the Kaizen methods to many areas of the company, and, in turn, in the year 2000, he was awarded the Shingo Prize for Excellence. One of the more recent successes the company had was the JAGM (Joint Air-to-Ground Missile) system. After that, he held many Kaizen conferences in order to make sure that the JAGM was manufactured as best as it possibly could.

The Lean Six Sigma

Even a method as broad and concise as Kaizen has its competitors. There is no denying that Kaizen has some flaws; every methodology does. It is only natural that someone would create an answer to said flaws. That is where Lean Six Sigma strategies come into play. Though one of Kaizen's greatest competitors, Six Sigma, can be considered a kind of Kaizen on its own. While it might seem strange at first, once you look deeper into it, it becomes plain to see. Similarly to Kaizen, Six Sigma aims to reduce waste and inefficiency. The methodology started in the 1920s. Its roots are the same as that of Kaizen, being inside Walter Shewarts mind. He took note of three sigma's that can be identified as key solutions in any problem. The idea saw little sunlight and development until the mid-1980s. Bob Galving, the chairman of Motorola, developed a measurement system for the methodology. This not only caused a cultural change but also gave us a way to measure efficiency.

Six Sigma has seen much acceptance among companies world-wide since the 1980s. It is often closely connected to Lean. Being born from the TPS, lean aimed to reduce waste in cost and time, lending itself well to Six Sigma. Furthermore, the methodology accepted the three areas that are targeted in TPS. The three areas being mura (inconsistency), waste (muda), and overburden (muri).

The TPS, on its own, relies on two pillars being present. The two pillars being "just in time delivery" and "automation with a human touch" (jidoka). As more and more people started welcoming TPS into their workplaces, the idea of Kaizen gained more and more prominence. Over time most companies replaced Six Sigma with Kaizen. This specific upshift can be seen within the food industry the most, as more and more CEOs started seeing the value in helping the employees cultivate a mindset of searching for problems and driving themselves to constant improvement.

Of course, like in every movement, proper leadership is one of the keys for Kaizen to succeed. This, however, does not mean that frontline employees should stay untrained. Many managers make the mistake of overlooking this. They forget that if your employees are not adept enough at using the tools you give them, then the improvement fails. Stateside Foods does not make this mistake. This UK-based company provided training to 430 employees with their own continuous improvement program, which they call "The Stateside Way."

The program aims to give the experience needed for using the tools of problem-solving through a series of interactive workshops. Here, some of the major emphasis is collaboration and teamwork. Stateside Food understands that in order for its employees to give it their all, they need help in figuring out how to do so. The company is more than happy to share the benefits of its program reaped. They allowed the teams to apply the approach to the workplace. The workers devised a practice of having a sort of boardroom meeting where they could discuss the performance that they have been giving lately and how it can be further improved. The workers are encouraged to find problems and give their own solutions to them. Of course, they are not given free rein over what is done to fix the problem. The decision falls to an administrative team that very closely communicates with all of the sectors in the company.

Another large business that shows a lot of interest in the Kaizen methodology is the Greencore Group. Greencore Group is a manufacturer of convenience foods that ships its products internationally. Specifically, they are interested in automating as much of the process as possible.

In the words of Greencore's business improvement manager, Jon Bremmer, continuous improvement requires you to remove as much variation as possible from the process. He sees automation as a solution that can lead to the least amount of variation due to the lack of human interaction. His goal with continuous improvement is to make room for more sophisticated automation within his sectors. The company does not see continuous improvement as an end-goal, rather a step that helps them ensure that they can afford to use the right tools for the job via automation.

The new trend of employing continuous improvement systems has grown so rapidly and went so wide that even Coca-Cola fell under its influence. In the year 2007, Coca-Cola requested from all of its bottlers that they start implementing the Six Sigma within their workplaces. The interesting part came up when they realized that their headquarters in Stockholm already had a great idea system. This gave experts in the field a unique opportunity. Never before had they gotten a chance to so clearly compare between two improvement systems.

The results were as expected as they were impressive. If reports are to be trusted, seven projects saved 2.5 million Swedish Kronor. With the implementation of 1 720 ideas they got from their frontline workers, they saved 8 million Kronor. The results spoke for themselves, and the company quickly started switching to the idea system. Over the next year, they managed to save 9 million Kronor. This greatly overshadowed what Six Sigma saved them, amassing only 1.5 million in saving.

The changes that they got from the projects were mostly minuscule, but they saved the bottler a lot of money. A unique example of how they did this was by adding a worker to the bottling line. The production line was working in such a way that half-liter bottles were first filled up. They were later capped and moved through a 90-degree curve. There, they would be tested by an electronic eye, and those seen as defective were pushed off the line. This often resulted in the bottle being pushed away, toppling others on the line, causing a lot of damage. With the simple addition of a person that oversees and helps the process, they saved 91.000 Kronor per year.

Chapter 3

How Can Kaizen Help My Business?

You have most probably heard of the "customer is the king" parole. In the market economy, this is almost a rule. Here, it is all about catering to the customer. You are expected to match their expectations when it comes to QCD (quality, cost, and delivery). This is something that you should always strive for in your business. These principles are applied by anyone invoking the Kaizen strategy.

We have already talked about the types of waste. After all, Kaizen is all about removing it from your system. But what does that mean? Well, Kaizen aims to save you as many resources as possible. It stops you from overproducing, saving you both time and money. It helps you balance out your work in order to reduce the time elapsed in waiting. It helps you get your transportation in line, as well, suggesting tactics on how to handle the moving of your inventory in the most optimal way. Excessive inventory is another targeted area of Kaizen. While an excess of materials will not hinder your production directly, it usually hides some problems that you should probably face as soon as possible on top of this aim to eliminate any unnecessary motion and over-processing. While moving from one place to another seems minuscule, it can save quite a bit of money over a prolonged period of time. What Kaizen aims at the most, however, is the complete elimination of defective manufacturing. Kaizen is all about quality, and nothing other than perfection will do.

As we have mentioned before, the principles of Kaizen are not something exclusive to the automobile industry. They are something that can be applied to any industry you might get yourself involved in.

In the automobile industry, for example, two very specific problems can cause a deterioration inefficiency. The first is the lack of supply on time, also known as the "external enemy" syndrome. The second problem is wastage due to a number of defects in printed sheets. This one is directly attributed to an improper way of storing and printing instructions. This, in turn, can be traced back to a number of employees.

How does Kaizen fix these problems? Well, three general steps can be taken here. These steps can be applied anywhere else, though with slight modification.

The first step is getting your employees to commit to continuous improvement. The Kaizen method shuns those that do this forcefully. You are not supposed to bear this upon your workers, rather give them encouragement to participate in the process of problem detection and solving. Your duty is to make sure that they are not only aware of this possibility, but also properly trained to tackle the responsibility.

The second step is to analyze the problem. If you do not analyze the problem completely, you will most likely not find a good solution. When a problem is detected, you need to consult as many employees as you can. The best insights can come from unexpected places. Ideas are what keeps the Kaizen methodology alive; thus you should make sure that you value every single one that you get.

The third step is implementation. In this specific example, the intervention was successful, and you should see a reduction in the waiting time, as well as defection rates within the sheet. This also has a positive long-term effect on your workforce, reinforcing their place in the company, and making them feel valued. One should never underestimate the effect morale has on the productivity of a workplace.

How Can Kaizen Help You?

Of course, you might be wondering what this means for you? Everything that we discussed up until this point has been very specific to the industry or a company. So what does it have to do to you? Well, while the examples might not be something that you can relate to, it was important to note the common principles that can be seen within every company in different industries that applied Kaizen. There are many reasons as to why Kaizen is great.

It places you into the mindset that no matter how good you are doing; you can do even better. There is always room for improvement. It drives you towards constant success, hugely changing the way you play the game over time. Of course, like any other change, this does not come easily. There are quite a few things to take into consideration before you start practicing Kaizen. You need to make sure that you can manage the time, consistency, and practice that it takes for the method to have a real effect on your work. Of course, it will help you save you time and money, but we will talk more about that later.

A good thing you can learn here, disregarding if you succeeded or failed in applying Kaizen, is critical thinking. One of the things that the method relies on is you never accepting assumptions. If you haven't put the research into something, do not do it. One of the traps of business is that it is easy to get trapped inside of a mindset unintentionally. When you see an idea working, you more often than not put far too much fate into it, sometimes causing you to suffer losses in the future. If you cannot adapt to the changing times and new problems, you cannot say that your system is working. Thinking outside the box is paramount to your success in this regard. It forces you to do some forward-thinking. This will do well by you, as a businessman, as well as your workers. You need to keep track of the innovations in the market you are working in and always think about the new things that you can bring or how you can surpass the old. In this way, you can compare the market to Mother Nature. Only those that evolve in the most efficient ways will survive. You will start seeing the value in even the tiniest improvements.

Another good idea that Kaizen implants into you are that it is okay to fail. It does not encourage it, of course, but it teaches you to dust yourself off when you fall and try again. "Failing forward" is a good learning process. You will learn from your mistakes, and you will start to find small successes, even in failures. In the words of Tomas

Edison, it is okay if you did not find a way to make a lightbulb. You found 999 ways to fail in doing so.

Again, tracing back to Toyota, it was noted that getting management involved with staff that made mistakes in order to help them out will encourage workers to start making their own actionable plans that will give your business more stability. It is always important to see the good in the bad. By finding the positives in negative situations, you will create a more healthy environment where constructive dialogue can bloom.

If you teach yourself how to fail forward, you will see risks becoming less and less costly. By researching trends carefully, you can open up new avenues for experimentation and, while failing forward, risks of wasting money will not be as high. By experimenting, you will decide if the trend works for you, and you will be able to find a way to implement it into how you do your job. If you see a trend that you think will work for you, go for it, even if everyone else saw it fail.

For the success of any company, it is important to nurture the main driving force - the workers. Creating a healthy work environment will not only boost your productivity but will also make your business feel more like home.

Kaizen encourages you to teach your teams how to work together. It is rather crucial in the methodology. Cooperation is the key to success. The Kaizen mindset values people much more than it makes money. It encourages you to improve your employees' job performance by educating them and giving them more confidence.

This brings us to lean leadership. Lean leadership is all about the workings of the company on an interpersonal level. The management sector of your company needs to get involved with your workers, getting to know them on a personal level. This helps your managers transcend from figures of authority to mentors and role models. Mentorship is a system as old as time. It is all about a more experienced member passing down their skills to the less experienced ones in order to help them grow every day. While managers collaborate with the workers to solve a problem, the workers will learn more about problem-solving, while management starts getting insights into the inner workings of the workplace.

When you apply Kaizen in a team environment, you will see how unity is slowly being built. You want to encourage and nourish this, as unified teams will be much more efficient. This is because cross-departmental projects are very important to the success of any business. And if your departments work together tidily, it is easier to play off of each of their strengths. To put it in numbers, this will make your productivity growth due to the healthier company morale, in turn gaining you greater profits.

Kaizen is not about reaching perfection. Though one of its main principles is striving to it, it is never really about reaching it. Rather, it is about chasing it, always improving. The Kaizen mindset is one where you abolish any lackluster ideas of perfection. By doing so and continuously improving, you create a very healthy atmosphere where new generations can learn and prosper.

I cannot stress enough how important it is to remember that Kaizen is not about making big changes quickly. Huge changes come over time as a result of smaller ones. The four areas you will often need to focus on are incremental gains, profitability, making better products, and customer service. The lean principles get everyone involved in the changes. Not only the managers and the workers but also the customer. A problem that you might have is that of the silo mentality. It is very easy to look at a single area at a time and work from that. However, in order to truly improve, you need to look at the company as a whole, as well.

Another thing that you have to know is that you do not have the luxury of getting out once the water gets cold. It is something you are going to have to stick with if you want to see it work. That being said, if everyone in your company accepts the Kaizen mindset, you will see it prove itself to be an amazing tool.

A mistake people often make is that they look at Kaizen as a method that can only benefit businesses that are struggling. This is highly untrue, however. While it is true that it is most often used by businesses that are aware of their bottlenecks. At that point, they call in a professional in order to help them apply this method.

However, you will note that Kaizen is working excellently in companies that have already seen great success. Toyota, being the giant it is right now, never stopped using Kaizen decades after they got out of the hole they were in. This helps them avoid complacency and keep the company on top of its game.

You can see a similar thing being done by professional athletes. They never look for a huge change as it may be damaging in the long run. The question they ask is where they can improve by one percent every day. And by doing so every day, they produce results.

You should do the same in business. Always look to achieve something every day, no matter how small it is. The change you are looking for might not happen in that single day, but by keeping up the good work and maintaining the attitude, you will build up towards success. No matter how well you are performing, always ask yourself how it can be done better. By doing so, you will see improvements in many areas.

Firstly, management performance will be drastically improved. The first step for the success of the Kaizen method is to get your management on the same track. Once you do, you will see the efficiency of management itself bloom. Start off by getting your managers to dedicate at least fifteen minutes every day to doing things the Kaizen way. Encourage them to keep asking, "Why?" until they reach the root. This is a technique commonly used to dig deeper into a problem and identify what the issue actually is.

Do not wait for life to give you a chance; take the chance yourself. It is better to make a tiny improvement than leave things as they are. Both you and your managers need to live by this parole. You do not have to make huge changes in order to prosper. It is best to focus on small, practical issues.

Opinions matter much less than facts. Once you accept this, it will be much easier for you to get your Kaizen events going. Keep your data as fresh as possible, and make sure that your managers do not solidify tactics on their personal beliefs. Doing so will hinder your productivity more often than not, as running a company is a group effort. You should always find the most agreeable solution, which is more often than not the objectively correct one.

Sometime after you begin practicing Kaizen, you will see a great improvement in Employee Performance. Kaizen makes sure that the company sees the value of employees and makes sure that they know that. Everyone that works for you has a voice. This helps your employees see their job as more enjoyable, making them more dedicated to doing it correctly. By expelling blame culture from the workplace, you will see an increase in productivity and morale in your facilities.

You do so by respecting everyone's ideas. If you want a more efficient cleaning system, it is often the janitors who have the best ideas when it comes to achieving that. Everyone has their own niche, and it is your job to find that niche and make them aware of it. You have to encourage your workers to show you how they think things can be improved.

This will also lead to your management staff and workers communicating more often and more easily. This change comes naturally, as you are essentially getting your workers involved in the management's job, almost forcing them to interact. This helps create an atmosphere of a partnership between the two groups, making a more friendly work environment. It also brings a sense of equality as everyone is speaking on equal footing, without the boss-underling pretenses. When applying Kaizen, it is the management's job to work on how they interact with the staff. Management needs to be aware of what the workers go through every day. If management does not appreciate the working force, then you can just scrap the system.

The main selling point of Kaizen is how much of an impact it will have on the efficiency of your processes and, by extension, your productivity. To put it in the simplest terms possible, Kaizen will help you weed out all of the flaws that your system may have one step at a time. You can apply this "process Kaizen" in a number of ways; however, the simplest and most common one is the PDCA cycle. It is important to stress how useful a tool the cycle is. It is an extremely easy system to understand and will, through a series of small changes, help you reap great benefits.

Of course, without a happy customer, a business cannot function, we can all agree on that. This is where the final and most important goal of Kaizen comes from. Everything you do in your corporation is aimed at providing your customers with as much satisfaction as possible. Efficiency comes in many forms, and with you failing to provide it in any way might cause your customers to turn their back on your business. This can happen in a plethora of ways. One example would be tardy delivery. While the customer will eventually get what they ordered, they are less likely to use your services again, meaning that you lost a lot of money. You do not want a customer that is not satisfied.

This "customer Kaizen" requires you to get involved with your customers in order to plan around their satisfactions or dissatisfactions. This helps you identify where the problems are. Once you get involved with your customers and get their input, you will get a better view of how to satisfy them. Recognizing the customers' values is a very important by-product of this process; however, the main benefits come from your customers feeling like you are really working for them, as well as gathering insight from a whole different source.

The main benefit of Kaizen, or more accurately, the most long-lasting one, is that it creates an atmosphere that encourages continuous improvement. After a while, Kaizen will become an integral part of your company. It stops being something that your workers need to do. It becomes something they do. At a certain point, you will stop having to invest resources into the methodology, as it will have become something your workplace runs on. This creates a company that almost improves itself on its own. It is obvious why this is good, no? So many companies have failed due to not being able to make a huge step after some time. You avoid running into this issue as your system does not require you to take such large steps. Rather, it walks steadily on its own. At the end of the day, that is what continuous improvement is about, what the Kaizen ethos is knitted around. Improving without treating it as an improvement. Making improvements is something that happens as a part of the production.

Chapter 4

Kaizen In Everyday Life

As I have mentioned numerous times, Kaizen is not just a way to increase your manufacturing output over a long period of time. It is a philosophy that can improve your life in many ways. As they say, a castle is built brick by brick. The same can be said for one's own happiness. While it is true that huge positive events bring incredible amounts of joy to your life, that happiness is only temporary. In both the east and west, there was always the belief that one can achieve true happiness only through self-improvement.

More often than not, however, self-improvement is something not only hard to achieve, but also to understand. One first needs to define what self-improvement is before thinking of how to achieve it. In the Kaizen philosophy, the form this self-improvement takes is that of striving for perfection. Of course, one first needs to be met with the realization that they will never achieve it. Though discouraging, this gives more virtue to the process itself. It boils down to you being better and better by setting up a new goal after reaching the previous one.

It encourages you to always aim for something above that which you have and go to it in small steps. Instead of improving by ten percent in a week, improve by 0.1 each day. If you pour a drop of water on a stone every day, the stone will eventually erode. While there is no text-book example of how you can introduce Kaizen to your life, there are some things that you can do to make it easier.

Keep your thoughts simple. When you put up a goal for yourself, you need to separate it into smaller, more chewable bits. When you ask yourself how you can reach the goal, you can often get stuck right there. That is because it is easy to forget that most goals require steps to be taken. You need to ask yourself questions like what the first thing is you can do to start getting there or how much time you a day can spare to do so. Keep the idea that nothing comes easy in the back of your head.

After thinking to yourself what needs to be done, you need to figure out how it can be done. Figure out a process that you can start executing immediately and organize it as well as possible and make it as repeatable as possible. Once you do so, examine it and decide if it gets you to your goal quickly enough. If not, remember that you do not have to stick with one thing. It is quite the opposite. Always be ready to innovate your approach.

Once you decide that your planned steps will help you get to the point where you want to be, decide in which order you will do them. It is easy to feel overwhelmed in such a situation, but in the true spirit of Kaizen, start with the smallest thing you can and go from there. Do not push yourself too hard, but drive yourself towards doing said actions consistently

Make sure that you are ready to give up the time required to put your plan into motion. Without time, even these small tasks will not be properly executed. Make sure to be realistic with your expectations and planning. Review your schedule as often as you can. Whenever you can find a slot to put an element of your plan into motion, do so. If something can be done tomorrow, do it today so you can leave tomorrow for another task.

Make sure always to keep your goals in sight. Always think about how you can achieve it and keep that picture inside of your mind every day, especially in the morning. Ignore the fact that you will see many hardships on the way. Think of it as a fun thing to do, which will make you stronger and stronger every day.

Make sure that you are aware of what you have achieved. Kaizen changes will happen slowly, but they will happen consistently. Make a way to track how effective you were at applying your plan. This can be in the form of a checklist or whatever else suits you the best. This will also help you make adjustments for the days to come. Remember that this is an ongoing process, so you will often need to act and plan at the same time.

As you open your eyes more and more to the Kaizen method, you will see more and more unnecessary things. Whenever you can, take a breather and decide if the value of the activity is worth the resources you are putting in. For example, going to language classes might be great, but doing so online can save you a lot of time. A similar case can be made about public transport versus walking or making your own food versus ordering it. This falls to your choice, however.

Kaizen is something that we subconsciously apply to our daily lives. While going from home to work, you always want to get there on time. If traffic is particularly bad, you will always try to find the quickest way, the best solution, the most efficient one. This is Kaizen. It is not only about changes; it is about decision making as well.

Cleaning up your room 10 minutes quicker is also Kaizen. It improves your life by giving you 10 more minutes that you can dedicate to yourself or your loved ones. Even things as small as getting the green light right on time can make a difference. Not a big one, but a difference, nonetheless.

It is about accumulating value over time. Those precious seconds that you save on small things can, over the course of the day, turn into minutes that you can use to read your book or take a quick nap.

There are many areas where Kaizen can help you accumulate said value. We have already discussed how it can save you time, but it is also important to note that it teaches you the value of time. People might often think that you can achieve results only by working long hours. Kaizen debunks this belief and teaches you how valuable even the smallest blocks of time can be. Even things like waking up 10 minutes earlier can feel big to you. It will give you time to water your plants or do a quick work-out before heading out to work. Similarly, going to sleep an hour earlier might have you feeling more refreshed in the morning. Kaizen rewards self-discipline as, if you can adapt to the changes you want quickly, you will also reap the fruits quickly.

While on the subject of changes, exercise and fitness are often a problem for many people. A lot of us want to get into shape but just cannot find the time or motivation to make the commitment. Giving an hour a day, not accounting for the time it takes you to move to get ready for exercising, might seem like a lot. By applying the Kaizen method, you will find that you can easily obtain your wanted results by starting now. If you have two or three hours of free time today, hit the gym, you will feel much better afterward. Even without that, sparing ten minutes every day to do push-ups will not do much for you right off the bat, but over time it will accumulate.

Remember, even the tiniest of changes matter. The "Zen" (for good) of Kaizen relies on you living in the present. While making plans on how you can hit the gym efficiently, you will often wander away from what is important at the moment. Think of how you can improve, but not how you can improve in a year, rather focus on today.

You need to experiment in order to find what works for you. Experimenting in your day to day life is something that most people recommend when they talk about obtaining happiness. This is especially true for Kaizen. Tracking back to the example of cleaning your room, Kaizen encourages you to think of techniques that will help you save even more time. This can be in the form of finding new space to sort things, or just getting a better broom. If you fail at first, do not be discouraged, there is a solution waiting for you somewhere.

The five whys, for example, are a great way to get to the bottom of any problem. You might want to go on a diet, but then you stop and ask yourself why you would want to do so. The answer will almost always be so you can lose some amount of weight. You then ask yourself why you want to lose weight. You figure that it will help you look and feel better. You have gotten to the root of the issue, and you don't have to go on to the next why. However, the Kaizen way urges you to do so. So you ask yourself why you would want to do that. The answer will usually be so that you can feel better in your own body and have more energy than you can spend on daily tasks. Quite simple, is it not?

On another note, the five whys can give you an answer that you are not satisfied with. When asking yourself why you want to lose weight, you might come to the conclusion that it is because your colleagues made rude comments about you. This, in turn, might prompt you to understand that losing weight might be a waste of time and effort as it will not enrich your life in any significant way. Understanding your own motivations can lead you to understand that some changes are not good. The name "five" in five whys is more of a placeholder relay. You will often need much less than five, while on the other hand sometimes you will have to ask yourself "why?" more than five times.

Of course, when Kaizen fails, the results can be pretty abysmal, like with anything else. You might forget where you stored something important. The broom might be too big for you to store efficiently, or your new organization might be hard to get used to. The clothes you stored inside of your closet might be impossible to take out without taking everything out. But that is fine. You need to accept your failures and see them as ways to grow. Your clothes might all fall out, but this is good. It gives you the chance to sort them more neatly, maybe even adding a pattern to your storage. You can start sorting them by color in order to find them more easily.

You might get the opportunity to get rid of some old, excess clothes that you might not even need anymore, freeing up some space. Of course, you can choose to ignore failure as an option, but that is unwise as it will often be a reality when experimenting with Kaizen. Another thing you should do is keep in mind that there is no such thing as an optimal solution. Finding something that works for you is nice, but it should never be an excuse to stop trying. There is always something better out there. There are just so many ways to interpret Kaizen, and it is up to you to find your own brand of continuous improvement.

This all might seem very daunting, and it often is. Setting up a new rhythm from that which you are used to is always quite difficult. Change is never easy, and that is why it is up to you to make it more bearable. Kaizen can be turned into something fun. You can think of it as a puzzle. While thinking about how you can clean your room, always try to find the spot where each piece fits. Have fun with it. Make plans. It is a good way to entertain yourself while wasting time. If you are thinking about a route you take to go to work, think about what you can get on the way. Is there a coffee shop in case you have not had breakfast yet? Is there a flower shop or a gift shop where you can purchase something for your partner if you are running late?

I recommend having a mantra. Yelling "Kaizen" whenever you find a way to do something more efficiently will get your blood pumping. You will feel a sense of achievement when you are faced with the recognition of a better way to do something, and vocalizing it will make it feel just that one bit more satisfying.

Do not forget that Kaizen requires you to be devoted to the cause. You owe it to yourself to follow the creed of Kaizen your whole life. It is, after all, a lifetime pursuit. Nobody can really say that their job is ever done. You will always find something to improve, and you owe it to yourself to improve it. It is a process that helps you grow and grows with you. Just when you feel like you got it, something might happen, forcing you to reevaluate again. Maybe you find just the right way to clean your room, but just as you do, you get the news that you are moving. Things like this can often be down heartening, but do not be discouraged; with Kaizen, it will all be better eventually.

Kaizen in Your Professional Life

The philosophy is not tied down to only a personal basis. You can take Kaizen into your professional life as well. Whatever field of work you might find yourself in, improving and being better than your competition will increase the chances of you staying in the game and making money off it. Living your life in a way that improvement is a norm for you, thus your success is guaranteed.

A very important thing Kaizen teaches you is consistency. We said that in order for Kaizen to work in a company, it is not something that you can just do whenever you feel like it. The same can be said here. Continuous improvement is not only about improvement. There is a reason why it is called continuous. It places you in the mindset where your goal is the main article on the agenda. It makes you think about how you are using your time and if your goal is something worth chasing. By doing this, you can really learn more about yourself. When thinking about how you can increase your own efficiency, first find the answers inside of yourself.

If you find that you are not a morning person, stay away from making important decisions before noon. If you find that you have the most energy in the evening, make sure that your schedule is set up in such a way that your most important tasks are done at that time. There is really no single correct way to do Kaizen. You need to find it yourself. Also, you should make a habit of not postponing things. While it might often be hard not to procrastinate, remember that procrastination is a kind of waste. Kaizen makes no room for such things.

Do not be afraid to ask for help on your journey. Again, going back to the room cleaning example. If you truly have no idea how you can store that pesky jacket well enough, do not be afraid to ask a parent. Feedback is very important in Kaizen, as collaborating with others may lead you to see things that you would not otherwise. Do not be afraid of bad feedback. Take it as a sign that you eliminated one bad option, and there is one less to choose from in the future. Never be stubborn. If you do not act on feedback, then it has no point.

The process of finding your own Kaizen is reminiscent of Michelangelo's thoughts on creating David. When he was asked how he had made the masterpiece, he said that it was simple. He just removed the stone that did not look like David.

With a wide scope of experimentation, you are also required to be flexible. Kaizen teaches you flexibility because the solutions you are looking for are often outside of the domain you are comfortable with.

This is true in both your personal life and professional. If you are a manager that has moved from one sector to another, you will have to change up your techniques as well as your toolkit. In a similar manner, you will not clean your kitchen as you would in your room.

You need to adapt your approach to the concept. If you are working with a group, you have to be able to adapt to that as well. If you have a colleague that focuses on the production process of your firm, you can make your partnership more efficient by focusing on the things around that. The environment in which you will find yourself will often change, and stagnation is your greatest enemy. Do not be afraid of change. That is the Kaizen way.

Of course, Kaizen is not all about saying "yes." While you are encouraged to seek out ideas from others, you should remember that it is up to you to reject those ideas if they are bad. The same can be said for your own needs and urges. If you have the need to leave work earlier, fight it. If you do not, your productivity will fall, and you will have betrayed the Kaizen way. If a colleague provides you with a solution that is misinformed, it is your duty to reject it and show them where they made a mistake. Saying no almost always takes a lot of courage. This helps build character in away. It can also help you get rid of bad habits.

This goes back to teamwork. Human interaction is very important for the success of Kaizen. If you want to bring Kaizen to your professional life, you are going to learn how to work as a part of your team efficiently. Remember that this will not always go according to plan. It is one thing to have a team of people all running under the Kaizen methodology. It is completely another thing to be the only one doing so. This will often require you to play off of the strengths and weaknesses of your coworkers and is also a good way to spread "Kaizen positivity" in your office. If what you are doing yields good results, some of your colleagues might pick it up, as well. This can be very beneficial for you in the future as their success helps your success. This aspect of Kaizen is very important in your personal life as well. You should always encourage people around you to do their best. It is even better if you can do so by being an example of this. If your friend is nervous about a speech he is supposed to hold, show him how it can be done. If there is maintenance that needs to be done in your home, get the whole family involved. This is a great bonding experience, as well as a way for all of you to learn. By doing this, you are giving your family the chance to gain new experience and skills while doing the job more quickly than you would yourself.

There is no denying that discipline is important in the professional sphere, perhaps even more so than in the personal. While you might believe that you are a hundred percent dedicated to your goals, some temptations that you find hard to reject might pop-up on the way. You should take Kaizen personally. If you fail at applying it, it is not an attack against Kaizen, but against yourself. Consider deadlines to be important personal goals. If you fail at remaining disciplined, that is completely on you. Even if you have the luxury to let lose a little bit, do not. If you told yourself that a specific task would be done by the end of the day, do it by the end of the day. Create a sort of inner drive that will constantly pull you towards making small steps and get you closer and closer to where you want to be. Once you get the drive going, it will be hard to stop it.

Every Kaizen enthusiast needs to have a healthy appetite for success. But what is success? According to Kaizen, success is not measured by profits, but by the quality of the work you are doing. You can view the people around you as quality circles. A quality circle is a group of people that gather around to discuss the issues you are facing and ask for advice on how you can solve them. It should be obvious that you should not be using any group for any problem.

You need to be certain that the people you are asking can give you useful insight into what you are talking about. In both the office and your personal life, you will see that consulting others is very important. To give a simple example, let's say that you want to find a way to spend more quality time together. After a month of planning and internalizing, you find a way. This will do you little good if your family is not ready or willing to make the changes that you want. This can be circumvented easily, however.

For this example specifically, you can just consult your family about this in order to discuss what are the best ways you can do this together. This is Kaizen, in a nutshell. You identify a problem, or in this case, an area that needs improvement, and you discuss the most efficient method to improve it while taking into consideration the feelings of everyone involved.

There is yet another point of interest that is shared by your personal and professional life. We mentioned how important morale is in the workplace. Everything is better if the environment you are in is positive. When we are talking about doing work, Kaizen encourages individuals to be recognized for their skillset. This boosts their drive and confidence. This does not change after working hours. If you did something you are proud of, no matter how small it is, congratulate yourself. Be proud of the little jog you did or for fixing a broken cupboard. Share the same kind of positivity with anyone else because they benefit from it as much as you do.

With Kaizen, it will always be important to be open to suggestions. Many businesses applied Kaizen unknowingly for decades. Suggestion boxes are a kind of Kaizen as they give the customer the chance to make the services they receive better by giving their own input. You should have a similar system in place. Your own suggestion box does not have to involve others; it doesn't even have to be a box really. A wall where you can pin notes for yourself will keep you focused on your goals. Make sure to follow your own recommendations after thoroughly analyzing them. Make sure that you visit these notes from time to time in order to remember what you wanted to achieve and see if you did so.

A Rarely Spoken Of Benefit

There's one benefit of Kaizen that is rarely brought up when talking about it- the adaptability it will instill into you. It's easy to miss this at first, but when comparing one's state of mind pre Kaizen and post Kaizen, you'll find that they adapt to new situations much better than before.

This is because most of the stress in adapting to different situations comes from the fact that you do not know how to deal with them. You don't know how to approach them, from which angle to come at them.

Kaizen gives you that framework. You no longer need to think about what you need to tackle; instead, you can just go straight at it.

This is because Kaizen makes you think in concrete terms. You're no longer uncertain about approaches or the results of your actions. You know what you need to do, and more or less how to do it.

It also provides a safety net in that it is an entirely iterative process, meaning that if the first time around you don't adapt to the issue correctly, the next time will have far higher chances of accomplishing it.

It isn't easy to achieve this with any other train of thought. Think about it, if you approach a new situation with a brand new way of thinking that just gives you more things to be uncertain about.

If, on the other hand, you approach it with an inflexible, old way of thinking, you'll encounter contradictions. These contradictions will then likely cause problems for you, either in adapting physically or mentally.

Chapter 5

Implementing Kaizen

Implementing Kaizen is not as easy as it might seem. When talking with people who follow it, they will often tell you that even though it was worth it, it was a grueling journey. This journey of long-term commitment might be overwhelming for many; however, there are a few general steps that you can make in order for your transition to be a bit easier.

You need to get buy-in inside of the organization you want to apply Kaizen to. The organization you are working for, or the organization you own needs to understand how important each Kaizen event is. Having the leaders' commitment is the first crucial step of successful continuous improvement. If you get higher echelons of the hierarchy to start working on this, most other people will follow. It is also very important that your employees get the proper support from the leadership. If they do not, there will be a lot of alienation between the efforts of each sector, and this will slow your changes down.

Make sure that Kaizen is not something that the people in your organization have to do. You need to make sure that they understand the benefits of applying it. They should not see it as a management tactic, rather a mindset that drives them forward and helps improve both them and their environment. Your employees should have a solid grasp on what the methodology is and how it benefits them. This stops your company from just being a company and turns it into a place of unity. An atmosphere of improvement and encouragement is both crucial for Kaizen and beneficial for the success of your business.

Your employees need to be empowered and aware of their value. After all, they are the closest to whatever problems your company might encounter. They are often also the ones with the best solutions from them as they have the most experience with handling their workplace. They are the most important element of Kaizen and are the key to your success. The first place to improve your manufacturing process is to help those who are the closest to the process obtain more skills that can help your business out. On top of this, it will boost the morale of your workers and make them feel happier about their place in your company.

Start with small changes. Kaizen is all about small changes, but it also requires planning ahead. Of course, you can avoid doing this right off the bat. Just test with implementing small changes and see how it works for you as you get better and better start thinking of Kaizen events that you can do in the future. By doing so, you can alleviate the pressure you feel when making a decision, as your decisions will always have lower stakes. Do not feel bad about taking things slow and small. One percent might seem small, but if you improve by that one percent every day, it accumulates greatly over the course of the year. It is also important to head straight to the root of the problem instead of first taking care of the side factors. This makes it so that the problem will be fixed much quicker with as little resources as possible expended.

Make sure to document your successes and failures. Keep track of how your performance and processes changed over time. Kaizen is not about working by feeling; it is about data and facts. You need to practice as much objectivity as possible, and the only way to do that is by standardizing and recording the existing procedures. You need to make a map of the original state of the process in order to identify what wastes can be eliminated and where it can be improved. By making this benchmark, you can come around to it later in order to compare the results with the original.

This will demonstrate how much you have improved and how much there is yet to improve. It shows you where your efforts were not as efficient as you might like, and it lets you make more strategic improvements in the future. Before doing so, you need to decide what metrics dictate if you have been successful. They may vary based on your priorities, but they will mostly revolve around waste management, profits, and product quality. Do not be afraid to set high standards for yourself. Even if they might seem unreachable, Kaizen is not about reaching them, but working towards them.

Standardize whatever part of your business that you can. If you want your improvements to last, they cannot be a one-time sort of thing. They need to be standardized and repeatable in order to work. This is very important for Kaizen as it creates a base level from which you can keep building up. If your improvements collapse after some time, what was the point of doing anything? Standardization will also help you increase productivity by reducing variability. The fewer unpredictable factors there are, the fewer problems you will see in the future.

Make your own Kaizen way. There is really no exact guide that you can follow, so do not be afraid to experiment. If something did not work for someone else, do not be afraid to try it. On the other hand, if something did work for someone else, do not take it as the status quo, as not every company works the same. Reflecting on your efforts and changing your approach with the new experiences will enrichen your Kaizen approach, further increasing the productivity of said efforts. The guidelines you make for yourself will change over time, and you should let them. Always strive for something more and never let yourself feel like you should stop improving.

If you want your improvements to last, you will have to stop your changes from regressing. When the going gets rough, it is easy to revert to your old ways and ruin the progress you have made so far. Enforce the changes that you have made so that your company can prosper in the long term. Check if your standards have been met as often as possible. Make sure that everyone is aware of the new changes and what needs to be done so that the benefits are maintained.

Always remember that Kaizen is not a line. It is a cycle. The cycle can be summarized in very simple terms: observe the workplace, find the problems, and find solutions. Observe your office both before you implement Kaizen and after. There can always be some waste that you did not identify originally. When you do so, be happy where you are at. By solving a problem, you found another one that has been hiding up until now. This is a great opportunity to start the cycle all over again. Only one person doing this will not save your company. There needs to be a sort of localized culture that revolves around continuous improvement.

Kaizen requires everyone to be responsible for their own improvement. This may often be hard to achieve as it requires a sort of awakening within the individual. An individual's will to help the workplace is directly connected to the love he has for the job. It is up to management to make sure that every worker knows that they are responsible for their own success and quality of life in the company by rewarding them and encouraging them. It is also up to the management to organize Kaizen Events. Any plan will go sour without proper execution. However, once the method starts to take its hold on your business, you will soon see workers taking the initiative and organizing events on their own.

This all might seem daunting, and it is. Living by Kaizen is not easy in the beginning, nor is organizing Kaizen events. It takes a lot of hard work and understanding. There is no real template that will tell you how you can convert the mentality of your workers into that of continuous improvement. There needs to be a sufficient amount of initiative on everyone's part of the project will be doomed.

Of course, the first thing you will do inside of your company is make the announcement that you are switching up the way that things are done. Let your employees know that things will not be the same as they were up until this point and ask them what they think needs to be done. This is a very valuable step in making sure that Kaizen catches on. Establish a relationship of openness and trust between your workers and you. Let them know that they will be heard.

This, however, will do you little good if you do not find a way that can help you efficiently receive these suggestions and properly analyze them. This is where Kaizen Corners come into play. According to Maasaki Imai, a Kaizen corner is a place where your employees can voice their opinions and findings. This can be done in a number of ways. You can go old school and set up a blackboard or a box where they can leave their thoughts. Alternatively, you can bring something new and modern into the process by making a website or doing it by email. According to Maasaki Imai, this can most efficiently be done through a series of three stages. During the first step, you take and evaluate the ideas you get from your workers. If you decide not to do as the employee suggested, it is always important to tell them why. This is in order to avoid a situation where the worker feels as if their opinion was tossed aside. They will not feel punished for wanting to help.

The second step is teaching your workers how the improvement system you want to set up works. This will give them a better grasp of how they can help and what they should be looking for. The third step suggests that you have a reward system that will show your gratitude to the employees who work hard on implementing Kaizen. This will help it feel like less of a phase and more of an actual commitment. Your workers can only handle so many technicalities, so it is extremely important to have a group of experts that have a technical background. This will help both you and the workers as it will set up a sort of a revision line that knows exactly what they are looking for. Once the cogs start turning and you have accumulated enough data, it is time to start planning out Kaizen Events.

If we take a breather from talking about the theory and philosophy behind Kaizen, we will see that it is made up of many tools that can be put into practice to improve your company. These are the tools that drive Kaizen forward and make up any Kaizen event.

The first tool that is worth mentioning is the Suggestion System. As discussed before, this can come in whatever form you may choose as long as it can be used to relate whatever information needs to be related from your employees to the higher-ups.

The second tool is the Quality Control Circle. To reiterate, every employee can give their input on how things should be changed around within the workplace; however, not all of them can make said changes. The QCC is a small team that you compose out of specialists in the field. They work on the analysis and proper implementation of solutions.

Total Quality Control can be compared to Business Process Management. TQM is an approach where everyone, no matter what job they are doing and in which office, gets to take part in the quality control of the company.

We talked about the PDCA Cycle, already. It is perhaps the most important tool in the Kaizen arsenal, and you will feel its benefits as soon as you start putting yourself through the cycle. Every time you start the cycle anew, you will see new things that can be improved due to the fog generated by other problems being lifted.

Business Process Mapping is yet another amazing hands-on tool. It is all about creating flow charts that are easy to follow and have well-defined goals and measures. This is important because it helps people visualize the process that they are about to partake in, making it easier for them to determine if they are doing their job right.

These are all the tools that you can use to have extremely beneficial Kaizen events. However, Kaizen events are not about picking up all the tools that you can and throwing them at the problems. You first have to organize the Quality Control Circle. We mentioned this previously. If we are talking about a company that has multiple layers, the QCC will be composed of people of all circles. The QCC will help you determine what the most important problem is currently.

Before you start Process Mapping, you are going to have to identify what needs solving as well as what changes you want to see. After doing so, you need to determine what metrics you are going to measure your success or failure with. If you do not identify the way things have changed, the whole process loses meaning. After this, you start thinking about solutions. Not all solutions need to be direct. After applying changes, you need to see if the Kaizen event achieved what you want. Compare the new metrics to the benchmark and see where you have succeeded and where your efforts are lacking. There are some problems you just cannot account for before you start working on it, so this is a good chance to pad out things like that. If the process you put in place is working sufficiently better than the original one, you need to start spreading it through your company.

This is a very difficult thing to do. It requires a lot of time and effort, as well as technical knowledge. There are ways to make this process much easier, however. We talked about how important planning is for the Kaizen method. Back in the day, this was all done by hand. Every time a process needed to be fixed, it was mapped on a piece of paper. This is what they would use for planning. Thankfully, we are not limited to this technique anymore. Rather, it has become redundant as there are so many quicker methods. There are digital ways of doing this. BPMS (Business Process Management Software) is an amazing tool to have when planning out your processes. There are many options in the current market, so you should do your research and see what kind of tool best suits you.

It will take a bit of time to get used to the tools as they are not exactly the easiest thing to master, however, once you put in the time, you will reap the benefits. It makes things so much easier. For example, when working with a larger group of people, it can often be hard to relay the process changes to everyone and, even then, there might be those who have a harder time understanding what the changes actually entail. Some might even forget about them. BPM software provides a platform that everyone can access in order to double-check if they got everything right, as well as one that is editable in real-time. This means that everyone will have a much easier time keeping track of the rapid changes, and that said rapid changes would be easier to make. We all know how hard it is to make drastic changes.

It is much easier to do things how you are used to and make excuses. However, BPM software leaves no room for excuses. Everything is as transparent as it can be, so nobody can claim that the instructions were anything but clear. One of the more technically difficult aspects of Kaizen is process analysis. Even when you have clear metrics, it is often hard to get a precise measurement of your changes quickly. The software itself, luckily, comes with analytic tools that will do the job much faster and with less room for error. This will make the job of keeping track of your progress so much easier.

I know that it might be a lot to take in, and it often can be. There is a reason why some companies avoid implementing Kaizen. It is difficult to do. However, remember that you can temporarily ignore the bigger picture and just go at it as hard as possible. In order to make it easier on yourself, think of it as a series of two steps.

First, you should start valuing small changes. This is one of the key tenets of Kaizen. Remember that improvement does not have to be big. It does not have to improve your profits by a large margin. The key is just to keep moving forward at your own pace. Think of it as accumulating value over time and see it as the seeds of a bright future. This is especially true if you are looking to improve the work culture of your company. This is where you need to especially take your time as it is a very sensitive aspect. These changes have to be gradual in order to succeed, no matter how trivial they may seem. Make "Rome wasn't built in a day," your mantra.

The second step you should take is seeking feedback. One of the best parts of Kaizen is that, since the changes are small and slow, you are more likely to see if they are going in the wrong direction. This will help you correct them if correction is needed. If you are at the front of a team, you should talk to as many people as possible in order to determine if the course of action you took was good. Feedback is a necessary part of the process. Getting feedback is not as important as how you respond to it, however. Not every piece of feedback you receive will be useful to you, so proper evaluation is necessary. If you do shoot down the feedback, you receive to make sure to tell the employee or colleague why.

The third step is eliminating as much waste as possible. That is the whole point of several pillars of Kaizen. By eliminating waste, you will inch closer and closer to your goals. By cutting down the time and resources you would spend in order to achieve nothing, you can instead redirect them towards the growth and improvement of your company.

The fourth step is focusing on improving processes. This can seem very trivial, but remember that, by doing so, Henry Ford reduced the time it took for a Model T to be produced by 87 percent. By introducing single work stations, he made it so that the production system flows naturally. This, as you might know, did wonder for him. This lowered princess improved working conditions, and lowered the prince of the product, in turn bringing a lot of profit to Ford.

This is what Taiichi Ohno used as a basis for the TPS.

The last step is to make sure that your team is working properly. They say that teamwork is dreamwork, and that much is definitely true for Kaizen. It is a group effort that requires everyone to be very aware of the philosophy and ready to work on it. Everyone needs to understand that placing blame for the problems that can occur will lead to nothing. Instead, the main priority needs to be working together in order to make it right. Ask yourself simple questions every day and improve based on them. Once you solve the first set of questions, it will be much easier to continue doing it.

Chapter 6

Kaizen Events

Kaizen Events are the backbone of continuous improvement. Companies that rely on Kaizen can make huge improvements only with a series of successful Kaizen events. So, what is a Kaizen Event? To put it as simply as possible, it is an event that is designed to improve something over a period of time. How long this takes and what it looks like differs from case to case. This depends on the company, what system needs to be improved, what kind of manpower is available, etc. A Kaizen event is not a one-time thing. Like everything else we have discussed so far, it is an ongoing effort. If a Kaizen event is successful, then you will see a drop in waste and an increase in productivity. Text-book Kaizen events usually revolve around lean manufacturing, following the principles of lean production; however, the philosophy is so broad that it can be applied to almost anything.

However, a Kaizen event does not only serve to eliminate waste but also to help everyone learn more about the causes for it and how it can be dealt with more efficiently in the future. If we follow the norm, an event will usually be targeted at one specific instance of waste inside of your company.

Of course, as with anything in the world of business, even the best courses of action will fail if they are not properly planned. The first step is planning out your event. As you might imagine, this includes identifying what waste needs to be eliminated, how it can be done, and what resources are needed for the task. Based on the types of waste, you will usually see different kinds of ways in which the problem can be addressed. The most common way is through process changes. If you, for example, want to cut down the time needed to make a product in your company, you might bring some automated tools or hire another worker so that you can spread out the work. Another way the same result can be achieved is by training your employees.

By teaching them the skills required to execute a task more efficiently, you will avoid the additional costs of buying machines or hiring additional manpower. With new skills, workers can find their own way to speed up production. A more simple way this can be done is by changing the layout of your facilities, for example, moving around machines in such a way that the space you are using is more passable. Even the small things like moving the bathrooms closer to a workplace can make quite a difference over a year. Standardization is a way to achieve higher productivity by making sure that everyone is doing their job as they should. This is very important as standardization is one of the main steps of successful Kaizen.

The second step that is required is identifying the scope of the event you are about to set into motion. If you are working in a granular environment, the small changes you make will seem even smaller, meaning that they can be done on the fly. An issue that you might identify here is the scope of the event being too large. You should not aim to fix everything with a single event. Focus on something significant but specific. Locate a process or area that can be improved and ask yourself how you can bring better value to your customers. Once you do so, you can look at this as a scope of the event.

Another thing you have to pay attention to is what team you are putting in the frontline of the event. In Kaizen, usually, the whole of the company will be working on the event. However, in cases that a team that leads the efforts is needed, make sure that the team is ready to tackle the job. Make sure not to appoint too few or too many people. If you have too many people on the job, the schematic you had in your mind can crack. Remember that you should not spread anything too thin. Make sure to have a representative of every party impacted on the team in order to round out the skillset and make sure that the skills they are bringing to the table fit the bill. When you gather up your team, there are several things that you should consider.

At least half of your team should be composed of individuals that will be the most impacted by the changes you are about to set into motion. When changing up how the storage facilities are working, you should get the delivery crew involved as well. People in related departments should be as numerous in the team as possible as well. Make sure to appoint as few leaders as possible as too many managers can limit how many solutions are being churned out by the rest of the team. Make sure that you have experts on the subject matter by your side. Professionals can often give you the most insight, as well as direct your efforts in a proper way.

Remember that what happens inside of your company does not just impact the people within them. If your products become cheaper or change in some way, that will affect your consumers as well. This is why you should have someone who can deliver the outside perspective as well. This will broaden your views, as well as help you eliminate some ideas. Make sure to involve someone who is not going to be impacted by the changes too. They will function as an objective third party that can detect oversights that most others miss. Their main and most valuable function is solving conflicts between other parties in the team.

A Kaizen event does not really have specific metrics on how long it lasts and can vary anywhere from an hour to a week. Every Kaizen event can be divided into specific phases. When you start the event, the facilitator has to explain to their workers the scope of the changes the company is about to go through. After this, a baseline needs to be established. This is what we compare the state at the end of the event. Gather as much data as you can, this will help you get a better feel of the problem, as well as allow you to see if the event was as fruitful as you planned it to be. The next step is finding the optimal solution.

An optimal solution needs to be as quick as possible and address everything you need it to address while expending as few resources as possible. Find the aspects of your system that add no value and find ways to remove them from your company or improve them in such a way that their presence benefits you. Before you implement the planned changes, however, they should first be tested. You can do this in simulations or on real machines. Here you need to look for any potential issues and eliminate them. Do not be afraid to completely redesign your approach until you get something that you are completely satisfied with. When you find a solution that satisfies all of your parameters, it is time to put in some elbow grease.

There are a few techniques and methodologies that are commonly used. Toyota's five "s" is one of the examples. It is a very simple but efficient method that can boost both your productivity and quality of service.

Another technique that is commonly used in developing a pull system. In production, we differentiate a pull from a push system based on one parameter. That is where the production starts or, to be more precise, with who. A push system is all about churning out as many products as you think you can sell. This makes sure that you attract more customers because you have a lower waiting time than you would with a pull system. A pull system, on the other hand, starts with the customer, as you get an order before you start building. This removes several types of waste. You do not waste time finding someone to buy the product. You do not waste resources on building excess products. By making more than you can sell, you make different kinds of waste, so always be mindful of that. A pull system will make sure that you waste less storage space, less time, and less manpower.

Equipment is also part of the workplace, so in order to increase productivity, one can also improve it through Total Productive Maintenance. The basic goal of TPM (Total Productive Maintenance) is to avoid any delays or errors by making sure that your equipment is in top-notch condition. It is a smaller branch of Kaizen than most, but it can be very important in some industries.

Improving the manufacturability of product design can help you churn out many more units of what you are selling in the same period of time. You can often spot imperfections or unnecessary things in your products. For example, a car maker would spend a lot of money on deluxe paint for his car. However, if the car is made to be a family vehicle rather than a luxury car, this is a waste of money as it adds nothing to its primary function. Make sure that your products are as efficient as your processes.

Remember that Kaizen does not target just the processes behind making a product. It goes much deeper than that. It targets many administrative processes. You can probably save a lot of time and money if you make sure that your papyrology department is running at top-notch efficiency.

As you can see, Kaizen events can target many parts of your company and, though some parts might seem irrelevant, do not underestimate how important a single nail is to a house. That being said, this teaches us that you can never be too careful and that there is no point in turning a blind eye to a problem, no matter how small it may be,

After the Kaizen event has been set into motion and eventually finished, the team is tasked with gathering as much data as possible. This data is compared to the baseline data. This is how you measure the success (or failure) of your Kaizen event. If you deem it lacking, the team gathers yet again. Of course, if the event was particularly long or difficult, holding a celebration is an option. This is a great training event, as well as a way to boost the morale of the company and get them more fired up about Kaizen.

While these are the general steps that most events follow, remember that there are quite a few more things to consider if you want to succeed. While it is true that Kaizen events are usually all about short-term brainstorming and implementing improvements, it can get a bit more complex than that. After all, there are often things that you will not be able to foresee, no matter how able or diverse your team is.

We can separate Kaizen events into two categories. Short-term Kaizen events and long-term ones. As we have mentioned, Kaizen needs to be at the forefront of all efforts within a company. It is not something you do to make your work easier; rather, it is a part of your work. This is what short-term Kaizen events are about. In order to create a Kaizen culture inside of your workplace, each worker needs to make it a part of their routine to improve what they can. Every time a worker finds a way to make his part of the job quicker is a short-term Kaizen event.

However, more often than not, larger problems will require more long-term approaches. In order to properly execute this kind of event, you will have to invest a significant amount of time. This goes for both you and your employees. These are extremely focused efforts that aim for improvement. However, not every problem will require either a long-term or short-term Kaizen event, but they will usually be the best tool for solving any problem you are given.

However, you need to remember, Kaizen is all about the mindset. There is no space for a colleague that is putting rain checks on improvement. Kaizen is not about finding something that you are unhappy with and fixing it. It is about fixing things for the sake of fixing them, improving something just because it can be improved. However, if not everyone is up to date with the new company motto, you might see a lack of short-term events. A large-scale Kaizen event can help your employees get unstuck and going. Your main team needs to get into the daily Kaizen events. They are the key to creating a healthy culture of continuous improvement inside your workplace. Showing your employees what kind of impact an event has on productivity will probably inspire them, so it is important to lead by example. Listening to your employees will also encourage them to do Kaizen and make them feel more important for the company. Nobody wants to see their workplace deteriorate, so they will start practicing the philosophy on their own.

In large companies, you will often see how hard it is to work with other teams. Cross-functional collaboration is a point where you might see quite a bit of dysfunction. Collaboration between departments has more potential complications due to the different priorities and leaders. When a Kaizen event is set into motion, it gives the different departments an environment where they can find a solution that fits all of their interests. They will often find a common goal, as well as a way to communicate it efficiently to the other side.

Often, people think that a Kaizen event is a one-time thing. They execute one and never do so again. However, in order to truly reap the benefits of Kaizen, you need to keep doing it. The system is all about continuous improvement, and if you return to the methodology of innovation, you might see deterioration in the changes that you have made with events.

What you can do to make your employees more Kaizen aware is to organize a Kaizen event whenever you get new team members. This is a great opportunity to introduce them to the concept of continuous improvement, but it also gets them into the general feel of the Kaizen spirit. As with everything, it is best to start as soon as possible.

Make sure that both you and your employees understand that there is not one specific way to implement a Kaizen event. While we discussed the general pattern, this does not tell you everything that you should know. It is not a thing of knowing, rather having a feel for it. Kaizen is all about data and facts, but you cannot remove the human aspect of it all. Instinct and luck are both parts of the game we call entrepreneurship.

Remember that Kaizen events are a process of its own sort. Improving the efficiency of your Kaizen is as beneficial as is improving any other process in your company. This can be done in a plethora of ways. The simplest would be talking to your employees about the company even when you are not planning an event. You can take a day of the week in order to run down a few key points of the previous week. This will help you see the issues more clearly. This can also be done non-verbally. Setting up a website will do the trick just fine. It will also prevent you from wasting any time that can be used for work. If you really want to go old-school, you can do this via a blackboard.

Forming a Kaizen committee will do wonders for the effectiveness of the events as well. Not to be mistaken with Kaizen teams. A Kaizen committee has a more permanent function. It is not tied down to only one event. This group of individuals can review the ideas and funnel only the useful ones to you and even help you decide which events need to be played out when. Having an extensive archive of each of your Kaizen events will help too. You might often encounter problems that are similar or even the same to those that you fixed in the past. If you have records of this, you can put your plans into motion much faster and know what to expect or avoid from the get-go.

Like every movement inside of an organization, a Kaizen event needs a leader. So, what is a Kaizen leader? A Kaizen leader is not someone who simply enforces Kaizen. Kaizen is not something that should be enforced in the first place. In order for it to succeed, the people of your company need to accept it of their own volition. There should not exist a person that can tell someone that they are using Kaizen wrong. Everybody needs to do their best. However, a Kaizen leader does not tell their worker what they should do. Rather the leader shows it to them. Leading by example is crucial here, as it almost evens out the playing field in the company. When the worker sees that their boss is doing the best they can, the worker will be encouraged to do so as well. What this means, other than making sure that your company succeeds is that the leader will care for their employees. In the Kaizen philosophy, an unhappy worker is a form of waste. You should not let morale in your company decline to the point where it is affecting the work done.

A Kaizen leader needs to be analytical and unbiased. While it is true that everyone sees what they want to see, a leader should want to see only the facts. Making a misinformed choice will not only hinder your improvement but will also make your workers trust you less. Make sure that you are properly informed about everything in your company. You need to be acquainted with every level and people in every function. You also need to be able to hear out what your workers have to say. The bottom line is that it is not easy to do this every day, but if you do, it will have amazing effects.

The Benefits of Kaizen Events

We talked to a great extent about what Kaizen does and how it does it, but we never specifically defined the benefits that you will reap. At this point, it is no secret that Kaizen will improve your productivity and profits. This is kind of the main thing it does and what it was designed for. Though it might seem very banal and menial, Kaizen has done miracles in different parts of the world. It saved some companies from shutting down, while it brought success to others, or, like in Toyota's case, both. It does so simply by stopping you from wasting resources that can be used for other more important things. All this talk of money and waste, however, might overshadow some more nuanced benefits that might just be as important in the long-run.

How most organizations, not just in the business sense, should ideally run is by having leaders that work on devising a strategy and staff that finds ways to implement said strategies. Finding creative ways to deal with problems noted by the executives is something that falls onto the worker. Most of the time, Kaizen events look like that. Whenever a Kaizen event is initiated that involves numerous teams, what you will usually see is the team appointing their most able members as strategic leaders. These leaders need to have extremely good communication with their teammates, as well as a great deal of trust in their abilities. It takes a great deal of knowledge to analyze the potential uses of every team member and then combine them to make a functional unit. What this does is it creates a bond of trust between the workers in the company. A chain will break if two links do not hold onto one another tightly enough. This also makes room for the growth and development of your workers. By having an extremely able group of people that know how to work together inside of your company, you are making sure that you have someone who can look after it while you are away.

We discussed at great length how important a hands-on approach really is. The best parallel that can be drawn is to that of a high-school chemistry class. While it might be simpler to sit down and learn how each chemical reaction works from a textbook, learning by mixing them up inside of a lab is much easier, more intuitive, and more enjoyable. Training your workers in the way of Kaizen will help both you and them greatly; however, letting them learn from experience will be both faster and more permanent. When a Kaizen event starts, the team members that have a particular set of skills have a chance to talk about how they can combine their efforts in order to make everything work as much as possible. A skill is not a skill if you do not apply it. By cooperating with different people with different skill sets, a person can grow exponentially, becoming more and more of a valuable asset.

Another great thing that your workers will learn is how to work together properly. In a Kaizen event, teamwork is very important. By accumulating the experience of working with other people in the events, the worker will come back to his post with the same attitude and knowledge. This makes them more flexible and ready to work with other people, even from other departments. The materials you ordered to be moved from storage to the factory will get there much quicker if both the delivery crew and the storage crew work on it together.

A great thing about Kaizen is that once it starts giving, it never stops. After the completion of a few Kaizen events, your workers will not only come out with new knowledge and skills but with a great deal of confidence as well. They will see how much improvement means and how they can contribute to it. They will also see that their bosses have a great deal of trust in them. This will make it much easier for them to have the courage to find flaws in the system on their own and give solutions that they think are the most fitting. They are both empowered and encouraged to practice Kaizen.

We have discussed to great lengths how important proper documentation is. This is especially true when it comes to the analysis of the baseline metrics. Indicating which performance metrics are going to dictate if you have been successful or not is a very sensitive process. You really need to have a knack for it or a great deal of experience behind you. Defining and documenting metrics is not a job that can just be given to anyone. However, this is a very important skill that Kaizen events allow your workers to practice.

With proper documentation of your metrics, comes an expanded repository of knowledge. The value of correct information has never been as important in business as it is today. This is why you should record not only Kaizen events but anything even barely important. Having a huge repository of knowledge makes it so that you avoid mistakes easier and you fix problems easier. It is also a great tool that can be used to introduce new members to the system they are about to enter. This will give them some useful knowledge from the get-go, and an awareness of what is expected from them and what they will receive in return.

While we are at the point of documentation, let us talk about Standard documentation. Standard documentation is often the target of Kaizen events. This set of rules and guidelines often needs to be updated when a Kaizen event of any kind is executed. Continuous improvement means nothing if it is not followed by continuous adaptation. To that point, the standard documentation needs to be up to date. It is important for the goal of making sure that more improvements will be happening in the future. Having many Kaizen events will make sure that your standard documentation is as accurate and comprehensive as possible. This is very important as it is probably the first thing your new employees, investors, and customers will learn about you.

Leadership is a word that has almost lost its meaning these days. Everyone wants to be a leader, but few understand what that really means. In Kaizen events, you will often see true examples of leadership. The best part is that anyone can try being a leader here. This is extremely beneficial for everyone as it does not only boost their confidence; it allows them to both grow as a person and obtain new skills in the fields of coordination, analytics, and communication. These leaders are not meant to be managers. In fact, managers are discouraged from taking part in this practice. It is there from the people low in the totem pole to have a chance to prove themselves and grow. Once a manager steps down, they might often be surprised at the leadership skills of some of their employees.

However, none of this would matter if the priorities of the company are not set straight. Suggesting a Kaizen event will often help you figure out how high in the list of priorities the problem is for the executives. While a Kaizen event is not a solution to any problem, it is important for people to have their priorities where they should be. Some problems are far too complex to be solved in a short period of time, however, suggesting a Kaizen event whenever you can give you some useful insight into how certain urgent problems are.

The thing that keeps employees making Kaizen changes inside of their workers is how closely they get attached to it. It is no secret that people tend to get attached to the things they help build. After a period of time, your workers will improve their work without being told. It will stop feeling like a responsibility, rather a place that they do out of love. Workers that get attached like this are a very valuable asset as they will usually not revert to their old ways. This means that they will stick to the new plan and improve it if given the opportunity.

The Kaizen toolbox is one filled with many incredible solutions for even the biggest of problems. However, the most important tool that also comes as a by-product of practicing Kaizen is practical problem-solving. Practical problem solving is a useful skill to have in your every-day life. Figuring out how to patch up a hole in your tire until you can get to a mechanic just might save you one day. The same can be said in business. Kaizen is about practicality if nothing else. It introduces you to a system of thinking that requires you to see golden opportunities in every moment of your work and make it yours. In order to do this, you must have a sharp mind and a willingness to see your errors. Once you get inside of that practical mindset, there is nothing you cannot achieve.

Chapter 7

Kaizen And Self Reflection

Self-reflection is the crux of Kaizen. This is also referred to as hansei. It is a central idea not only in Kaizen, but Japanese culture in general.

Hansei or self-reflection means to acknowledge that you have made a mistake and to pledge that you will improve. This principle has been compared to the old German proverb "Selbsterkenntnis ist der erste Schritt zur Besserung," meaning "Insight into oneself is the first step to improvement."

So far, we've already looked at some examples of self-reflection; however, this final chapter is dedicated to helping you absolutely master it. We'll be looking at the ways you can use self-reflection, as well as some helpful tips on how to achieve it.

The Hansei Process
- Place emphasis on what went wrong- If you are to improve, you must understand what went awry in the first place. You must ensure that you aren't underestimating what went wrong. Taking responsibility is the first step of hansei. You

need to do this at all times, and perpetually admit new mistakes.

- Understand that no problem is a problem- At Toyota, they have hansei-kai, which translates to reflection meetings. This is where they do a comprehensive review of everything that went wrong. If a manager says that there were no problems with the project, that is taken as a problem. This is because that means the situation wasn't very well researched. There is always room for improvement, and failing it to see it is a big problem. The lack of any problems shows a lack of challenging oneself.

- Improve- All of this means nothing if you don't improve in the end. For this, you need to take steps to ensure each of the problems you've found doesn't repeat.

- Rinse and Repeat- This is an iterative process, meaning you'll want to repeat it over and over again until it becomes second nature.

A good example of hansei is how Japanese politicians involved in corruption treat it.

They publicly state their involvement, apologize for it, and remove themselves from politics. By doing this, they give themselves enough time to reassess, to understand where they went wrong, and how they can prevent it from occurring again.

Then, once they've delved through the process, they may resume their career without being sneered at by the public. This helps both fester a better political climate, as well as helping the people involved rehabilitate, rather than punishing them.

For a more mild example, let's look at what usually happens when a regular worker makes a mistake. Now, in a western country, the worker might get fired or chewed out.

On the other hand, in Japan, the manager would take the blame publicly, while the worker simply fixes the issue in private. Japanese culture isn't perfect either, though, so naturally, sometimes these issues are tackled differently.

Like most Japanese terms, hansei also has a variety of meanings. The concept of hansei also takes the concept of greeting success with modesty.

In other words, rather than making a massive fuss over your next big thing, maybe just chill out with your friends for a night or two? This is done in order for one never to get the false idea of superiority,

The idea of superiority breeds conceit, which, in turn, halts progress. As we've already concluded, they who stop progressing are already doomed. With hansei, you can ensure that you are always kept aware of the exact amount you have yet to grow.

Working On Kaizen And Self-Reflection

Self-reflection isn't easy to achieve. Especially when you're starting from a typical Western viewpoint, this is because we are taught from an early age not to reflect upon our mistakes, but to either hide them or simply deny them.

This is especially common in the workplace, where office politics are all too often a dominant presence. If you want to run a company, you must know that this is inherently toxic to its growth.

To combat this, we'll be looking at some ways that you can prevent yourself from getting caught up with it.

Understand What You Need To Reflect Upon

You need to know where the target is before you shoot. You can't self-reflect about every waking moment, as it's simply not possible. Identify the things that are important to you and start asking questions about them.

For example, let's say I am running a football club and want to self-reflect. I would look at questions such as:

- Did I treat that player right last time?

- Was there something I could've done better last game? How about the last 5?

- How can I get more excellent players in the club?

- What is my biggest folly as a coach?

Using questions like these will help you get closer to the exact areas you need to reflect upon. Furthermore, by asking the questions often, you'll get used to immediately looking for at least one answer, which will make self-reflection more instinctual for you.

Make It A Routine

In a way, routines are what makes you, you. The routine to think about certain things at certain times, when you get out of bed, when you read, when you work.

Doing these things at an allotted time is much better than simply winging it. If you make self-reflection a routine, soon enough, you'll be doing it without even thinking about it.

Because of this, you should use the questions you came up with above, and ask yourself them every single day.

Ideally, you should set this to be a specific time around midday. This is because that's when your brain is most alert.

Then, run through a list of questions. You'll be used to doing this in no time!

A more advanced technique you can try is to use questions of different scales at different time intervals.

For example, you could self-reflect about basic, simple questions every day. Let's say you set apart 15-20 minutes for that.

You could self-reflect about bigger, more long-term questions every week. And then you could have one big roundup of your progress every month.

It's important to acknowledge progress when it happens. That way, your brain stays motivated to practice.

Meditate

Now, meditation is very useful when it comes to focusing on all manner of things, but especially self-reflection.

You don't need to be used to meditation, or even good at it to start off. Just relax, sit in silence, and think of nothing. If that's too difficult, think about your imperfections and your virtues.

What could you do better? What do you do well?

Take notes of the thoughts that pop up during meditation, as they can be quite indicative of your progress.

Jot It Down

Writing things down helps greatly in remembering them. If you've got a hard time thinking of what you want to self-reflect on, and you're only getting one idea every now and again, just write it down!

I suggest having a journal of sorts just for it. That way, your thoughts won't get jumbled across different books.

Furthermore, having a checklist of what you've addressed, and what is a work in progress will help you garner a feeling of accomplishment much easier.

When writing, be specific! Don't just write, "I want to self-reflect on my car dealership." Write down, "I want to reconsider the initial pitch I approach potential buyers with."

This way, when you go into your daily allotted self-reflection time, you'll already have a clear-cut idea of what exactly you want to do, rather than just having a rough idea.

With that being said, writing it down is a good idea for pretty much every step of your Kaizen journey.

Read

While reading might not be the first thing that comes to mind when it comes to realizing Kaizen, it's actually a crucial step.

You see, improvement hardly happens without seeing how to improve, without thinking about which axis to do so on.

Reading material like this very book does more than just make you think about Kaizen, however. It also makes you expand your horizons to other potentials. Reading is simply good for the mind, and any such activity would be ill-advised to forego it.

Now, I'm not saying all you should be reading is Kaizen related material. Naturally, you want to read a variety of different books that help you with what you want. For example, if you want to work in finance, you might start with reading the economist, and wind up with college textbooks sooner rather than later.

Think Systems, Not Goals
Chances are you want to achieve something in life, much like every other human being on earth. On the other hand, consider that over 80% of New Year's resolutions go unfulfilled.

This is purely because people usually think, "I want to do X" not "I want to make progress towards X." So, let's think about this using one of the most common ones out there- going to the gym 3 times a week.

A person that thinks about goals would set the goal "go to the gym 3 times a week" and start on the 1st of January. Through a week or two, they'll most likely quit because it's too much of a toll on their body, and they simply aren't used to that kind of routine and activity,

On the other hand, a Kaizen-oriented individual is going to posit a system that tends towards a more abstract end. For example, "I will go to the gym once a week for a month, then twice a week, then thrice a week." Soon enough, our Kaizen user is not only going to the gym as much as the goal-oriented one wanted to but is surpassing them rather heftily.

Because of this, it's crucial to keep a system-oriented mindset. As long as you better yourself every day, eventually, you'll be among the best. This is much like the tale about the turtle and the hare, except here, the turtle doesn't move slower, it just takes time to accelerate.

Don't worry too much about how large every increment you make is, what is important is that it is kept going perpetually.

Always Be Specific

Kaizen doesn't like it when you're vague. Saying something like "I'll exercise a bit more every day" does not follow Kaizen.

This is because it is not specific or measurable enough. If you said, "I'll exercise 20 seconds more every day." That would be what Kaizen wants of you.

To take a business look at things, instead of completely overhauling all of your sales strategies, try improving one part with a specific method. For example, try boosting the engagement of younger audiences by using social media they enjoy.

If you're instead working in an organization, this method makes it much easier to bring change. If you said, "We're going to stop using paper at the office today," you'd probably be laughed out. But if you said, "let's use 5 leaves of paperless each month," that would sound a lot more reasonable.

This is the way that Kaizen enhances your chances of success even in the short-term.

Minimize Excess And Waste

Kaizen says that one of the best ways to get a process to another level is to access the things that are wasted within it. Reducing wasted time and resources can lead to a large boom in productivity.

Let's take a personal example here. Let's assume you want to improve the way you manage your time. The first thing you'll need to do is find out how exactly you spend your time.

So, after plotting an approximate graph of your day, evaluate what each activity brings to the table when it comes to improving your life.

To make this easier, you can use a 1-10 scale. Then by simply taking the ratios of the two numbers, you can find which aspects of your day aren't contributing as much as they perhaps should. Then all you need to do is cut them out a bit.

Note that the goal here isn't for every single second of your life to be perfectly optimized towards productivity. The impact that something has on your quality of life is equally important, if not even more so.

With that being said if you can streamline your leisure time, why not do it? For example, if you find that you gain more relaxation from playing table tennis than video games, you might want to cut down on the latter and do the former more often.

Think Less, Do More

A lot of us like to think about how we would change our lives. This is even shown in the very fact that you bought this book in the first place.

On the other hand, taking actual action is a lot more strain, and work than simply thinking about things is.

Because of this, it's important to take action as soon as possible. Waiting for tomorrow might as well be tantamount to waiting for a day that will never come.

You should also entirely abandon the very concept of excuses. Arguing for why something cannot be done is merely a waste of breath. Kaizen principles implore you to, instead, look at how it can be done, ignoring the initial dilemma.

You Need Not Work Alone

Even if you aren't in a company setting, you can still get help from others. For example, you could work together with your peers on how you could kick a lousy old habit.

If, on the other hand, you are in a company setting, this becomes so much more important. Even in a small enterprise, there are simply too many decisions made every day, and too many issues to keep up with individually.

Rather than simply placing all of the responsibility on yourself and applying Kaizen there, you should teach it to your employees and actually listen to their advice when they offer it.

No man is an island; if you are contemplating whether or not it would be better to call upon more people or fewer, you are almost always correct to call on them.

Point Out Other's Mistakes

This one mostly refers to applying Kaizen in a team environment. If you want to do this, you'll obviously first have to get everyone on the same page. With that being said, people are swift to jump on the Kaizen boat, but they are then shocked when it leads to people actually calling them out for mistakes.

Make sure that you start pointing out mistakes as soon as you start because this will help people get much more used to what you're doing. In order to properly apply Kaizen, we need to get rid of some of the social boundaries that prevent us from calling our higher-ups out on their mistakes.

You should also encourage this to go the other way around. Give the people around you a good example, and react well to criticism. You should ensure that every time you're called out for something, you react to it positively and with an improvement-friendly mindset.

Start In Only One Area At First

At first, you'll want to focus on only one area of work. If you suddenly start applying Kaizen to every single facet of your life and/or business operation, you can bet that it'll be a burning pile of chaos in no time.

For Kaizen to work properly, you'll need to narrow down at first and ensure that you're getting progress from the system that you're changing. If you aren't, then you'll need to reevaluate.

If you start with multiple areas immediately, the results might be chaotic and interfere with one another. Taking it to step by step is the best way to get to a functional application of Kaizen.

Make A Timeline

You'll want to make a timeline/schedule of sorts. Map out everything that you need to do. In addition, make benchmarks that you'll test your progress with. Using just your own perception as a gauge of progress is okay when it comes to something simple, but more complex matters like the company pipeline need an objective look.

For example, let's say you want to bring down paper consumption in the company. Rather than just relying on your perception of whether you are using less, look at objective metrics.

Jot down on your timeline how much you're planning to lessen your consumption over time. Then when those days come, check the metrics out to see if your expectations hold up.

Always Be Ready To Scrap It

Applying Kaizen isn't always easy. Sometimes, you'll try to do it, but in the process, you'll cause more harm than good. This is even more likely in a larger operation, as with more people being involved, the chances of something messing up is higher.

Because of this, you need always to be ready to scrap your approach and try out a different one. For example, let's say that the above paper consumption method didn't work out. You're not meeting your metrics, and even the people at the company aren't noticing the change.

In this case, what you'll want to do is take an entirely different approach. If the way you tried doing it this time was restricting everyone on how many papers they can print in a day, try making a per-printer limit. This way, you'll be able to ensure that every printer is only printing as much as to meet your metrics.

Don't Change For Change's Sake

A lot of people, when they first start applying Kaizen, change some things they didn't need to. While change can be good, and Kaizen is good for bringing it, there are things where you don't need to bring a drastic change.

For example, if you've been on a workout plan for a few months, and it's working alright, you won't want to start a completely new one. In fact, that simply wouldn't be following Kaizen, as you have no reason to believe it will work better than the last one.

Instead, try focusing on the one you're currently on. Is there something you can change? Something that'll help you improve its effectiveness?

Helping A Business Self-Reflect

Now, when you read the term "self-reflection," you're probably thinking of someone contemplating their flaws and virtues in a dimly lit room. While that is one kind of self-reflection, a business is also capable of it.

Now, this isn't done in the traditional sense where the business itself grows a brain to think with. Rather, a business that self-reflects involves everyone in the business reflecting on it, what is good about it, what is bad about it.

This isn't very easy to do, especially in today's Western climate, where jobs are simply avenues for making money. This is a self-perpetuating idea that turns businesses into nothing more than money-making machines as well.

People connect to businesses less; this extends not only to its operations but also to bosses and coworkers. Japan has a completely different idea, where some of your closest friends are likely to be coworkers, and chances are you've gone to get drinks with your boss a couple of times.

Point Out The Benefits Of Kaizen

This works especially well on small companies, but pointing out how big companies have been using Kaizen to gain the upper hand on their competition is a great way to ensure that your company starts using it as well.

In case you're the company owner, then you'll want to be doing this to your own workers. To start with, simply talk about the benefits it brings to the company, and how that translates to benefit them. Remember, it's quite likely that they're looking at the job as a way to make money, and that's okay.

Hold Kaizen Meetings On A Weekly/Monthly Basis
Something that will help you instill Kaizen into the work culture at your company is holding Kaizen meetings regularly. Now, you might be thinking that it'd be ideal for holding these every single day. Unfortunately, this isn't the case, and Kaizen itself would show you this.

Simply put, unless you're running a high-risk startup, there simply aren't enough things happening for daily Kaizen meetings.

On the other hand, weekly or monthly meetings are on the table. You want everyone at these meetings to contribute. Their rank at the company doesn't matter for this short period of time. Everyone has to find issues with the things they themselves did.

There are a few different ways you can make these meetings, but there are two main ways.

The first is for everyone at the company to be there. If you're a small company without many employees, then this is feasible. This is good for increasing the connections within the company. The people will build and strengthen relationships in addition to all of the usual benefits of Kaizen. Furthermore, this will get you more in tune with the company's processes at all levels.

The second is to rely on this process on multiple levels. For example, you would have it with the managers, and then the managers would, in turn, have it with the people under them. If your company has more levels than this, just rinse and repeat. While this is certainly doesn't let you get as close to everyone at the firm, it lets you do it at a manageable pace.

Conclusion

We've come to the end of the line! By now, you should understand Kaizen in its entirety. We've covered every step of the way, from introducing you to Kaizen, to how to incorporate it and self-reflection into a business.

So, let's recap some of what we've learned, shall we?

- You've learned what Kaizen is, as well as how businesses in Japan often credit it for their success.

- There's a variety of different kinds of Kaizen, and you've probably singled out the best one for you by now.

- The history of Kaizen, how it has come from the 21st-century Western world to Japan and back all the way from the '30s.

- The inner machinations of Kaizen, how it works, and how you can implement it.

- We did a study on Toyota's take on Kaizen. While it is neither the only nor most ideal(theoretically) take, it does show that massive companies are using Kaizen on a day to day basis.

- You've learned of lean six sigma, an attempt to fix Kaizen's "flaws."

- We've gone over the ways that Kaizen can benefit your business and help your endeavors flourish.

- We analyzed how Kaizen helps people not only in their business lives but that applying Kaizen to one's private life leads to more happiness and success.

- We went over how Kaizen can help you in your relationships as well as your professional life if you aren't the CEO of the business.

- Next, we went about ways to implement Kaizen. While it's never easy to do so, knowing these ways will make it much easier for you to do in the future.

- We talked about Kaizen events, and how you can use them to your advantage to get ahead in life.

- Finally, we discussed how Kaizen and self-reflection are connected, and I gave you some tips on applying Kaizen and self-reflection.

All of this and more is what you've learned in the short time that you've been reading this book.

A wonderful thing to realize is that even the very act of reading this book is your first step towards applying Kaizen to your life. If it is even a small improvement in your life, you've succeeded. In the same vein, if it's a small improvement in your life, I've succeeded as a writer.

Now, you don't need to remember everything you've read in this book. After all, who's going to remember 80 pages in a row?

The good thing is- you don't need to. All you need to do is start applying Kaizen to your life. If you want to remember everything in this book, then go for it! Just remember to start with one page and improve one at a time.

The benefits of Kaizen are so vast that we haven't even covered them all, such as their impact on innovation. Note that if you're planning to incorporate it into your company, you don't even need to be at the management level to do so.

It's important to lead by example, so if you use Kaizen in your day to day life and show its capabilities, more and more people will flock to it.

If I could leave you with one message, it would be "don't give up." No matter how much a method or system like Kaizen makes improvement easier, it'll always be reliant on one's willpower.

Because of this, the most important thing to applying Kaizen to your life is nothing other than your ability to persevere and not give up, no matter how hard the challenge ahead might seem.

If you can collect yourself and resist the urge to fall to your knees and give up, then you have a bright future ahead of you.

I hope you succeed on your road to improvement. May Kaizen treat you well.

CPSIA information can be obtained
at www.ICGtesting.com
Printed in the USA
LVHW081515080921
697346LV00011B/636